CHOKE POINTS

T0341750

Wildcat: Workers' Movements and Global Capitalism

Series Editors:

Immanuel Ness (City University of New York)
Peter Cole (Western Illinois University)
Raquel Varela (Instituto de História Contemporânea (IHC) of Universidade Nova de Lisboa, Lisbon New University)
Tim Pringle (SOAS, University of London)
Peter Alexander (University of Johannesburg)
Malehoko Tshoaedi (University of Pretoria)

Workers' movements are a common and recurring feature in contemporary capitalism. The same militancy that inspired the mass labor movements of the twentieth century continues to define worker struggles that proliferate throughout the world today.

For more than a century, labour unions have mobilized to represent the political-economic interests of workers by uncovering the abuses of capitalism, establishing wage standards, improving oppressive working conditions, and bargaining with employers and the state. Since the 1970s, organized labour has declined in size and influence as the global power and influence of capital has expanded dramatically. The world over, existing unions are in a condition of fracture and turbulence in response to neoliberalism, financialization, and the reappearance of rapacious forms of imperialism. New and modernized unions are adapting to conditions and creating class-conscious workers' movement rooted in militancy and solidarity. Ironically, while the power of organized labour contracts, working-class militancy and resistance persists and is growing in the Global South.

Wildcat publishes ambitious and innovative works on the history and political economy of workers' movements, and is a forum for debate on pivotal movements and labor struggles. The series applies a broad definition of the labor movement to include workers in and out of unions, and seeks works that examine proletarianization and class formation; mass production; gender, affective and reproductive labor; imperialism and workers; syndicalism and independent unions, and labor and Leftist social and political movements.

Also available:

Just Work? Migrant Workers' Struggles Today
Edited by Aziz Choudry and Mondli Hlatshwayo

Wobblies of the World: A Global History of the IWW
Edited by Peter Cole, David Struthers and Kenyon Zimmer

Southern Insurgency: The Coming of the Global Working Class
Immanuel Ness

The Spirit of Marikana: The Rise of Insurgent Trade Unionism in South Africa
Luke Sinwell with Siphiwe Mbatha

Working the Phones: Control and Resistance in Call Centres
Jamie Woodcock

Choke Points

Logistics Workers Disrupting the Global
Supply Chain

Edited by Jake Alimahomed-Wilson
and Immanuel Ness

PLUTO PRESS

First published 2018 by Pluto Press
345 Archway Road, London N6 5AA

www.plutobooks.com

British Library Cataloguing in Publication Data
A catalogue record for this book is available from the British Library

ISBN 978 0 7453 3725 8 Hardback
ISBN 978 0 7453 3724 1 Paperback
ISBN 978 1 7868 0190 6 PDF eBook
ISBN 978 1 7868 0235 4 Kindle eBook
ISBN 978 1 7868 0234 7 EPUB eBook

This book is printed on paper suitable for recycling and made from fully managed and sustained forest sources. Logging, pulping and manufacturing processes are expected to conform to the environmental standards of the country of origin.

Typeset by Curran Publishing Services
Printed and bound by CPI Group (UK) Ltd, Croydon, CR0 4YY
Simultaneously printed in the United Kingdom and United States of America

Contents

Introduction:
Forging Workers' Resistance Across the Global Supply Chain

Jake Alimahomed-Wilson and Immanuel Ness

The shipping container, or box, has become one of the most recognizable symbols of modern global capitalism.[1] The standardized shipping container revolutionized global trade by making it possible for intermodal transportation—the ability to move goods across different modes of transport (ships, trucks, and trains) without their ever having to be unloaded or reloaded. This, in part, contributed to a massive decline in global shipping costs becoming a key element in the subsequent logistics revolution.[2]

Today, there are over 20 million shipping containers scattered around the world. On any given day, approximately 6 million of these containers are circulating the global supply chain on massive container ships, moving in and out of the world's ports, or on trucks and trains. Despite the fact that the ubiquitous shipping container has become a mainstay on our roads and highways, most people rarely ever think about the workers who move these containers across the global supply chain. Although containers are seemingly everywhere—hiding in plain sight—they remain an enigma for most consumers, and in some sense obscure the economic and power relationships inherent in global capitalism. Despite the increase of interest in logistics by academics, the stories and struggles of logistics workers remains an understudied component of logistics in contemporary capitalism.

Who moves the goods?

The vast majority of industrial production relies on the hyper-exploitation of manufacturing workers in the Global South.[3] After a consumer product is assembled in a factory in, say, China—the largest export economy in the world—it is typically packed on a pallet and subsequently loaded onto a shipping container, where it is then hauled by a truck driver who moves the box to the nearest warehouse, rail yard, or port. Once the container makes its way to the port, longshore workers (or dockworkers) use large cranes to unload the container from the truck's chassis and onto a massive container vessel. Approximately 90 percent of all commodities are shipped across the world's oceans by container vessels.[4] From there, seafarers (the workers on the giant shipping vessels) ensure the movement of the container over thousands of miles across the world's oceans en route to their destination port. This work is very dangerous for millions of seafarers in the world. The vast majority of these logistics workers are men from the Global South. Upon arrival at a port, the container will once again be offloaded from the ship by longshore workers, and typically placed on either a truck or train, before heading to a warehouse or distribution center, where the goods are processed and sorted by warehouse workers, then sent back out to retail stores via truck, or increasingly sent directly to a consumer's home by a third party logistics provider thanks to e-commerce. So before a product arrives at a retail store, or appears on a person's front doorstep from an e-retailer, that product touches the hands of numerous transportation and logistics workers. It is precisely these 'invisible workers' that this volume seeks to make visible by placing their struggles at the center of our analysis.

The strategic location of logistics labor

So who are the world's logistics workers? Typically, they are longshore workers (dockworkers), warehouse and distribution center workers, seafarers, railroad workers, and truckers (both port truckers and long haul). Collectively, these workers represent a key group of laborers who are on the front lines of critical workers' struggles around the world. Logistics workers are uniquely positioned in the global capitalist system. Their places of work are also in the world's choke points—critical nodes in the global capitalist supply chain—which, if organized by workers and labor, provide a key challenge to capitalism's reliance on the "smooth circulation" of capital. In other words, logistics remains a crucial site for increasing working-class power today.

Logistics workers are facing immense challenges in exercising (or maintaining) working-class power around the world. Collectively, they are confronted with a combination of the following factors: the systematic assault on logistics and transportation unions; deteriorating working conditions; a rising tide of contingent employment relations and third-party employment systems; wage theft; anti-worker legislation; employment misclassification; precarity; automation and technological control over their workplaces; racialized forms of exploitation; alarming safety hazards and workplace dangers; and the privatization of their industries. Taken together, these conditions can be overwhelming—but all hope is not lost. Realizing the strategic nature of the transportation sector, labor organizers have long known and successfully focused on organizing transport workers for many decades as a result of their propensity for militancy and collective action. Many of these unions are fighting just to hold on to what they earned. Others are trying to organize industries in the new economy. As this volume demonstrates, transportation and logistics workers are actively engaging in resisting exploitation across many of the world's choke points. As capitalism has shifted away from the mass production Fordist model to a logistics-driven "flexible" capitalism, labor organizers and unions have also had to adapt and shift labor-organizing strategies.[5] In this process, there have been some key victories achieved by workers and organized labor, but there have also been failures (and everything else in between). One thing remains clear: corporations and states are heavily invested in fragmenting logistics workers from one another. These workers, although connected in the global supply chain, largely remain divided across region, nation state, industry, and job sector. In light of this, linking these global struggles remains an important task in developing strategies of resistance.

Identifying both the victories and challenges of these workers is also an important step toward building stronger workers' movements. As industrial investments have spread throughout the Global South, new workers' movements have emerged across critical industries, thereby challenging the hegemony of state, capital, and traditional union policies, which have in many cases weakened the collective interests of the majority of the global working class. This has certainly been the case for global transportation workers throughout the South. Transportation workers across Africa, Asia, the Middle East, and Latin America, are engaged in struggles for dignity in the face of vast exploitation and economic violence. Logistics workers in the Global

North are also engaged in struggle. Drawing connections between these previously fragmented struggles provides an essential blueprint for building stronger coalitions of workers who have been divided by nation state borders, unequal transnational trade agreements, or neoliberal policies.

Tracing the rise of retailers such as Walmart, the world's largest big box retailer, and Amazon, the biggest e-commerce company, plus other major contractors for industrial goods like Alibaba, can also provide insight into the broader structural forces that have occurred in global capitalism in connection with the restructuring of the global logistics industry. Global changes in the ways goods are produced, stored, transported, and moved have had immense deleterious consequences for workers, workers' movements, and trade unions. While the global capitalist system is certainly not defined by the practices of two individual corporate entities, contextualizing the rise of Walmart and Amazon within the logistics revolution helps identify a critical framework for understanding the changing nature of global production and distribution, including its negative impact on workers around the world. Indeed, Walmart's rise in retail power, and Amazon's uncompromising technological control of its warehouse workers, are directly linked to the preeminent neoliberal paradigm and technocratic 'science' of supply chain management.[6] As corporations, governments, and universities collude to increase the scope and power of controlling the global capitalist supply chain through the exploitation and suppression of global logistics workers, unions and workers are left to fend for themselves.

Toward an unmanageable supply chain

The chapters in this volume center the resistance struggles, challenges, and issues facing logistics workers across many of the world's logistical choke points. Moreover, the chapters also represent a critical intervention into the academic study of logistics, which lately has become increasingly obsessed with a detached academic tone and infatuation with the seamless circulation of global trade. The exploitive material conditions inherent in global trade become lost when workers' perspectives, conditions, and struggles are ignored.

This volume also represents a challenge and opposition to the collusion of universities and academics with corporations in the growing business-driven managerial field of supply chain management. While the business literature theorizes labor control strategies that enhance the exploitation of transnational logistics workforces by emphasizing avoidance of "disruptions" on the supply chain, the chapters contained in in this book implicitly call for the resistance to the so-called managerial disciplining of the supply chain by identifying the critical areas and issues facing logistics workers. Drawing connections becomes an essential ingredient in strengthening logistics workers' unions, and developing new strategies for increasing labor power across the global supply chain. In this regard, global logistics workers must become unmanageable.

Today, global "logistics management" has become a burgeoning career field and many universities are rapidly moving in this direction, thereby aligning with the interests of capital—not workers—in order to produce more and more supply chain managers whose purpose is to further squeeze workers across the logistics industry. Take, for example, the rise of educational institutions adopting neoliberal supply chain management principles in their curricula. One of this book's co-editors, Jake Alimahomed-Wilson, teaches at California State University, Long Beach. His university office is just a few miles away from the largest port complex (the neighboring ports of Los Angeles and Long Beach) in the United States, and is at the epicenter of roughly 600,000 logistics-related jobs scattered throughout the Southern California region. In recent years, Cal State Long Beach, along with countless other universities around the world, has developed a number of degree and certificate programs including degrees in Global Logistics and Supply Chain Management, operated under the auspices of the College of Business Administration. Absent from the curriculum in supply chain management programs like these are courses on logistics workers, unions, and labor. Yes, "jobs" are discussed, but what kind of jobs are they talking about? Are these union jobs? Are they safe jobs? Are these permanent jobs? Do these jobs pay living wages?

It is not just universities that are looking to jump on the supply chain management bandwagon: high schools, trade schools, and community colleges, especially in port cities, are also developing programs and "partnerships" with private corporations in order to grow the field of supply chain management. For example, in 2016 the Port of Long Beach, in collaboration with the Long Beach Unified School District, launched the Port of Long Beach Academy of Global Logistics at the mostly working-class Cabrillo High School with great fanfare. Even the local community college in Long Beach, Long Beach City College, now offers a program in Supply Chain Logistics. The program is partly funded by a grant from the Walmart Foundation, so that students can be trained in warehouse and distribution center supply chain logistics, some of the most precarious jobs in the region. Both the curricula and the philosophy of academic supply chain management programs fail to seriously consider the perspective of labor or workers. That is, these programs generally approach logistics within an anti-worker pro-capitalist paradigm, which teaches students (the future managers) the latest and most efficient strategies of controlling labor, maximizing profit, and ensuring the smooth circulation of capital.

In light of this, this volume seeks to identify the key labor struggles in the global logistics system to advance dialogue and connections between disparate workers' struggles, which are too often fragmented from each other by borders, regions, or the long supply chains. What, then, do Walmart's warehouse workers in the Inland Empire region of Southern California have to do with the organizing strategies of Amazon's warehouse workers in Poland? What linkages can we draw between workers' strikes in the ports of China and the privatization of Greece's ports? What have been the successes and failures of labor organizing across various supply chains around the world, and how can we connect these struggles? What can the history of dockworkers using their labor power from South Africa to the US West Coast teach us about the power of solidarity in choke points? What do longshore workers in Mumbai have in common with truckers in Occupied Palestine? This volume seeks to answer these questions by bringing together a group of experts from a diverse range of perspectives.

The authors include an international group of logistics workers, activists, union and labor organizers, academics, graduate students, and researchers. The chapters in this volume collectively analyze both the past and present struggles facing logistics workers across various choke points in the global supply chain. The authors provide a diverse exploration into the unique circumstances shaping the working conditions of logistics workers throughout various ports, warehouses, and logistical hubs around the world. The themes highlighted in the book include both the historical and contemporary role of solidarity actions, unionization and workers' resistance struggles, attacks on workers and unions, the effects of neoliberalism and technology in the goods movement sectors, among other areas. While it is critical to highlight the unique social, political, and historical forces shaping the various struggles in the goods movement sector around the world, taken collectively, the works contained in this volume also implicitly draw together some important lessons that can, in some sense, help unify a divided global supply chain. The chapters explore and identify critical organizing challenges and strategies facing logistics workers, while offering insight into the key role that these workers have played, and will continue to play, in building capacity for worker's resistance in the global struggle against exploitation.

Chapters in the volume

The chapters are organized thematically as follows: Part I: Building Labor Power and Solidarity Across the World's Choke Points; Part II: Disruptions: Logistics Workers Resisting Exploitation; Part III: Neoliberalism and the Transformation of Ports; and Part IV: New Organizing Strategies for the Global Supply Chain.

Part I (Building Labor Power and Solidarity Across the World's Choke Points) contains four chapters and begins with Chapter 1, Labor and Social Movements' Strategic Usage of the Global Commodity Chain Structure, authored by Elizabeth A. Sowers, Paul S. Ciccantell, and David A. Smith. In this chapter, Sowers, Ciccantell, and Smith argue that by focusing on global commodity chains (GCCs), along with key nodes related to logistics and transportation, we can gain insight into the potential for resistance by labor and other social movements. The authors argue that a "lengthened" GCC approach, beginning with extraction and focusing on global logistics, offers critical insight into the ways that workers, unions, and other social movements can exploit various choke points to resist the power of capital and states. In light of this, the chapter explores how transport systems can link various nodes and choke points around the world, ranging from containerized shipments of goods through seaports, to the movement of raw materials such as coal or oil, which is often via railroads, tankers, or pipelines. Finally, the authors explore some case studies of disruptions by commodity chain workers. Some of the key vulnerabilities shared by the cases stem from the global integration and capital intensiveness of each commodity chain. In terms of integration into the global economy, the importance of containerized consumer production and oil to the vitality of today's global economy is significant, and suggests that choke points are indeed places that logistics workers, and workers in commodity chains generally, have a crucial role to play in the broader struggle for social justice.

Chapter 2, Across the Chain: Labor and Conflicts in the European Maritime Logistics Sector, is authored by Andrea Bottalico. This chapter provides an overview of the working conditions and conflicts along the European maritime-logistics chain, with a special focus on dock labor in the port sector and the container shipping industry. Bottalico identifies critical fragility points of the European transport chain, especially the transhipment system—the shipment of goods to an intermediate destination before moving to another destination. The transhipment revolution since 1990s and the increasing size of vessels increased the rigidity and therefore the fragility of the maritime logistics chain. As Bottalico argues, the relationships between the European logistics workforce and transnational companies along the logistics chain should be read with awareness of a structural power in the hands of a variegated, fragmented workforce involved in a common structure of exploitation. The challenges for the future, in other words, have to be faced by looking at the potential common struggles to be disseminated at both the national and international levels, across the overall European logistics chain.

Part I concludes with Chapter 3, Durban Dockers, Labor Internationalism, and Pan-Africanism, authored by Peter Cole. Cole provides an excellent historical analysis of the ways in which dockworkers in Durban, South Africa, have historically (and into the present day) wielded power and solidarity in support of anti-racism and other international working-class and/or anti-colonial struggles around the world. Cole demonstrates how Durban dockworkers combine their leftist and anti-racist ideologies into the practice of solidarity by utilizing direct action tactics in the form of boycotting ships. The commitment to Pan-African freedom struggles by Durban dockers, in addition to other anti-colonial causes such as the Palestinian freedom struggle against Israeli apartheid, remains a critical reminder of how logistics workers can potentially utilize their strategic location within a region, node, or the global economy, to extend solidarity with struggles against oppression and exploitation. Indeed, as Cole notes, despite the ongoing assaults on logistics workers and port communities around the world, (Durban) dockworker power still exists. Understanding the historical and present-day contributions and activism of Durban dockworkers remains a crucial component in the global struggle for social justice.

Part II (Disruptions: Logistics Workers Resisting Exploitation) begins with Chapter 4, Worker Militancy and Strikes in China's Docks, authored by Bai Ruixue and Au Loong Yu. In this chapter, Ruixue and Yu provide an important overview of the major struggles facing logistics workers throughout China's major ports. The authors argue that "logistic workers in China occupy a very strategic position not only for China but also for the world, if they know how to make use of their power." The chapter links China's economic rise as the "world's factory" to the rapid expansion of ports and overall restructuring of the logistics infrastructure throughout the country. Indeed, China's export-led growth strategy has relied on significant investment into expanding the capacity of China's ports, both inside the country and in its efforts as a major investor in overseas port construction. This, of course, means that China's logistics workers have faced a high degree of exploitation, poor wages, unsafe working conditions, and a host of other structural challenges, including automation. Across various logistics sectors throughout China, the authors analyze some of the key strikes and workers struggles throughout one of the world's largest choke points.

In Chapter 5, "Work Hard, Make History": Oppression and Resistance in Inland Southern California's Warehouse and Distribution Industry, Ellen Reese and Jason Struna provide an overview of both the warehouse industry in inland Southern California—a region known as the logistics capital of the United States—and workers' efforts to improve their working conditions in the region. Just east of the port complex of Los Angeles-Long Beach, the region is home to about 1 billion square feet of warehouses. Like elsewhere in the United States, the region has been impacted by the "Amazon effect" as e-commerce and home delivery have expanded the demand for goods movement and inventory space in the logistics and warehousing industries. Reese and Struna argue that despite rhetorical and discursive claims that seek to make the industry appear attractive and innovative—embodied by one of Amazon's employee mottos, "Work hard, make history"—the region's warehouse workers, most of whom are Latinx, earn poverty-level wages, are commonly hired through temporary agencies, and are frequently subject to wage theft and health and safety violations. Furthermore, the types of management-by-stress schemes addressed by other researchers pervade the industry, even as automation threatens to make large segments of already precariously employed workforce redundant. Even so, since 2008, warehouse workers have organized and fought to improve their working conditions through the Warehouse Workers United (WWU) campaign, which involved a series of workers' strikes and other collective actions including a 50-mile public march, as well as a series of legal complaints, many of which targeted Walmart and its contractors. WWU's efforts won millions of dollars of back wages for workers who experienced labor law violations, and contributed to the passage of a new state law to better regulate the industry. Together with other members of the transnational "Making change at Walmart" campaign, WWU members also obtained an agreement with Walmart to improve its safety standards and to better monitor the labor conditions of its contractors.

Chapter 6, Stop Treating Us Like Dogs! Workers Organizing Resistance at Amazon in Poland, provides a first-hand account of workers' resistance and organizing strategies in Amazon warehouses in Poland. The chapter is collectively authored by Amazon warehouse workers, in collaboration with activists from a grassroots union and the co-organizers of Amazon workers' meetings. This group has participants from several European countries. The chapter begins with an overview of the working conditions at an Amazon warehouse in Poland, including an analysis of the various forms of worker control such as technology, and some of the detrimental effects on workers' health and well-being. The authors provide a detailed account of the various mechanisms of exploitation present in Amazon warehouses while simultaneously documenting the various strategies and tactics that Amazon workers have developed in order to build workers' power and resistance in one of the largest logistics-driven corporations in the world. In doing so, the chapter delves into both the successes and challenges that the workers faced in resisting exploitation and empowering themselves. Finally, sharing the stories of struggle across the global supply chain, like the story of Amazon warehouse workers' resistance in Poland, remains a key and necessary step in order to build alliances in the global struggle against capitalist exploitation.

Part II concludes with Chapter 7, Decolonizing Logistics: Palestinian Truckers on the Occupied Supply Chain, authored by Jake Alimahomed-Wilson and Spencer Louis Potiker, which analyzes the role of logistics in shaping Israel's colonial occupation of Palestine. Alimahomed-Wilson and Potiker argue that Palestinian logistics and transportation workers labor in one of the most violent supply chains in the world today. The chapter focuses on the structural conditions facing Palestinian truckers who move goods to and from Israeli-controlled security checkpoints and military crossings throughout Gaza and the Occupied West Bank. These workers face an intense combination of logistical capitalist exploitation, colonial violence, and anti-Arab racism, largely structured by Israel's dehumanizing supply chain security apparatus. Despite the seemingly insurmountable colonial conditions inherent in the occupied supply chain, Palestinian logistics workers are actively resisting such dehumanizing conditions. The chapter also highlights the role that international logistics labor unions and workers movements have played in supporting the call by Palestinian workers and trade unions to boycott Israeli goods across the global supply chain.

Part III (Neoliberalism and the Global Transformation of Ports) begins with Chapter 8, Decoding the Transition in the Ports of Mumbai, authored by Johnson Abhishek Minz. The chapter provides an in-depth study of the port of Mumbai (formerly known as Bombay), located on the west coast of India. The port of Mumbai remains one of the oldest and most important ports in India. Minz argues that the Indian port sector is going through a major transition. He analyzes the impact that global trade and the broader restructuring of the Indian economy has had on India's port workers. The chapter also examines various themes that affect port labor in India, especially the governance model of the ports and the trend of containerization. Finally, the chapter analyzes the challenges that port labor unions have faced amid the restructuring of the ports across India.

Chapter 9, Back to Piraeus: Precarity for All! authored by Dimitris Parsanoglou and Carolin Philipp, provides an in-depth account of the impact of privatization on the port of Piraeus in Greece. As Parsanoglou and Philipp note, in less than two years following the outbreak of the global financial crisis in 2008, Greece became an exemplary case study of the ongoing and growing crisis extended from finance and sovereign debt and its impact on labor, unions, and logistics workers. One of the central issues at stake has been the neoliberal readjustment—including use and ownership—of critical logistics infrastructure, especially ports, in increasing efforts by capital to make goods and commodities move in more efficient ways. The chapter begins with an analysis of how the privatization effort of this formerly state-controlled port was initiated and completed prior to the Greek debt crisis. The firm of Cosco, based on Chinese capital, purchased a concession through 2051, thereby controlling 67 percent of the state-owned harbor.

Chapter 10, Contested Logistics? Neoliberal Modernization and Resistance in the Port City of Valparaiso, authored by Jorge Budrovich Sáez and Hernán Cuevas Valenzuela, focuses on a case study of Valparaíso, the historic port city located in central Chile, just 118 kilometres from the capital, Santiago. Because of the radical nature of the economic and labor reforms implemented and the depth of the social and political changes experienced there, the city provides an opportune case study for observing the operations of capital and the resistance that these generate in society. Budrovich Sáez and Cuevas Valenzuela argue that the changes and development of Valparaíso can be best understood using three concepts: neoliberalization, extraction, and logistics—three master logics that govern or structure social processes in Valparaíso.

Part III concludes with Chapter 11, Logistics Workers' Struggles in Turkey: Neoliberalism and Counterstrategies. Authors Çağatay Edgücan Şahin and Pekin Bengisu Tepe explore the current challenges facing logistics unions in Turkey. Drawing on extensive data including interviews with militant logistics workers and union leaders, the authors provide a thorough analysis of the challenges facing logistics and transport workers (and their unions) in neoliberal Turkey. Şahin and Tepe contextualize their chapter with an overview of the impact of neoliberal policies on the logistics and goods movement sectors in Turkey. The authors supplement their analysis with an in-depth glimpse into some of the logistics struggles on the ground—in the ports, ships, trucks, and warehouses—from the perspective of militant Turkish logistics workers and trade unionists themselves. The chapter concludes with a discussion of possibilities and strategies for the future of organized logistics labor in Turkey.

Part IV (New Organizing Strategies for the Global Supply Chain) begins with Chapter 12, "The Drivers Who Move This Country Can Also Stop It": The Struggle of Tanker Drivers in Indonesia, authored by Abu Mufakhir, Alfian Al'ayubby Pelu, and Fahmi Panimbang. This chapter discusses the struggle of fuel tanker drivers in several cities throughout Indonesia, with a special focus of the Plumpang depot in Jakarta, the largest fuel terminal in the world. The authors provide a comprehensive overview of the circumstances behind the organizing of the fuel tanker drivers, which led to the formation of the fuel tanker drivers' union. The chapter highlights both the organizing strategies and the building of solidarity between tanker drivers across Indonesia in order to exert their collective influence to attain their rights. Although a series of industrial actions by the drivers was not quite successful in bringing about significant change, their collective action was a remarkable experience and the start of a journey, which led to where they are today. The collective experience of strikes and resistance has taught them that grassroots labor organizing is necessary for success in the union's political struggle.

In Chapter 13, Lessons Learned from Eight Years of Experimental Organizing in Southern California's Logistics Sector, Sheheryar Kaoosji, the founder and current co-director of the Warehouse Worker Resource Center, reflects on his eight years of organizing and research experience in the Southern Californian logistics sector. Over the past eight years, the unions at Change to Win (CTW) established organizing efforts among goods movement workers throughout Southern California, the hub through which $500 billion in goods pass through each year—accounting for approximately 43 percent of the goods that enter the United States. These efforts were resourced with strategic researchers and experienced organizers, and supported by motivated community partners. While significant impacts were made on the way the goods movement sector operates, Kaoosji maintains that these efforts fell short of the ambitious original vision of sparking the organizing of production and retail workers using the power of the supply chain. In light of this, this chapter analyzes the experiences of these two distinct yet related efforts, with the perspective of eight years of lessons learned from somebody who worked on both projects and remains committed to organizing in the goods movement sector of Southern California. These two projects were intended to make significant, strategic changes in a sector that is critical to our global economy. While the optimism of these projects at their outset was not realistic, according to Kaoosji, the central strategy was correct, and this chapter examines both the victories and challenges of these efforts in order to offer a path for moving forward in organizing the supply chain.

Chapter 14, Struggles and Grassroots Organizing in an Extended European Choke Point, authored by Carlotta Benvegnù and Niccolò Cuppini and drawing on approximately 30 interviews with workers and labor organizers, traces the evolution of grassroots workers' organizing in the logistics and warehousing sector in Northern Italy. In doing so, the authors also examine the changes in the logistics labor force, including the rise of migrant workers in the warehouse sector in Northern Italy, which today constitute approximately 80 percent of the warehouse workforce in some regions. In a context where traditional trade unions are encountering increasing difficulties in organizing contracted-out and precarious workers in the low-wage services sector, Benvegnù and Cuppini argue that the cycle of labor struggles that occurred in Northern Italy provides an important case study in order to understand how dynamics of resistance can emerge in a sector characterized by anti-union policies, the precarious status of the workers, and ethnic segmentation and divide-and-conquer strategies that challenge labor organizing and unionization. This logistical conflict also provides a concrete example of how alternative strategies can be put in place by grassroots organizing in a sector characterized by high fragmentation and where traditional trade unions seem to fail.

Part IV concludes with Chapter 15, Beyond the Waterfront: Maintaining and Expanding Worker Power in the Maritime Supply Chain, which is authored by Peter Olney, a labor organizer with over 40 years' experience and the retired organizing director of the International Longshore and Warehouse Union (ILWU)—the union representing dockworkers in the Western United States. In this chapter, Olney examines the power that longshore unions, particularly the ILWU, hold over major maritime ports. The ILWU and other dockworker unions have been trailblazers in the past in standing with world-wide revolutionary people's struggles and in strengthening the domestic power of their sisters and brothers in the working class. While dockworkers still wield power at the point of production, according to Olney it is incumbent on them to recognize new structural and employment realities and adjust their strategies accordingly. The chapter argues that strategic choke points are not static and forever lasting since class conflicts, along with new technology, preclude any strategic position from becoming permanent. As a result of the increasing automation of port labor, coupled with anti-union legislation and the constant assault on dockworker unions, these workers face the challenge of preserving their power in the face of these challenges. Thus, Olney argues that working-class strategies cannot be static or frozen in time irrespective of the shifting terrain, and the ILWU provides an ideal case study for understanding how dockworker unions can respond to such challenges in the global supply chain.

Notes

1 Marc Levinson, *The Box: How the Shipping Container Made the World Smaller and the World Economy Bigger* (Princeton, N.J.: Princeton University Press, 2016).

2 Edna Bonacich and Jake B. Wilson, *Getting the Goods: Ports, Labor, and the Logistics Revolution* (Ithaca, N.Y.: Cornell University Press, 2008).

3 Zak Cope, *Divided World, Divided Class: Global Political Economy and the Stratification of Labour Under Capitalism* (Montreal: Kersplebedeb, 2015).

4 Rose George, *Ninety Percent of Everything: Inside the Shipping Industry that Puts Clothes on Your Back, Gas in Your Car, and Food on Your Plate* (New York: Metropolitan Books, 2013).

5 Jake Alimahomed-Wilson, *Solidarity Forever? Race, Gender, and Unionism in the Ports of Southern California* (Lanham, Md.: Lexington Books, 2016).

6 Deborah Cowen, *The Deadly Life of Logistics: Mapping Violence in Global Trade* (Minneapolis, Minn.: University of Minnesota Press, 2014).

Part I

Building Labor Power and Solidarity Across the World's Choke Points

Labor and Social Movements' Strategic Usage of the Global Commodity Chain Structure

Elizabeth A. Sowers,
Paul S. Ciccantell, and David A. Smith

A key issue of this volume is whether there are identifiable "choke points" where workers and solidarity movements can gain the leverage necessary to disrupt the global capitalist supply chains. We are sociologists who work in a political economy of the world-system framework who conceptualize the world-economy as defined by the far-flung sinews of global commodity chains. We believe that by focusing on these chains—and particularly on key nodes related to logistics and transportation—we can gain great insight into the potential for resistance by labor and other social movements.

Global commodity chains (GCCs) are defined as a linked set of processes by which a series of inputs become tradable consumable goods: in the case of clothing this might involve "the manufacture of the cloth, the yarn, etc., the cultivation of the cotton, as well as the reproduction of the labor forces involved in these productive activities."[1] These chains are very complex, socially embedded processes; in-depth understanding of them requires a knowledge of the details of the particular materials and transformation sequences. Gary Gereffi is a key scholar who developed the GCC framework—and if taken seriously, his approach opens up a new paradigm for conceptualizing global development and inequality, since it shifts our attention on "national" development to the activities at particular loci on these long global chains of production and exchange.[2] This perspective emphasizes "on the ground" (or, in some cases, underground!) activities at particular places of extraction and production—and a key challenge for local actors is how to "upgrade" various processes to generate more surplus in particular places.

From a wider global angle, the GCC view seeks to understand "the unequal distribution of rewards among the various activities that constitute the single overarching division of labor defining and bounding the world economy."[3] This is a critical approach, grounded in political economy (and neo-Marxist notions), which is rather different from the focus on "global value chains" (GVCs) and "supply chain management" (SCM) that seems to have subsumed much of the initial scholarly energy behind this field. Jennifer Bair provides an overview of the way that the GCC approach gradually seems to morph into a more "practical" business and managerial focus on value chains, which shares many characteristics with the SCM literature that is popular today, exemplified by a well-known journal, graduate degree programs, and so on.[4]

In this chapter we argue that a "lengthened" GCC approach (which begins with extraction and focuses on global logistics) offers insight into ways that workers and social movements can exploit choke points to resist the power of capital and states. Indeed, there are well-known historical disruptions that fit our rubric, in particular some famous global coordinated actions by dockworkers in the twentieth century. Perhaps the most familiar attempt of active cooperation between port workers and extractive workers was a week-long national dock strike in the United Kingdom in solidarity with coal miners in 1984 and in opposition to the anti-labor positions of the Thatcher government. The strike fizzled out—largely owing to flagging solidarity at the ports (and maybe because there was no broader global coordination)—and the British coal industry was decimated.[5] But actions by longshoremen on the US West Coast in the 1930s opposing Nazism and fascism by refusing to unload German and Italian goods, and more recent coordinated anti-apartheid actions by maritime workers in the United States and Australia who effectively blocked South African shipping cargo in and out of ports beginning in the 1960s through the mid-1990s, were quite successful.[6] Strategic mobilization at GCC choke points has worked in the past and may be a potent weapon in the future.

The supply chain management versus the GCC/world-system approach

At first glance the goals of the SCM approach seems consistent with the GCC perspective. For instance, a 2001 review article which sought to clarify the meaning of SCM notes that supply chains themselves are defined as networks of actors: almost always firms, but sometimes including consumers, and that there is an emphasis on the unimpeded flow of goods and the strategic actions that firms undertake in these efforts.[7] But the key difference is that the ultimate goal of SCM is to analyze firms' efficiency across the supply chain, particularly maximizing efficiency in the use of capital. So a recent popular book on SCM is unequivocal: the objective is to "serve customers in the most cost-effective way" and to "reduce or eliminate buffers" to the smooth and effective functioning of supply chains.[8]

To some degree, Gary Gereffi himself seems to have incorporated some of these assumptions. Beginning in the late 1990s he segued from describing his focus as on "commodity chains" to one that examines "value chains."[9] In contrast, the goal of our theoretical model of lengthened GCCs is to reclaim the original foci that Terence Hopkins and Immanuel Wallerstein, and Giovanni Arrighi and Jessica Drangel, lay out: we want to emphasize that, while GCCs as constitutive of the world economy generate inequalities and asymmetries, they also may provide openings for labor and social movement organizations (SMOs) to resist, disrupt, perhaps even reshape firms' supply chain strategies.[10]

So despite our interest in the key role of corporate global sourcing in the contemporary world-economy and the immense heft this provides to logistics and transportation industries, our analytic emphasis is very different. In the SCM model, labor is a cost to be minimized and an obstacle to the efficient use of capital—it is an object of research attempting to model and quantify the (pernicious!) impact of various "disruptions" in supply chains, including those caused by labor interests.[11] Any form of resistance by workers or SMOs is something to be avoided or minimized.[12] In contrast, we place this resistance and contestation by labor and SMOs at the center of our analysis.

Interestingly, a recent special edition of the *Journal of Supply Chain Management* focused entirely on the concept of "power" in supply chains and how it is operationalized by various actors. The key theme was how buyers or suppliers use power, and its influence on firm performance—labor interests are mentioned only in passing, if at all.[13] We don't dispute that buyers and suppliers are important and powerful actors in supply chains. But we believe that workers and other organized civil society actors (environmentalists, consumers, local residents) are also actors who can potentially wield power in global supply/value/commodity chains—and make an impact.

As we shall show in the following sections, our lengthened GCC theoretical model both permits us to improve our understanding of firms' strategies and actions, and offers another angle to probe the role of workers and SMOs as key actors in the world economy.

The role of labor in commodity chains

In order to place labor at the center of our analysis of the world economy, we must first determine just how workers in commodity chains derive their power and assess its potential as leverage for workplace gains. Labor scholars extensively discuss workers' bargaining power, not only in broad terms, but specifically as a result of their structural positions in economic activities.[14] The key question is not only what this sort of "positional power" of workers entails, but how it can translate into concrete gains in the workplace.

Positional power, in Luca Perrone's classic exposition, refers to the "varying amount of 'disruptive potential' endowed on workers by virtue of their different positions in systems of economic interdependencies."[15] Michael Wallace and his colleagues extend this definition by specifying the spatial locations that labor interests might disrupt: their own local workplace, or industries "upstream" or "downstream" in the production network. In this framework, positional power is thought to be greatest when it has disruptive potential beyond the local context of work.[16]

From the beginning of this discussion, scholars were quick to acknowledge that positional power, formulated as workers' "disruptive potential" in a particular spatial arena, is not always indicative of the actual tendencies of these workers to participate in strikes or other labor actions, or of success in these actions. Empirical studies have tried to show the conditions under which positional power is acted upon by workers, as well as specifying when it leads to concrete gains in the workplace. For instance, Perrone (1984) finds that the positional power of workers predicts intersectoral wage differentials, but not strike behaviors, while Wallace and colleagues (1993) find that positional power leads to higher wages, particularly for workers who are able to disrupt the labor process in the "upstream" direction (for instance, among those workers who receive large quantities of goods or services from previous stages in the production process). In a historical perspective, Silver discusses how workers endowed with positional power successfully disrupted production specifically in the automobile and transport sectors over the longer historical period across the world system (1870–early 2000s).[17] However, it is not only actual labor actions that matter. Andrew Martin, in his discussion of the bureaucratization of social movements, notes that formalized labor and social movements rely on the threat of strike, rather than actual strikes, to achieve concrete workplace gains.[18]

Where commodity chains are concerned, it is easy to see the potential utility of the concept of positional power. For instance, Ashok Kumar and Jack Mahoney describe how labor actions in the garment industry, combined with a collegiate boycott of Fruit of the Loom, resulted in massive gains for labor in a specific case.[19] A general critique of global production network scholarship is that it is firm-centric and not attentive enough to the role that labor plays in co-determining economic development.[20] Explorations of the vulnerabilities in critical capitalist commodity chains, and the role of labor and political movements within them, as we provide here, help fill this gap by focusing on the actions of labor as constitutive of commodity chains.

Dispersed production networks encompass many groups of geographically separated workers, all of whom are linked through the central capitalist interest guiding the functioning of the entire chain. This suggests a great opportunity for exercising positional power. Workers can not only disrupt production in their own local workplace, but potentially have the power to do so in the upstream direction (on those workers who receive inputs from other ones) or in the downstream direction (on those workers who provide inputs to other ones). Generally, the functionally integrated nature of the chains endows workers with the ability to disrupt on a large (global?) scale, potentially in all three of those spatial locations. This could lead to successful outcomes for workers—particularly since the interests of capital in global commodity chains require that each stage of the process seamlessly flow into the next one, providing a substantial amount of financial leverage for disruptive actions (or the threat of such) by workers.

A theoretical model of lengthened GCCs

The theoretical and methodological model of raw materialist lengthened GCCs brings together the GCCs model[21] and "new historical materialism", or to put it more bluntly, raw materialism.[22] This perspective begins by exploring the material process of economic ascent in the capitalist world-economy. The key problem for rapidly growing economies over the past five centuries has been obtaining raw materials in large and increasing volumes to supply their continued economic development in the context of economic and geopolitical cooperation and conflict with the existing hegemon and other rising economies. The competitive advantages created by organizational and technological innovations in generative sectors and by subsidies from peripheries lead to global trade dominance. The most successful cases of national ascent restructure and progressively globalize the world economy, incorporating and reshaping economies, ecosystems, and space. The historical sequence of rapidly ascending economies, from Holland to Great Britain to the United States to Japan, led to dramatic increases in the scale of production and trade, building generative sectors in iron and steel, petroleum, railroads, ocean shipping, and other raw materials and transport industries that drove their economic ascent while impoverishing the peripheries that provided their raw materials.[23]

The relative decline of US power in the global economy since the early 1970s is widely acknowledged, as is arguably the most important change in the economic and geopolitical structures of the capitalist world-economy: the rapid ascent of China.[24] The economic ascent of China in the past three decades is the most dramatic change in the capitalist world-economy of the late twentieth and early twenty-first centuries. China utilized a global system of raw materials supply created earlier by an ascendant Japan, which utilized a variety of innovations in technology and social organization of steel production, ocean shipping, and raw materials supply agreements.[25]

The lengthened GCC model begins analysis of any commodity chain by focusing on raw materials extraction and processing, and on the transport and communications technologies that link the multiple nodes of the chain, from its raw materials sources through industrial processing to consumption and eventually waste disposal.[26] This approach contrasts sharply with most work in the GCC tradition, which focuses on industrial production and consumption, and pays little attention to the upstream parts of commodity chains.[27] It offers a lens to examine spatially based disarticulations and contestations over extraction, processing, transport, consumption, and waste disposal across these chains.[28] It highlights the role of contestation and resistance to the construction and reproduction of a particular commodity chain in particular places, as for example labor movements and social movement organizations seek to achieve their goals despite resistance from firms and states that oppose these goals, such as port worker conflicts and the battle over the Keystone XL pipeline and oil sands extraction.[29]

Overall, this lengthened GCC approach provides an integrated approach to assess the likelihood or propensity for labor or SMOs to disrupt global production networks—and it should allow us to look at potential and empirical cases of contestation and resistance in a wide variety of GCCs varying in time and place. There are various possible vulnerabilities in particular GCCs: (1) the nature of the transport system(s), the material state of the commodity (liquid, solid, gas, and its fragility), the difficulty of storing the commodity, technical issues in operating transport systems, and the existence of choke points in the logistic network; (2) economic aspects, including the capital intensity and total cost of each node and link in the chain, and whether the firms involved are privately held, listed on the stock market, or state-owned; (3) political dimensions linked to world-system geopolitical contexts, the type of regulatory regime, political regime type, effects of multiple levels of jurisdiction, laws and the legal system, and indigenous rights; (4) social dynamics including the existence or non-existence of public support for the commodity and local production, and the ability of labor or SMOs to attract attention and allies in their struggles; and finally (5) labor power itself, including the degree of labor organization across the chain, contract terms between capital and labor, and so on.

The transport systems that link the nodes of GCCs are particularly important potential choke points. GCCs vary in terms of the transport systems that fit their material characteristics. For containerized manufactured goods, a high value/volume ratio and easy storage of solid matter in containers make it possible to use a wide range of transport technologies, including trucks, railroads, container ships, and airplanes. In contrast, while coal is solid matter and is easy to store, its very low value/volume ratio constrains transport options to railroads and bulk shipping over longer distances. Oil, however, is quite different because of its liquid state and its very difficult to store in nature, so transport options are constrained to railroads, tanker ships, and pipelines.

In turn, these transport systems present very different characteristics in terms of shipping facilities, ports, and the existence of potential physical choke points. An oil pipeline under construction is in essence mile after mile of potential points of disruption for opponents. Once it is completed and hidden underground, choke points are limited to loading and unloading points and pumping stations, unless a significant leak occurs to provide a new site of vulnerability during remediation and repair. Railroad networks are more visible and therefore seem more vulnerable, but the multiple shipping routes available on a well-developed network make it relatively easy to reroute cargoes, leaving choke points mainly at loading and unloading facilities. In some cases, particularly in extractive industries with only one rail route from mine to port (such as at the world's largest iron ore mine in the Brazilian Amazon), the lack of alternative routes does make it possible to use the railroad as a choke point (and a number of indigenous groups have done so over the years while seeking compensation for damages and claiming land rights). Ocean shipping, airplanes, and trucks all have multiple potential routes, leaving mainly loading and unloading facilities as crucial nodes.

Case study examples

We use this lengthened GCCs model to examine a variety of commodity chains and their vulnerability to labor and SMOs in terms of using their positional power to achieve economic, environmental, or other goals. For steel-based GCCs, the scale of investment and operations, capital intensity, and technologies of extraction and processing combine to make these chains vulnerable to upstream disruption by coal and iron ore mining, railroad, port, shipping, and steel mill workers. Strong unions emerged in many countries in these industries because of the use of positional power by workers in these networks. For firms in these industries, it has often been cheaper to buy peace with unionized workers than to risk disruption of the massive GCCs, given the high cost and rapidly mounting losses when facilities are left idle by strikes. This concern has motivated extensive efforts by steel firms and their home core states to develop new, less unionized nodes for the chains in coal and iron ore (such as in coal mining in western Canada and iron ore mining in the Brazilian Amazon) to reduce the risk of disruption, even when it reduces overall efficiency of the GCC by increasing the distances raw materials must be transported, or raises extraction and production costs.[30]

There is a long history of severe disruptions by workers to containerized manufactured goods commodity chains. Particularly noteworthy examples include the 83-day West Coast longshore strike of 1934, in which port workers found support from outside their ranks (for instance, from other maritime workers and seamen) and which brought about broad unionization of longshore workers on the West Coast, and East Coast longshore strikes in 1907 and 1919, when New York longshore workers shut down the port for more than a month in each instance.[31] Currently, the positional power of workers in the third party logistics sector is exemplified by the latest strike at the port of Long Beach/Los Angeles, which graphically illustrates the potential vulnerability of port nodes in the global containerized shipping system.

As the fifteenth strike waged by port truck drivers in the last four years, the current strike builds off recent efforts among port drivers, beginning in Southern California and spreading elsewhere, to challenge the persistent (mis)classification of port truck drivers as "independent contractors" and to raise allegations of egregious wage theft and other labor abuses.[32] While these drivers are classified as independent contractors, so-called "captive leases" require them to lease trucks from the companies that hire them while restricting them from working for any other firm, and recent journalistic investigations highlight other exploitative and restrictive actions engaged in by companies, such as prohibiting drivers from returning home each night and forced overtime. The combination of these issues has led to the portrayal of these drivers as "modern-day indentured servants."[33]

While previous strikes were short-lived and did not win any direct concessions, in 2015 Los Angeles Mayor Eric Garcetti took a public stance against the persistent misclassification of truck drivers, calling it a "battle cry of a systemic problem that must be addressed."[34] Since then, truck drivers have won other similar legal victories, some of which are so large that companies sought bankruptcy protection. Others paid out large sums to workers, including a $228 million victory for 2,300 FedEx drivers who were wrongfully classified.[35] This was one of the largest settlements of this nature recently, and constitutes a compelling labor-led victory in the industry. More recently, XPO Logistics and its subsidiaries, after it acquired major trucking companies in the United States and Europe, became the battleground for strikes and legal challenges to the owner-operator status among its truck drivers.[36] While the outcome of the present strike remains to be seen, the attention drawn to the systemic nature of the abuses against port truck drivers via their misclassification as independent contractors is another way that labor can gain enhance its organizing power in the logistics industry.

One of the most important GCCs in both volume and value is petroleum, the single most critical raw material for the everyday functioning of the capitalist world economy. Three competing types of chain constitute this industry: conventional oil production, oil sands, and "tight oil" produced from shale formations by hydraulic fracturing, mostly in the United States. Conventional oil production is the cheapest and least technologically sophisticated, and can vary in scale from one well to large fields with thousands of wells. Fracking is typically somewhat more expensive and technologically sophisticated, and ranges in scale from a few wells to thousands of wells in a field. Oil sands production is invariably large in scale, highly technologically sophisticated, and the most costly. Crude oil prices are notoriously volatile.[37] This price volatility, and the resulting booms and busts in profits and investments, present severe challenges for firms.

For conventional oil in the Middle East and Africa, ocean shipping is the primary link to markets in Europe, Asia, and the United States, with a very large scale of shipping, high capital intensity, low cost per ton because of scale, minimal labor costs, a very low degree of labor organization, and highly cyclical prices and profitability.[38] The criticality of oil and the capital-intensive, global network of inter-firm cooperation and competition in these GCCs create the potential for vulnerability to labor and SMOs. However, labor organization is typically very limited or state-controlled in producing regions, and labor in the global shipping industry is unorganized and highly unlikely to be organized in the foreseeable future.[39] The shipping and loading/unloading facilities are extremely technologically sophisticated and require very little labor, further enhancing the ability of firms to avoid labor disruptions. Downstream processing facilities in core countries are typically heavily organized by labor unions, but the lack of unionization in producing regions and in the transport system severely constrain any potential for exerting power over this commodity chain.

For the oil sands and for tight oil produced by fracking, the two transport options are pipelines and railroad tank cars. Pipeline shipment is cheaper per ton than rail shipment but construction costs are high.[40] In geopolitical terms, these transport systems have a tremendous advantage in stability and predictability. This geographic proximity, reliance on pipelines and railroads rather than ocean shipping, and high degree of unionization across the commodity chain create an important opportunity for labor organizations to take advantage of numerous vulnerable nodes in the chain at the extraction, transport, and processing stages. However, the highly politicized battle over the Keystone XL pipeline created important divisions between the United States and Canada, and between labor, environmental groups, and other social movements in North America, sharply constraining this potential opportunity. But these SMOs have had no practical impact on the scale of oil sands extraction; only low oil prices in recent years because of excess capacity have slowed oil sands development. The potential vulnerability of many nodes in this chain is in practice neutralized by sharp divides between labor and environmental SMOs.

Lessons for labor and social movements

Our animating question in this chapter involved whether labor and social movements can capitalize on interrupting flows of commerce at the points of extraction, processing, or transportation. In other words, are there "choke points" in GCCs that can be exploited to disrupt those chains and possibly either win benefits or force reconfiguration of those production networks? Our lengthened GCC approach provides a guide for some key factors that might make disruption possible—and we offered a brief overview of how this might work in global oil production (highlighting distinct types of extraction within this sector), as well as specific examples for logistics (in particular, recent labor actions at the ports of Long Beach and Los Angeles. Not surprisingly, the real-life examples provide evidence of both vulnerabilities on which labor and social movement organizations could capitalize and challenges that might impede their organization.

Some of the key vulnerabilities shared by the cases we examine stem from the global integration and capital intensiveness of each commodity chain. In terms of integration to the global economy, the importance of containerized consumer productions and oil to the vitality of today's world-economy is significant, and suggests choke points could be places of power. The increased reliance on "just in time" delivery for goods that flow through US ports doubtless provides workers at those nodes with added leverage. Capital intensiveness and technological sophistication offer both a challenge and an opportunity for labor/SMO interests. Oil pipelines, massive ports, and other large infrastructural investments represent vast sunk investments which are much more difficult to relocate than factories or other processing facilities. This offers physical fixed choke points in some GCCs that might be eminently vulnerable. Of course, this presupposes that the logistics workers at these key crossroads are knowledgeable about solidarity issues and willing to put their own narrow economic interests on the line.

Long commodity chains, however, do present some challenges to insurgents bent on using positional power for disruption. In the contemporary world GCCs are complex and far-flung, involving many disparate groups of workers in spatially distinct locations. That makes concerted and coordinated action a challenge. Further, the relevant workforces are not evenly organized: some may be unionized, others subcontractors or "independent contractors," still other workers on the chain may be contingent or even informal workers. While it is rather easy to see the potential for shared concerns between human rights SMOs and labor, tensions between labor and those who want to defend the environment might be an obstacle to solidarity. And of course, politics at various levels can cross-cut various alliances and conflicts. Trying to organize during the Trump administration (with a loud "climate denier" in charge and enthusiasm for any oil pipeline ever considered, along with very little sympathy for labor) is likely to be a challenge, despite significant environmental and political opposition to that regime's agenda, even at ostensible vulnerable choke points in these chains.

This short chapter is just a suggestive beginning. More studies are called for in the sectors we highlight here (and some others we are examining). We also would hasten to point out that logistics and extraction, however vital in today's world-economy, are not the only sectors to investigate. Scholars should also home in on other possible vulnerable networks. Business/tourism/travel and the extraction and processing rare earth minerals, for instance, might be promising places to locate other choke points for labor and movements to effect change.

Logistics workers, and workers in commodity chains generally, have a crucial role to play in the broader global struggle for social justice. Of course, this presupposes that the logistics workers at these key crossroads are knowledgeable about solidarity issues and willing to put their own narrow economic interests on the line. Past experiences (for instance, of the radical longshore workers in the United States and Australia) suggest that they could be critical catalysts for wider global struggles.

As an industry, logistics plays a crucial role in linking up the systems of global production and consumption, which means the logistics workers are central not just to their own immediate work in distribution, but to these social arenas as well. Because of this, they have potential impacts far afield from their immediate contexts of work, and potential allies in struggles for social justice aside from their co-workers as conventionally defined. For instance, workers involved in extraction and manufacturing, as well as retail workers, and ultimately consumers, are all embedded in the same containerized manufactured goods commodity chain, and are subject to various mechanisms of exploitation at the hands of the capitalist interests controlling this commodity chain. Because of this, logistics workers might have a crucial role in interfacing with these broad categories of social actors and uniting with them in focused struggles against capital. Of course, the objective interests of these various groups and constituencies are not always in alignment, and perhaps that is the biggest challenge logistics workers face in forming alignments with other groups struggling for social justice.

How can groups of social actors in disparate places and industries come to recognize that their problems—as differently as they may manifest—have a common origin? Doubtless effective communication and coordination between these groups is essential, but that is much less of a challenge in today's highly electronically connected world. There is also a need to educate logistic workers about the benefits of labor solidarity in a ruthlessly competitive global capitalist system which tends to promote "race to the bottom" policies for labor whenever and wherever those can be implemented. Raising consciousness is not a trivial matter, but the centrality of workers in logistics and commodity chains generally suggests they have a potential important role to play in the resistance to the status quo in the world-economy.

Notes

1 Terence Hopkins and Immanuel Wallerstein, "Patterns of development of the modern world-system," *Review* (Fernand Braudel Center) 1(2) (1977), p. 128.
2 Gary Gereffi "The organization of buyer-driven global commodity chains:

how U.S. retailers shape overseas production networks," pp. 95–122 in Gary Gereffi and Miguel Korzeniewicz (eds.), *Commodity Chains and Global Capitalism* (Westport, Conn.: Praeger, 1994).

3 Giovanni Arrighi and Jessica Drangel, "The stratification of the world-economy," *Review* (Fernand Braudel Center) 10(1) (1986), p. 16.

4 Jennifer Bair (ed.), *Frontiers of Commodity Chain Research* (Stanford, Calif.: Stanford University Press, 2009).

5 R. W. Apple, "National dock strike ends in Britain," *New York Times*, September 19, 1984.

6 Howard Kimmeldorf, *Reds or Rackets? The Making of Radical and Conservative Unions on the Waterfront* (Berkeley, Calif.: University of California Press, 1988), pp. 114–15; Peter Cole and Peter Limb, "Hooks down! Anti-apartheid activism and solidarity among maritime unions in Australia and the United States," *Journal of Labor History* 58(3) (2017), pp. 303–26.

7 John T. Mentzer, William DeWitt, James S. Keebler, Soonhong Min, Nancy W. Nix, Carlo D. Smith, and Zach G. Zacharia, "Defining supply chain management," *Journal of Business Logistics* 22(2) (2001), pp. 1–25.

8 Martin Christopher, *Logistics and Supply Chain Management*, 5th edn, ch. 1 (London: Pearson, 2016).

9 Gereffi and Korzeniewicz (1994).

10 Hopkins and Wallerstein (1977), Arrighi and Drangel (1986).

11 Seyed Hessameddin Zegordi and Hoda Davarzani, "Developing a supply chain disruption analysis model: application of colored petri-nets," *Expert Systems with Applications* 39(2) (2012), pp. 2102–11.

12 Sunil Chopra and ManMohan S. Sodhi, "Managing risk to avoid supply chain breakdown," *Managerial Economics and Decision Sciences* 46(1) (2004), pp. 53–61.

13 See Renate P. Brito and Priscilla L. S. Miguel, "Power, governance, and value in collaboration: differences between buyer and supplier perspective," *Journal of Supply Chain Management* 53(2) (2017), pp. 61–87; Sangho Chae, Thomas Y. Choi, and Daesik Hur, "Buyer power and supplier relationship commitment: a cognitive evaluation theory perspective," *Journal of Supply Chain Management* 53(2) (2017), pp. 39–60; Russell T. Crook, Christopher W. Craighead, and Chad W. Autry, "Hold back or held back? The roles of constraint mitigation and exchange diffusion on power 'nonuse' in buyer–supplier exchanges," *Journal of Supply Chain Management* 53(2) (2017), pp. 10–21; Isaac Elking, John-Patrick Paraskevas, Curtis Grimm, Thomas Corsi, and Adams Stevens, "Financial dependence, lean inventory strategy, and firm performance," *Journal of Supply Chain Management* 53(2) (2017), pp. 22–38; Huo Baofeng, Barbara B. Flynn, and Zhao Xiande, "Supply chain power configurations and their relationship with performance," *Journal of Supply Chain Management* 53(2) (2017), pp. 88–111; Felix Reimann and David J. Ketchen, "Power in supply chain management," *Journal of Supply Chain Management* 53(2) (2017), pp. 3–9.

14 Erik Olin Wright, "Working-class power, capitalist-class interests,

and class compromise," *American Journal of Sociology* 105(4) (2000), pp. 957–1002.

15 Luca Perrone, "Positional power and propensity to strike," *Politics and Society* 12 (1983), p. 231.

16 Perrone (1983); Luca Perrone, "Positional power, strikes, and wages," *American Sociological Review* 49(3) (1984), pp. 412–21; Michael Wallace, Larry Griffith, and Beth Rubin, "The positional power of American labor, 1963–1977," *American Sociological Review* 54 (1984), pp. 197–214.

17 Beverly Silver, *Forces of Labor: Workers' Movements and Globalization Since 1870* (New York: Cambridge University Press, 2003).

18 Andrew Martin, "Bureaucracy, power, and threat: unions and strikes in the United States, 1990–2001," *Mobilization* 15(2) (2010), pp. 217–37.

19 Ashok Kumar and Jack Mahoney, "Stitching together: how workers are hemming down transnational capital in the hyper-global apparel industry," *Working USA* 17(2) (2014), pp. 187–210.

20 See Andy Cumbers, Corinne Nativel, and Paul Routledge, "Labor agency and union positionalities in global production networks," *Journal of Economic Geography* 8(3) (2008), pp. 369–87; Al Rainnie, Andrew Herod, and Susan McGrath-Champ, "Review and positions: global production networks and labor," *Competition and Change* 15(2) (2011), pp. 155–69; Ben Selwyn, "Beyond firm-centrism: re-integrating labor and capitalism into global commodity chain analysis," *Journal of Economic Geography* 12(2) (2012), pp. 205–26.

21 Hopkins and Wallerstein (1977), pp. 11–145; Gereffi and Korzeniewicz (1994); Jennifer Bair, "Global capitalism and commodity chains: looking back, going forward," *Competition and Change* 9(2) (2005), pp. 153–80; Bair (2009).

22 Stephen G. Bunker and Paul S. Ciccantell, *Globalization and the Race for Resources* (Baltimore, Md.: Johns Hopkins University Press, 2005); Stephen G. Bunker and Paul S. Ciccantell, *An East Asian World Economy: Japan's Ascent, with Implications for China* (Baltimore, Md.: Johns Hopkins University Press, 2007).

23 Bunker and Ciccantell (2005, 2007).

24 See Givanni Arrighi, *The Long Twentieth Century: Money, Power, and the Origins of Our Times* (London: Verso, 1994); Giovanni Arrighi, *Adam Smith in Beijing: Lineages of the 21st Century* (London: Verso, 2009); Bunker and Ciccantell (2007).

25 Bunker and Ciccantell (2007).

26 David A. Smith, "Starting at the beginning: extractive economies as the unexamined origins of global commodity chains." pp. 141–57 in Paul Ciccantell, Gay Seidman, and David Smith (eds.), *Nature, Raw Materials, and Political Economy: Research in Rural Sociology and Development*, Vol. 10 (2005); Paul S. Ciccantell and David A. Smith, "Rethinking global commodity chains integrating extraction, transport, and manufacturing," *International Journal of Comparative Sociology* 50 (3–4) (2009), pp. 361–84; Elizabeth Sowers, Paul

Ciccantell, and David A. Smith, "Comparing critical capitalist commodity chains in the early twenty-first century: opportunities for and constraints on labor and political movements," *Journal of World-Systems Research* 20(1) (2014), pp. 112–39.

27 Smith (2005); Ciccantell and Smith (2009).

28 Jennifer Bair and Marion Werner, "The Place of Disarticulations: Global Commodity. Production in La Laguna, Mexico," *Environment and Planning A* 43(5) (2011), pp. 998–1015.

29 Ciccantell and Smith (2009); Sowers, Ciccantell, and Smith (2014).

30 Bunker and Ciccantell (2005; 2007); Elizabeth Sowers, Paul Ciccantell, and David A. Smith, "Are transportation and raw material nodes in global commodity chains potential places for worker/movement organization? *Journal of Labor and Society* (forthcoming 2017).

31 Rod Palmquist, "Labor's great war on the Seattle waterfront: a history of the 1934 longshore strike" (2008), http://depts.washington.edu/dock/34strikehistory_part1.shtml (accessed July 10, 2017); Calvin Winslow, "Longshoremen's strikes 1900–1920," pp. 547–58 in Aaron Brenner, Benjamin Day, and Immanuel Ness (eds.), *The Encyclopedia of Strikes in American History* (Armonk, N.Y.: M. E. Sharpe, 2009).

32 Jack Flemming, "L.A. and Long Beach port workers begin striking," *Los Angeles Times*, June 19, 2017; Brett Murphy, "Rigged. Forced into debt. Worked past exhaustion. Left with nothing," *USA Today*, June 16, 2017.

33 David Jaffee and David Bensman, "Draying and picking: precarious work and labor actions in the logistics sector," *Working USA* 19(1) (2016), pp. 57–79; Flemming (2017); Murphy (2017).

34 Asia Morris,"New drayage trucking company to hire drivers as employees and promote 'labor peace' at ports," *Long Beach Ports*, May 4, 2015, https://lbpost.com/business/trade-transportation/2000006010-new-drayage-trucking-company-to-hire-drivers-as-employees-to-promote-labor-peace-at-ports (accessed September 4, 2017).

35 Robert W. Wood. "FedEx settles independent contractor mislabeling case for $228 million," *Forbes*, June 16, 2015.

36 Loretta Chao, "Union targets XPO Logistics," *Wall Street Journal*, May 11, 2016.

37 Daniel Yergin, *The Quest: Energy, Security and the Remaking of the Modern World* (New York, Penguin, 2012).

38 Martin Stopford, *Maritime Economics*, 3rd edn. (London: Routledge, 2009); Daniel Yergin, *The Prize: The Epic Quest for Oil, Money and Power* (New York: Free Press, 2008).

39 Yergin (2012), Stopford (2009).

40 See James Conca, "Pick your poison for crude—pipeline, rail, truck or boat," *Forbes* (2014), http//onforb.es/1isyiqs (accessed September 4, 2017); Congressional Research Service, U.S. rail transportation of crude oil: background and issues for Congress, Washington, DC (2014), www.crs.org (accessed September 4, 2017).

2

Across the Chain: Labor and Conflicts in the European Maritime Logistics Sector

Andrea Bottalico

This chapter presents an overview of working conditions and conflicts along the logistics chain. To achieve this aim, the structure of the supply chain is illustrated and integrated with additional items. The premise of this approach relies on the purpose of investigating working conditions and struggles through the observation of both the variety of labor regimes in the maritime-logistics chain and the overall frame within which labor is embedded. The perspective of this analysis allows us to grasp the common trends, taking into account the management of the chain, global factors, and power relationships, with a focus on dock labor in the European port sector and the container shipping industry. Part of the information in this chapter has been collected through a detailed review of specialized newsletters, and from ongoing comparative research into dock labor issues in the European ports.

The structure of the chapter is as follows. After an overview of the working conditions and the conflicts across the maritime logistics chain in the last years, in the second part hypotheses are formulated. The structure of the supply chain from which the hypotheses derive is illustrated. The third part discusses the relationship between global factors and logistics labor, linking some trends that cross each leg of the chain, and focusing on the port sector. The conclusions provide a summary of the conceptual operations together with the partial confirmation of the hypotheses. This approach offers the possibility of verifying the following claims. Given the structural and institutional constraints partly common to the cases, partly specific to each of them, labor in the logistics chain remains a significant variable in value production. Nevertheless, there is a general trend towards the growth of contingent labor. The slow erosion of the institutional basis suggests an ongoing transition dictated by external pressures.

Labor and conflicts in the maritime logistics chain

On September 17, 2016, a demonstration took place in Piacenza, northern Italy, after the death of Abd Elsalam Eldanf, a 50-year-old Egyptian porter knocked down by a truck outside a GLS warehouse used by Montale.[1] Among the protesters were members of a migrant workforce that had been committed from 2008, together with independent unions, to struggles over conditions at the Veneto, Lombardy, Emilia Romagna, and Piedmont warehouses.[2] On that night of September 14, Abd Elsalam was protesting at the gates of the warehouse with a group of workers whose contract had expired. The reason for the picket was a deal signed by the contractor of the labor force, Seam Srl, which belongs to the subcontractor consortium Natana Doc, a service provider at Gls. In Italy in 2016, third-party logistics reached a turnover of €80 billion.[3]

The European Commission proposed to present by the end of May 2017 a package of rules that would address the gap between countries such as Poland, that benefit from low road transport costs, and those that do not, such as France and Germany. The latter are implementing measures that have been contrasted by the European Union itself, such as banning drivers from taking their statutory weekly rest hours in the cabin of their vehicle, and obliging them to ensure that the wages of foreign truck drivers are adjusted where necessary to match the national minimum wage.[4] Italian trade unions have also launched a strike, announcing that they will picket outside the port gates. According to the statements of the union leaders, these new enhanced rules will legalize social dumping.[5]

In March 2017 a dispute at Spanish ports reached a turning point. The European Commission had instigated an infringement procedure against Spain related to its dock labor scheme. The consequence was a port reform proposal quickly submitted by the government, without any negotiation, only to be rejected by the parliament on March 16. A few months after the defeat in parliament, a new port reform proposal in line with the requirements of the European Commission was submitted and approved by the majority. The Spanish port unions announced a series of strikes. Europe is effectively subjecting Spain to economic blackmail, in the form of a fine of €15 million, with the addition of a daily penalty of €150,000, to be paid until the port labor reforms have been realized. In the meantime, workers at ports all over the world have shown solidarity with the Spanish workers. To avoid interruptions, Maersk diverted container ships from Algeciras (Spain) to Tangier (Morocco) and from Barcelona to Fos-Marseille (France), although French dockworkers refused to unload those ships. Belgian dockworkers affiliated to the ITF (International Transport Workers' Federation) and ETF (European Transport Workers' Federation) protested on the dockside in Antwerp against the arrival of the world's second biggest container ship, the *Maersk Madrid*, in solidarity with their Spanish colleagues who were taking action against the port labor reforms.[6]

Belgian ports have also had differences with the European Union for reasons similar to those of their Spanish counterparts. Belgium has been subject to an infringement process initiated by the European Commission since 2014, because the scheme that has regulated the organization of port labor since the 1973 was judged to be incompatible with the principles of the European Treaty on freedom of establishment and freedom to provide services (Article 49 of the Treaty on the Functioning of the European Union, TFEU). (This was the core issue in Spain too.) After months of talks, a compromise was reached in 2016, when social partners proposed a process of port reform to the European Commission, to be implemented in the coming years. The delicate point is to trigger a gradual process of change through negotiations, without strikes. A shutdown in a Belgian port like Antwerp, the second biggest logistics hub in Europe by volume of cargo handled, would cause a huge amount of unwanted disruption for stakeholders such as terminal operating companies, shipping lines, logistics providers, forwarders, other multinational companies of the petrochemical cluster in the port area, and hinterland transport companies.

After a long wait, the solution proposed by the Belgian government was positively assessed by the Commission in the middle of May 2017 and the infringement procedure was withdrawn. However, what seemed to be the end of a path is actually the beginning of a new phase for the European ports.[7] The consolidation process and the oligopolistic nature of the shipping/logistics industry have transformed the overall landscape both at sea and on the land. The strategies taken by the main players along the maritime logistics chain in a search for economies of scale have increasingly produced an unbalanced bargaining power between the actors involved, posing new challenges for workers.

In 2016 an unprecedented number of mergers, acquisitions, and alliances occurred in the shipping sector. The result was to strengthen the bargaining power of shipping lines and port authorities, together with terminal operators. Dockworkers and their unions are negotiating now not only with the terminal operators but also with their customers and shareholders (the shipping companies). In the same year Hanjin declared bankruptcy, creating the biggest economic failure in the history of the maritime industry. The container shipping sector is currently dominated by shipping companies that have created three major strategic alliances over time. Some of the main players manage a substantial share of capacity.[8] These processes have changed the structure of the market, while the financial results of the key players do not seem to be positive.[9] The shipping companies, to compensate for their falling profitability, apply pressure along the entire logistics chain.

In the winter of 2007 a Filipino sailor, Glenn Cuevas, was crushed to death by an 8 ton container on a ship sailing under the flag of Antigua and Barbuda and moored in the port of Rotterdam. The tragedy occurred while the crew members were lashing the containers to the deck. The sailor's death brought attention again to the working conditions of seafarers and the dangers of the semi-legal procedure of self-handling. (This refers to the ever more common practice of requiring the ship's crew to lash and unlash goods while the ship is moored.) This practice has become increasingly common because of commercial pressures, but these tasks were traditionally carried out by dockworkers, and not by sailors, for safety reasons.[10]

Hundreds of workers belonging to ITF and ETF affiliates protested against self-handling at the beginning of December 2016 outside Unifeeder's logistics offices in Denmark. The union inspectors had found that Unifeeder ships did not use organized lashing gangs in the European ports.[11] The action was part of a campaign led by the unions to claim that lashing must be left to dockworkers, in compliance with an ITF collective agreement, which states that "lashing and securing operations on board of the ships are a matter for dockworkers, and the crewmembers should not be asked to carry out this task. Shipping companies, captains and officers who request seafarers to conduct lashing and unlashing operations without permission violate this contract."

The complex structure of the maritime logistics chain

These examples are drawn from research into dock labor issues in Europe. I chose these specific cases after reviewing the specialized press and analyzing the results. I collected other information during fieldwork. I then classified the examples I had uncovered, in a sequence aimed at mapping the geography of the variety of contiguous as well as distant working regimes throughout the logistics chain as a whole. From this perspective, it is possible to sketch out not only a general overview of the conditions and struggles across the chain, but also an outline of the interdependencies, tensions, and connections between each leg and the central nodes (choke points, in the term proposed by C. Chua[12]). Observing the entire logistics chain brings home the complexity of the structure for distributing goods, its multi-scalarity, its dynamism, and the labor that is incorporated in and crosses it. Although labor in the logistics chain remains a significant variable in value production, this approach offers the possibility of assessing a general trend to the growth of contingent labor across the chain, given the structural and institutional constraints that are in part common to the cases. The slow erosion of the previous institutional basis for handling labor suggests an ongoing transition dictated by exogenous factors.

The reasons underlying this approach are based on the structure of the supply chain elaborated by some maritime economists.[13] According to these authors, compared with the past, when shipping companies and ports were the main source of competition, competition now takes place all along the logistics chains that connect origins to destinations, and involves a multitude of actors, not just shipping companies or ports. However shipping companies or ports still constitute the central link in the chain. The interest of the economists remains competitive advantage and the coordination of all activities carried out by both public and private actors, in order to ensure the smooth flow of goods from the ship to the port's hinterland and vice versa.

For this reason, ports experienced a paradigm shift in the 1990s. It was no longer feasible to view them in isolation: they had become elements in value-driven chain systems, links in the supply chains and global production networks.[14] Containerization, linked to economic globalization, was emblematic of this change.[15] If logistics has firmly integrated transportation and production, breaking the spatial link between production and sales, the role of containers in production and distribution has marked the constitutive revolution of the maritime logistics chain. The reasons relate firstly to the function of inter-modal transport as a glue between the various nodes of the productive network into which a commercial enterprise can be broken down.[16]

The current configuration of competition is therefore along the whole logistics chain, which is generally formed by three integrated dimensions: the maritime activities, the handling of goods in the port area, and the transport services in the hinterland. Two major forces affect the port sector: changes in port organizational structures as a result of privatization or deregulation processes, and the efforts of shipping companies to control the whole logistics chain. Empirical studies have shown to what extent shipping lines have sought greater integration among the players in order to leverage economies of scale and gain greater control over the entire chain. To understand the new challenges, hence it is necessary to consider their totality.[17]

Despite the different purposes of various authors, from this perspective is possible to analyze the complex structure of the supply chain, the visual angle of the anonymous goods moved into the container. We should start here if we want to understand how value is created and distributed in the global supply chain sequence. This view also reveals the social embeddedness, the power relationships between the actors, and the pressures that run through the logistics chain, whose structure is represented in Figure 2.1.

The main actors are the cargo owners and shippers, the shipping companies, intermediaries such as agents and forwarders, terminal operating companies in the ports, and hinterland transport companies. Some of these actors are particularly influential: the owners of the goods, forwarders, and shipping companies. The economic performance of the terminal operating companies will depend on the decisions made by those three parties, but at the same time the operating companies are obliged to invest over long periods.

The dotted lines in the figure indicate alternatives to direct paths that could be undertaken, involving one or more intermediaries. The owner of the goods or shipper chooses a shipping company with or without the mediation of a forwarder, as shown in bold lines. In the reverse case, marked with non-bold lines, the receiver of the goods makes that choice. In turn, the shipping company will opt for a specific route and then for a port of call, either in collaboration with the shipper or independently of them. On arrival at the port, with or without an agent's mediation, the shipping company chooses a terminal operator. The final stretch of the route requires the choice of a logistics operator and of intermodal transport in the hinterland. This decision might be made by the shipper (in bold) or the receiver of the goods (not in bold), or the shipping company. Distribution centers, in dotted boxes, can be used in the land stretch. The main issue is to organize this complex context so that market forces can ensure the flow of unhindered goods through the logistics chain in the most efficient way.

Labor in the logistics transport chain: common trends

The structure of the supply chain should be enriched with additional elements, in order to introduce the crucial questions of how the way the organization of the labor incorporated into the logistics chain is changing, and which kinds of conflict arise as a result. It is therefore appropriate to place into this analytical framework some exogenous variables (such as global factors and European regulations) and endogenous variables (such as labor, conflicts, and national regulation). The integration of these items, coupled with the examples illustrated earlier in the chapter, allows us to highlight some general observations based on the starting hypotheses.

As we have seen, along the logistics chain there is a variety of labor regimes. They organize a heterogeneous workforce with different features, contractual conditions, and positions occupied in the various segments. In order to avoid rough generalizations, labor processes and the diverse intensity of conflicts should be defined in detail, placing them within the overall structure. Focusing on details is a useful exercise, for instance to detect the extent to which conflict has not yet emerged in a specific leg of the chain. In the strict sense, logistics deals with the management system whose main objective is to reduce the costs of storage and distribution of goods. The appropriate definition of a physical internet emphasizes the close relationship between logistics and the digital economy through the support of information technology.[18] From here we have to start to study the logics, articulations and operating mechanisms. Although logistics has become a privileged access point for the critical analysis of contemporary capitalism, economic sociologists seem to ignore it. A "logistical gaze,"[19] though necessary, is not in itself enough to enable us to understand the complexity behind this word.

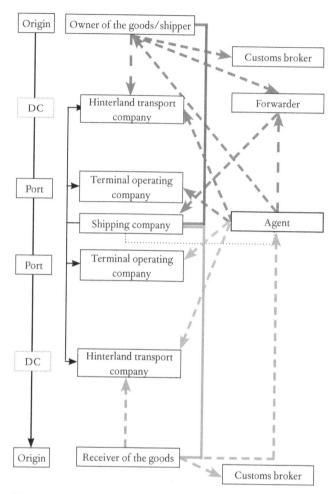

Figure 2.1 Structure of the supply chain.

Source: redrawn from Meersman et al. (2009) (see note 13).

The efficacy of using logistics as the lens through which to interpret the present must be associated with in-depth empirical studies that observe labor within the logistics chain in all its complex composition. Such an approach is much more necessary with respect to indistinct or endorsed approvals over the ongoing struggles in a specific leg of the chain. It is important to understand how workers' actions can alter the dynamics of the logistics chain, affecting business decisions, policies at national and supranational level—and how social research must foster these processes. For this purpose, it is useful to know the articulation of the chain, synergies, value creation, and the logic of exploitation of the logistics workforce. There is room for labor studies and approaches that question those who are directly involved, without underestimating the social role of the economic actors and the structure of the supply chain within which they act.

From the perspective of the logistics chain, it is possible to observe the consequences of neoliberal policies. The cases of European policies in the trucking industry as well as in the port sector, where the forms of protection from external tensions to which dock labor is subjected are conceived as "restrictions" to the free market, are crucial. For the European institutions, the goal is to liberalize the last knot that remains to be dissolved in the maritime logistics chain: the central one. To echo W. Streeck,[20] if Durkheimian institutions exercise a public authority, Williamsonian institutions are conceived by market players as ways to increase the efficiency of trade and reduce transaction costs. The ongoing liberalization processes in the maritime logistics chain can be seen as a gradual transition of modern capitalism, which leads from Durkheimian institutions to Williamsonian institutions.

The fragility of the transport chain, first discovered by the workforce, incorporates the power of the latter.[21] The typical example is the transhipment system. In the maritime leg of the logistics chain, economic globalization and the increasing size of vessels have imposed a structure of the container shipping service based on the development of some hub ports for the transhipment of cargo. Figure 2.2 illustrates the main transhipment systems. "Hub and spoke" refer to the transhipment of cargo from mother vessels to feeder ones, "relay" from an east–west route to north–south routes, "interlining" among different liner services. The transhipment service structure affects both the maritime and port stretches. Shipping companies focused the traffic on the main routes; main ports have emerged—touched by the main routes—together with "ancillary" ports, in which international traffic is provided by smaller vessels. The transhipment revolution since 1990s and the increasing size of vessels increased the rigidity and therefore the fragility of the maritime logistics chain.

In the literature on supply chain management, the concept of *disruption* refers to any major breakdown in the production or distribution nodes that comprise a supply chain, from natural to human-made factors such as labor strikes. Disruption causes a wide range of impacts on the maritime supply chain. Specifically for transportation networks, these impacts can be very negative. Although stakeholders continuously strive for solutions, the magnitude of these impacts is correspondingly set to grow. Major transport gateways such as ports are generally considered to be critical infrastructure,[22] given that owing to their key roles they are particularly liable to disrupt supply chains should there be any interruption to their smooth functioning. The relationships between workers and transnational companies along the transport logistics chain should be read from this perspective.

The real force of economic globalization is the declining cost of international transport—and the same force is moving the inshoring process. In the maritime leg of the logistics chain, a Greek owned vessel, built in Korea, may be chartered to a Danish operator, who employs Filipino seafarers via a Cypriot crewing agent, is registered in Panama, insured in the United Kingdom, and transports German-made cargo in the name of a Swiss freight forwarder from a Dutch port to Argentina, through terminals whose concessions have been granted to port operators from Singapore.[23] For this reason, it is cheaper to ship freshly caught fish from the West Coast of the United States to China to be deboned and filleted by Chinese workers and then shipped back again, than it is to pay for the cost of that work under US labor regulations.[24] Liberalization and globalization of the maritime industry has led to a reduction in transport costs.

The profitability of the maritime leg of the logistics chain does not seems to have increased. Shipping companies impose many constraints on ports, terminals, and hinterlands; both ports and operators have to meet these requirements to stay competitive, compelled to follow the pace of an apparently unlimited volume growth. The empirical studies about the impact of megaships emphasize the pressures on terminals,[25] and their obligation to invest in new facilities and infrastructure. However, such studies have not shown pressures along the central nodes and the social costs. The most significant transformations in ports are driven by the unstable dynamics of the maritime industry. The increasing size of vessels has had strong effects on the market structure in terms of oversupply, decreasing freight rates and profitability. Some issues linked to the impact of the megavessels on ports and terminals, such as overcapacity, congestion, increasing peaks in the demand for labor, shrinking of the operational time, and fierce competition among

Hub and spoke:

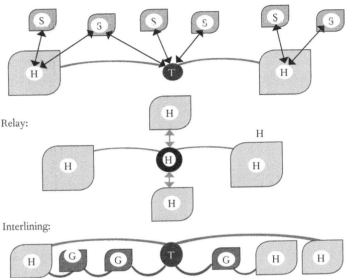

Relay:

Interlining:

Figure 2.2 Transhipment structure.

Source: redrawn from Rodrigues et al. (2015) (see note 21).

Note: circles represent ports, rectangles represent hinterlands, H represents main ports, S represents spoke ports, and T, transit ports.

ports and terminal operators, have shown how tight is the link between ship size and port operations.

Empirical evidence from the port of Genoa, for example, shows to what extent the work organization in container terminals and the national regulation of port labor are influenced by global factors and European regulations. The consolidated strategies of shipping companies produce systemic pressures on the container terminals, and this in turn fosters the further flexibility of the workforce. The ever-increasing role of interim agencies and the slow erosion of those structures that have formed over time to protect working conditions in ports suggest a shift dictated by exogenous pressures which cross the entire chain. Working conditions in the port of Genoa are influenced by the strategies of a multiplicity of actors across a variety of spatial scales, with a cascading effect that leads from the global container shipping industry to the social organization of labor at the quayside. The institutional transition process seems to support such dynamics, calling into question the interplay between national labor regulations, the social role of transnational companies, and the European regulations.

Conclusion

This chapter analyzes the working conditions and conflicts across the logistics chain, through a gaze that tries to shed light on the details of each segment, as well as the overall structure of the transport chain. To address this approach, profiles of diverse array were presented sequentially, and the structure of the supply chain that shows the mobility of goods, with the actors involved, has been illustrated (Figure 2.1). As the term "maritime logistics chain" suggests, competition is no longer at the level of individual ports or shipowners, but along the entire chains.

Two classes of variables introduced into the framework enriched the structure of the supply chain, enabling us to investigate the relationship between global factors, European regulations, and labor. Particular attention has been paid to the container industry and to European dock labor in the framework. Starting from the hypothesis of a tendency towards rising contingent labor along the logistics chain and a transition of institutional structures dictated by exogenous variables, I have argued that we can discern some background tendencies. Linking this view to the working conditions along the chain offers the possibility to partly verify the starting hypotheses, beyond the structural and institutional constraints commonly shared in the cases considered.

There is ample room for further studies. A total confirmation of the hypotheses requires more investigations into the multiple arrangements of labor regimes along the logistics chain, including questioning the actors directly involved, without losing sight of the complex structure within which labor and conflicts are embedded. From this particular perspective, it is possible to assess how the fulcrum of power affecting logistics workers has changed over last few years—moving across the chain—and to consider its potential for further change in the future. When we consider the oligopolistic consolidation of the shipping/logistics industry, together with the resulting imbalance in bargaining power, we reveal an unprecedented scenario, with new challenges for workers, whose power is questioned despite the rise of conflicts in specific legs of the chain. On the other hand, it is important to highlight the increasing fragility and rigidity of the transport chain, which was illustrated here through the example of the transhipment revolution. In light of this, workers must play a central role in creating social justice and challenging the exploitation inherent in the global supply chain. How can logistics workers align with other workers in other industries and/or social justice struggles?

The concept of *disruption* embodies in itself part of the answer. Although stakeholders continuously strive for solutions to render their supply chains leaner, for instance through automation processes, the structure of the maritime logistics chain reveals that they still have to deal with the workers and their agency. The relationships between the logistics workforce and transnational companies along the logistics chain should be read with the awareness of a structural power in the hands of a variegated, fragmented workforce involved in a common structure of exploitation. One of the crucial points for the coming years, therefore, is to go beyond the differences, to boost the exchange of practices among workers who are geographically dispersed, and to favor cooperation in dealing with the increasing conflicts between logistics workers across the chain, despite the variety of labor regimes and working conditions. The challenges for the future, in other words, have to be faced by looking at the potential common struggles that will be disseminated at both national and international level, across the overall logistics chain.

Notes

1 GLS is an acronym for General Logistics System, a global transport company with its headquarters in Amsterdam. See www.gls-italy.com/

2 For the Italian chronicle of the demonstration, see A. Bottalico, "Perché è morto Abd Elsalam? I lavoratori della logistica in piazza a Piacenza" (Why did Abd Elsalam die? Logistics workers on strike in Piacenza), *Napoli Monitor* (2016), http://napolimonitor.it/perche-morto-abd-elsalam-lavoratori-della-logistica-piazza-piacenza/ (accessed April 16, 2017).

3 D. Debernardi, "Logistica conto terzi conferma la crescita" (Third-party logistics confirms growth), TrasportoEuropa, November 11, 2016, www.trasportoeuropa.it/index.php/logistica/archivio-logistica/15541-logistica-conto-terzi-conferma-la-crescita (accessed November 23, 2017).

4 TrasportoEuropa, "Violeta Bulc anticipa provvedimenti UE su auto trasporto" (Violeta Bulc anticipates the EU provisions on road transport), April 27, 2017, www.trasportoeuropa.it/index.php/home/archvio/9-autotrasporto/16387-violeta-bulc-anticipa-provvedimenti-ue-su-autotrasporto (accessed November 23, 2017).

5 There are no recent studies on working conditions in the trucking sector. I go back to G. Crespi, "Camionisti, La ristrutturazione del trasporto merci in Italia" (Truck drivers, The restructuring of freight transport in

Italy), Franco Angeli (1986). See also Z. Conway, "Ikea drivers living in trucks for months," BBC News, March 15, 2017, www.bbc.com/news/business-39196056 (accessed November 23, 2017).

6 ETF (European Transport Workers' Federation), "ITF/ETF dockers take actions to back Spanish colleagues," http://mail.statik.be/t/ViewEmail/r/0A2C2C54BBB162082540EF23F30FEDED/A4DBAF6E BADB6BDD6B5BE456C00C2519 (accessed November 23, 2017).

7 ETF, "Open letter to Transport Commissioner on the reality of port work," Dockers' Section news, May 12, 2017, www.etf-europe.org/files/extra net/-75/47503/ETF%20Open%20letter%20VB.pdf (accessed November 23, 2017).

8 C. Sys, "Is the container liner shipping industry an oligopoly?" *Transport Policy* 16 (2009), pp. 259–70; G. Alexandrou, D. Gounopoulos, and T. Hardy, "Mergers and acquisitions in maritime industry", *Transportation Research Part E*, 61 (2014), pp. 212–34.

9 See the 2016 annual report of AP Møller Mærsk: press release, February 8, 2017, www.maersk.com/press/press-release-archive/annual-report-2016 (accessed October 15, 2017).

10 D. Sacchetto, *Fabbriche galleggianti. Solitudine e sfruttamento dei nuovi marinai* (Milan, Italy: Jaca Book, 2009). This is a study on the working conditions of seafarers. A movie directed by Axel Koenzen, *Deadweight* (2016), deals with the topic of self-handling.

11 ITF (International Transport Workers' Federation). "Reclaiming lashing" (2016), www.itfglobal.org/en/transport-sectors/dockers/in-focus/reclaiming-lashing (accessed November 23, 2017).

12 C. Chua "Logistics, capitalist circulation, chokepoints," *The Disorder of Things*, September 9, 2014, https://thedisorderofthings.com/2014/09/09/logistics-capitalist-circulation-chokepoints/#more-9011 (accessed November 23, 2017).

13 H. Meersman, E. Van de Voorde, and T. Vanelslander, "Scenarios and strategies for the port and shipping sector," pp. 143–60 in H. Meersman and E. Van de Voorde (eds.), *Future Challenges for the Port and Shipping Sector* (London: Informa, 2009).

14 R. Robinson, "Ports as elements in value-driven chain systems: the new paradigm," *Maritime Policy and Management* 29(3) (2002), pp. 241–55.

15 M. Levinson, *The Box. La scatola che ha cambiato il mondo* [*The Box: How the Shipping Container Made the World Smaller and the World Economy Bigger*] (Milan, Italy: Egea, 2013 [2006]); S. Bologna, "Di camion e di porti," in Cesare Bermani (ed.), *La rivista Primo Maggio, 1973–1989* (Rome: Deriveapprodi, 2010a).

16 See S. Bologna, *Le multinazionali del mare. Letture sul sistema marittimo-portuale* (Milan, Italy: Egea, 2010b); Bologna (2010a).

17 E. Van de Voorde and T. Vanelslander, "Trends in the maritime logistics chain: vertical port co-operation: strategies and relationships," pp. 121–40

in T. Vanelslander and C. Sys (eds.), *Port Business: Market Challenges and Management Actions* (Antwerp, Belgium: University Press Antwerp, 2014).

18 S. Bologna, "The creation of surplus value in logistics," In VV.AA., *Bodies, Logistics, and Labor* (Nero edizioni, 2016).

19 S. Mezzadra and B. Neilson, "Extraction, logistics, finance. Global crisis and the politics of operation," *Radical Philosophy* 178 (2013).

20 W. Streeck, *Re-forming Capitalism: Institutional Change in the German Political Economy* (Oxford: Oxford University Press, 2009).

21 S. Bologna, *Tempesta perfetta sui mari. Il crack della finanza navale* (Rome: Deriveapprodi, 2017); A. Rodrigues, C. Ferrari, F. Parola, and A. Tei (2015), "Competition issues in liner shipping. Note by the secretariat," OECD, DAF/COMP/WP2(2015)3.

22 T. Liu and S. L. Lam, "Impact of port disruption on transportation network" (2012), www.fas.nus.edu.sg/ecs/events/pe2012/Lam_paper.pdf (accessed April 26, 2017).

23 S. Kumar and J. Hoffman, "Globalisation: the maritime nexus," in C. Grammenos (ed.), *The Handbook of Maritime Economics and Business*, 2nd edn (London: Lloyd's List, 2010).

24 Chua (2014).

25 OECD and ITF, *The impact of megaships* (2015), www.itf-oecd.org/sites/default/files/docs/15cspa_mega-ships.pdf (accessed April 14, 2017); C. Sys, G. Blauwens, E. Omey, E. Van de Voorde, and F. Witlox, "In search of the link between ship size and operations," *Transportation Planning and Technology* 31(4) (2008), pp. 435–63.

3

Durban Dockers, Labor Internationalism, and Pan-Africanism

Peter Cole

A ghostly galleon plies the seas
that give and take, build and break
on Africa's ex-colonies
on Mozambique, Namibia,
(sometimes mild and sometimes wild),
Angola and South Africa.

Bang, bang, bang, the *An Yue Jiang*
is looking for a port,
but workers on the Durban docks
said, "Nothing of that sort"!

"Take your AKS somewhere else,
your mortars and grenades;
they'll use those bullets on working folk …" [1]

On April 21, 2008, the Chinese ship *An Yue Jiang* docked in Durban, "Carrying three million rounds of ammunition for AK-47 assault rifles and small arms, 3,500 mortars and mortar tubes as well as 1,500 rocket propelled grenades." Zimbabwean President Robert Mugabe, of South Africa's landlocked neighbor, purchased this arsenal to retain power amidst a highly contested election during which his military and police beat thousands and killed hundreds of Zimbabweans. Mugabe's forces also brutally assaulted his political rival, who had won the election's first round and served as secretary-general of the Zimbabwe Congress of Trade Unions. Instead of unloading, the Durban branch of the South

African Transport and Allied Workers Union (SATAWU) embargoed the ship in solidarity with Zimbabwean workers opposing Mugabe. Subsequently, dockers in other southern African ports joined this boycott and the ship returned to China with its deadly cargo. This action was not the first time that Durban dockers used their position at a choke point in support of social justice in another nation, and it echoed their earlier efforts in the long struggle against apartheid. Their history provides further evidence of the power of logistics workers to leverage strategic niches in global trade to agitate on behalf of working-class movements. While no one can deny the global reach of neoliberalism and the decline of unionism, Durban dockers demonstrated that downing tools remains workers' greatest power.[2]

Labor internationalism and pan-Africanism

Dockworkers are quite international-minded, more inclined than most to see local struggles in larger contexts due to the nature of shipping—moving goods, people, and information around the seven seas. Dockers interpret their work and world through a global lens. In Durban and many other ports, they deploy their power to advance internationalist, anti-authoritarian ideals. Global labor historian Marcel van der Linden uses the term "labor internationalism" for actions like the one described above, and defines it as "the collective actions of a group of workers in one country who set aside their short-term interests as a national group on behalf of a group of workers in another country, in order to promote their long-term interests as members of a transnational class." In doing so, they challenge the notion that workers are powerless to shape their world.[3]

Dockers in Durban belong to an international community of maritime workers with a centuries-long history, part of what Peter Linebaugh and Marcus Rediker name the "hydrarchy." In their classic *The Many Headed-Hydra*, Linebaugh and Rediker use this concept to describe "the self-organization" of maritime workers who "had ways of their own—their own language, stories, and solidarity." Shipping was "both an engine of capitalism," they write, "*and* a setting of resistance."[4] The Left generally also understands capitalism as a global phenomenon, and hence advocates a global movement of workers. In the First World War era, for instance, sailors belonging to the anarcho-syndicalist Industrial Workers of the World (IWW or Wobblies) spread their ideas around the world, including South Africa. From

Cape Town, where the Industrial and Commercial Workers Union (ICU) arose out of a 1919 dock strike, the Wobbly motto "an injury to one is an injury to all" traveled the subcontinent. Many Durban dockworkers embrace(d) the hydrarchy and worker solidarity[5]

Many dockworkers also upheld the ideals of pan-Africanism, an ideology and movement of politically conscious black people who believe themselves connected to all people in Africa and its diaspora. Jeffery Bolster documents how well represented black men were at sea in the early modern era, but Linebaugh explains the significance: "the ship remained perhaps the most important conduit of Pan-African communication before the appearance of the long-playing record."[6] Recently, historian Russell Rickford has revived the term "Left pan Africanism" to describe a subgroup of pan-Africanists who identify capitalism, imperialism, and racism as a triple-headed threat, but these sentiments go back centuries.[7] "The power of transatlantic Pan-Africanism," Linebaugh and Rediker write, "frightened the slaveowning ruling class; in response, Charleston's rulers immediately passed the 1822 Negro Seamen Act, which permitted the sheriff to board any incoming vessel and to arrest any black sailor for the duration of the ship's stay."[8] This fear was justified since black sailors boasted about the Haitian Revolution which, as Linebaugh and Rediker suggest, must be understood as "the first successful workers' revolt in modern history."[9]

Similarly, Risa Faussette analyzes the "working class radicalism" of West Indian longshoremen in the early twentieth century.[10] The most famous West Indian ever to work dockside was legendary pan-Africanist Marcus Garvey, about whom Robert Trent Vinson writes: "Many black sailors, students, laborers, and other travelers from Africa, the Caribbean, and the Americas were in London at the time [1912–14]. As Garvey worked on the docks in London, Liverpool, and Cardiff, he listened to their stories of racial subjugation."[11] The solidarity actions of black dockworkers in Durban, hence, must be understood in this long tradition of pan-Africanism among black mariners, who acted against the Italian invasion of Ethiopia, a *cause célèbre* of both labor internationalists and pan-Africanists.[12]

Early waves of solidarity

Durban dockers first downed tools in solidarity with fellow Africans in 1935, in a truly fascinating strike. That year, fascist Italy invaded

Ethiopia, the last African nation free of imperialism's grip. Anti-fascists and leftists worldwide condemned the invasion and sought to support Ethiopia; not surprisingly, many of the most vociferous and active supporters were black themselves. Indeed, black leftists in Africa, Europe, North America, and the West Indies—often in conjunction with communist unions and political parties—took the lead. For instance, the International Union of Seamen and Harbour Workers (ISH) and the International Trade Union Committee of Negro Workers (ITUCNW), both part of the Communist International, organized global protests against Italy as well as against fascist Japan for invading China. Durban dockers would have talked regularly with black and other sailors sympathetic to the Ethiopian cause; historian Gopalan Balachandran brilliantly documents the experiences of Indian sailors, some of whom possessed anti-imperialist and socialist views.[13] Perhaps it was Indian seamen who first informed Durban dockers about the Ethiopian invasion, though they could have read about it in *The Negro Worker*, the ITUCNW's monthly. Linebaugh writes of this "revolutionary newspaper, *The Negro Worker*, on which George Padmore worked, [that] was passed from hand-to-hand by Black sailors in Hamburg, Marseilles, and African and North American ports."[14]

In response, Durban dockers refused to load frozen meat aboard the *Perla*, intended for Italian troops in Ethiopia. When asked by a *Natal Mercury* reporter why they stopped work when the Italians would "civilize" the natives, one docker countered, "It would be civilisation for the financial gain of Italy at the expense of the Native." This worker continued, "you can be sure that the Native would get a very small look in anything which was being done for the apparent benefit of the country."[15] Similarly, the Durban Committee of the South African Communist Party declared, "If we, workers of South Africa, allow this food to be sent to East Africa, we shall be helping Mussolini to conquer and enslave the people of Abyssinia."[16] Though the possibility of being replaced amidst a labor surplus did not intimidate the dockers, the police did. They only agreed to load the *Perla* after police forcibly dispersed a picket line. Dockers in Cape Town also refused to load cargo meant for Italy's army. *The Negro Worker* reported that black dockers in Luderitz Bay, South West Africa (now Namibia) refused to work an Italian vessel too.[17] These actions reconfirm that dockers were well informed about international affairs and opposed European colonialism. Alas, only in the 1970s does evidence emerge of further transnational activism.

In 1969 and the early 1970s, Durban dockworkers repeatedly struck to improve their wages and in opposition to apartheid. Their actions helped shape and launch the Durban strikes of 1973 which marked the return of mass resistance to apartheid after nearly a decade of relative quiet (because of pervasive repression in the early 1960s). As historian Robinduth Toli concludes, "the Durban dock worker strikes were a forerunner of the 1973 strikes and foreshadowed a reawakening of black worker struggles in the 1970s."[18] These events also belonged to a renewed push for freedom, led by black workers, across southern Africa. Loet Douwes Dekker and others forcefully argue for the centrality of worker activism in the 1970s: "in a political system as tightly controlled by a dominant minority as in South and South West Africa, one of the few points of leverage at the disposal of the dominated majority lies in the use of what here can be roughly be termed as 'labour power'."[19]

Concurrently, the armed struggle for independence in neighboring Mozambique and Angola, both Portuguese colonies, reached a crescendo. Hence, it comes as no surprise that the South African state feared a dockworkers' resurgence in Durban, where ships regularly stopped before steaming to the Mozambican capital of Lourenço Marques (now Maputo).

The impending liberation of Mozambique, in 1975, greatly concerned the South African government, although ultimately Durban dockers did not strike. The previous year, however, South African activists planned a series of rallies to celebrate the announcement of Mozambican independence; the South African Students' Organization (SASO), co-founded by Black Consciousness leader Steven Biko, declared it "a revelation that every bit of Africa shall yet be free." Before it could occur, local and national authorities undermined a SASO rally in Durban in support of Mozambican independence. In 1975, the apartheid regime continued monitoring black South Africans who might celebrate in solidarity with Mozambique, which everyone understood was also a cry for freedom in South Africa. R. F. Drew, acting manager of Bantu Affairs in Durban's Central District, sent a confidential memo to divisional heads regarding "Rumoured strikes." His agency feared dockers and other black workers would down tools "on or around 26th June 1975, to coincide with Mozambique independence day." The report warned that activists might use this celebration "for the distribution of subversive literature," and urged authorities to report any issues "immediately to the South African Police."[20] Another special meeting of the city's Bantu Affairs' Sub-Committee on Labour and Transport reiterated that what transpired among Durban harbor workers "was of national importance in bringing in foreign capital." Their alarm was understandable considering Samora Machel, the first president of the People's Republic of Mozambique, soon declared, "we will provide all necessary assistance to the ANC-led people's liberation struggle and the South African people's resistance to this inhuman form of racism known as apartheid, so that they can attain complete economic and social emancipation." The apartheid regime's concern of Durban dockers continued despite containerization which, in the late 1970s and 1980s, drastically reduced their numbers and weakened them.[21]

Boycotting for Zimbabwean democracy

In the twenty-first century, Durban dockers renewed their commitment to working-class power in Africa. Though fewer in number, dockers remain a powerful and militant component of SATAWU, the dominant union for transportation workers—maritime, road, and rail. SATAWU represents dockers in every port including Durban, still the busiest port in the country and in sub-Saharan Africa. Most dramatically, Durban dockers boycotted a ship on behalf of Zimbabwean workers and democracy, in what South African scholar-activists Patrick Bond and Ashwin Desai call "foreign policy, bottom-up."[22]

In 2008, the political crisis in Zimbabwe boiled over as many South Africans looked on with interest and sympathy. Elected after independence in 1980, President Mugabe held power until November 2017, though increasingly he was condemned for refusing to relinquish power. The truth, not surprisingly, is more complicated, especially in the context of left internationalism and pan-Africanism.

First, the two nations share a border along with countless cultural, demographic, economic, historical, and political ties. Second, Mugabe and the Zimbabwean people provided much assistance to opponents of apartheid including Thabo Mbeki, a long-time African National Congress (ANC) leader in-exile and the South African president in 2008. Third, throughout his reign Mugabe claimed to act on behalf of the black masses; for example, the major land redistribution program, in which wealthy white farmers lost "their" lands, was praised by many black Zimbabweans and other Africans albeit it was attacked in the West. Nevertheless, over time Zimbabwe's economic decline and lack of democracy resulted in rising opposition in his country as well as South Africa. When Morgan Tsvangirai, leader of the Movement for Democratic Change (MDC) and a trade unionist, won a plurality in the 2008 presidential election, Mugabe unleashed terror. A Human Rights Watch report documented that the "government was responsible, at the highest levels, for widespread and systematic abuses that led to the killing of up to 200 people, the beating and torture of 5,000 more, and the displacement of about 36,000 people." This conflict particularly concerned South Africans and the several million Zimbabwean immigrants and refugees there. Worldwide, people looked to Mbeki to mediate, but his efforts at "quiet diplomacy" (behind closed doors) failed.[23]

Less than three weeks after the election, Durban dockers sent shockwaves across the globe by refusing to unload weapons intended for Mugabe's regime. SATAWU members in the Planning Department of Transnet, the South African port authority, provided essential information including which ship carried the cargo, when it arrived, and where it docked. SATAWU general-secretary Randall Howard coordinated with provincial secretary Joseph V. "J. V." Dube, who sprang into action. "I called a meeting of the 20 shop stewards and they got word out to the workers" via text messaging. SATAWU quickly declared, "Our members employed at the Durban Container Terminal will not unload this cargo. Neither will any of our members in the truck driving sector move this cargo." Word spread to community activists, Zimbabweans and South Africans, who picketed in solidarity. The ship remained in harbor for several days, its decks loaded with containers holding millions of rounds of AK-47 ammunition, thousands of mortars, and thousands of rocket-propelled grenades (RPGs), as confirmed by Inspector Sprite Zungu of the International Transport Workers' Federation (ITF).

The South African government, meanwhile, attempted to wash its hands of the affair. The BBC quoted South African Defence Secretary January Masilela, "If the buyer is the Zimbabwean sovereign government and the seller is the Chinese sovereign government, South Africa has nothing to do with that." SATAWU's Howard countered, "The South African government cannot be seen as propping up a military regime." This standoff continued for several days until the *An Yue Jiang* raised anchor in search of another port. A great many people in South Africa, across southern Africa, and worldwide considered it a great victory for Zimbabwean democracy, though Mugabe remained in power.[24]

SATAWU acted in solidarity with fellow African workers. In Dube's words, "Our members are very well informed. We opposed what was happening in Zimbabwe. Trade unions have no rights. There is no freedom. Union leaders are victimized, kidnapped, assaulted and arrested. We've been supporting the refugees coming into our country from Zimbabwe, fleeing the repression there."[25] Breaking down Dube's comment, first, many South Africans followed the Zimbabwean crisis and sympathized with the opposition. They appreciated Mugabe's and other Zimbabweans' support during the anti-apartheid struggle, so regretted the irony of a revolutionary ally acting in anti-democratic ways. This author's interview with Dube and Bhekitemba Simon Gumede, a Transnet shop steward, reiterated their knowledge that Zimbabwean unions had partaken in the anti-apartheid struggle, as had other unions outside South Africa. Second, the SATAWU educational program for its members proved effective at motivating solidarity actions on behalf of other workers' struggles. The slogan of SATAWU, not surprisingly, is the old Wobbly one, "an injury to one is an injury to all."[26]

Many individuals and organizations supported and praised SATAWU. The Anglican Church, with millions of South African and Zimbabwean members, actively supported the dockers, particularly the Anglican Bishop of Natal, the Right Reverend Rubin Phillip—who had grown up in an Indian township, belonged to the Black Consciousness Movement, and served as deputy president of SASO. Phillip spearheaded legal action to prevent the movement of military supplies through South Africa, in the event dockers had been forced to unload the vessel. Zimbabwean refugees and South African allies demonstrated at the Durban harbor and Chinese embassy in Pretoria. During and after the boycott, congratulatory emails and letters poured into SATAWU headquarters from Angola, Australia, Canada, China, Germany, Italy, Thailand, the United States, and particularly Zimbabwe. One Zimbabwean woman emailed, "Thank you for your involvement in trying to stop arms from making their way to Zimbabwe. We appreciate it because their arrival here would only mean further loss of lives. God bless you." Sandile Gasa, a Durban shop steward, echoed this sentiment, "As South Africans, by standing up and refusing to off-load these arms, we are proud that we have not contributed to increasing the violence in Zimbabwe."[27]

SATAWU also used its networks, particularly the ITF, to expand the boycott. SATAWU quite actively participated in the ITF, Durban hosted its 41st Congress in 2006, and SATAWU Secretary-General Howard served as ITF President, coincidentally, in 2008. Unions in Mozambique and Angola also belonged, so Howard's advocacy fell on sympathetic ears. As noted, dockworkers in Maputo and Luanda refused to touch the *An Yue Jiang* which ultimately returned to China having failed to deliver its cargo. ITF unions throughout the world, including Australia, New Zealand, and the United States, praised this outcome. ITF general secretary David Cockcroft declared, "For over two weeks, working men and women have kept these bullets and bombs out of the hands of Mugabe's killers."[28]

Of course, neither SATAWU nor the Congress of South African Trade Unions (COSATU) have the capacity to engineer regime change in Zimbabwe or elsewhere. Undeniably, South African unionists have had limited success in promoting democracy in Zimbabwe and Swaziland, the last absolute monarchy in Africa, where unionists lead opposition to its king. Accordingly, scholars Geoffrey Wood, Pauline Dibben, and Gilton Klerck denote the "limits of transnational solidarity," providing myriad reasons why COSATU actions failed to create democracy. Unfortunately, they completely ignore the Durban boycott, which offers one possible tactic that COSATU and these academics might (re)consider—direct action on the job, particularly by logistics workers. As with the global movement to support South African liberation, apartheid ended only when a mass movement, in-country, made South Africa "ungovernable." While COSATU cannot democratize a foreign country, that is quite a high standard for judging transnational solidarity.[29]

What this incident also suggests is that, despite containerization and casualization, Durban dockers remain a vital force. Scholar Bernard Dubbeld thoughtfully chronicles the devastating impacts of containerization in Durban, but his research stopped in the early 1990s, resulting in his concluding that dockers were permanently weakened. Clearly, that proved incorrect. Similarly, while casualization's harmful impacts on South African workers are clear, Durban dockers have managed to weather that storm, too.[30] Scholar Franco Barchiesi makes a powerful case about the increasing precariousness of work (and life) in contemporary South Africa. Without contesting his overall thesis, this chapter argues that Durban dockers' actions in 2008—years after Barchiesi conducted his interviews, none with dockers—are quite impressive and demand consideration for the proposition that dockworkers in many ports still hold surprising power.[31]

Solidarity with Palestine

Durban dockworkers have also taken up the cause of Palestinian statehood. From 2009 to 2014 Durban dockers protested against Israeli-owned ships, to express discontent over Israeli military campaigns that largely killed Palestinian civilians and pressure Israel to recognize a Palestinian state. Their actions—and similar protests by other dockers—suggests the labor internationalism of dockers persists.[32]

In 2009 Israel bombarded the largely defenseless population of Gaza for three weeks, killing over 1,000 civilians. In response, SATAWU announced its Durban members would not unload the *Johanna Russ*, an Antiguan-flagged ship sailing on behalf of the Israeli shipping company Zim. A COSATU press release criticized Israel's "flagrant breaches of international law, the bombing of densely populated neighborhoods, the illegal deployment of chemical white phosphorus, and attacks on schools, ambulances, relief agencies, hospitals, universities and places of worship," and declared that "the momentum against apartheid Israel has become an irresistible force."[33] The use of the term "apartheid" is noteworthy, if contested. Many sympathetic to Israel point to numerous differences between the Israeli treatment of Palestinians and South African apartheid. Nevertheless, many South Africans consciously make this comparison, including Ahmed Kathrada, a legendary anti-apartheid activist who spent twenty-six years in prison and counted Nelson Mandela among his closest friends: "A South African who is not white does not need more than one day's stay in Palestine to be thrown back to pre-1994 and realize that apartheid is very much alive under Israel as a colonial power." While COSATU prematurely predicted Palestinian independence, its stance typified dockworker solidarity with Palestinians.[34]

Conclusion

This chapter has explored how—to this day—Durban dockworkers periodically wield their power on behalf of black freedom and working-class struggles in other nations. They demonstrated their ability to act for transnational causes, rooting their actions in the context of freedom and power. "Solidarity is important," declared Bushy Shandu, a Durban shop steward, regarding the Zimbabwe action, "we urge people of Africa and abroad to do the same in saving people's lives who are still oppressed by their countries."[35] In 2008, Durban dockers engaged in transnational solidarity to further their democratic, anti-racist agenda. According to South African journalist Azad Essa, "The actions of COSATU and its affiliate SATAWU suggest a dramatic shift back to the social movement unionism that defined the union movement at the height of the liberation struggle." He quotes SATAWU's Howard who claims, "I don't think COSATU has ever shifted away from the community issues. We always knew that our role was always going to be more than merely workplace based issues."[36] Patrick Bond, a prominent activist-scholar, agrees: "COSATU's philosophy of internationalism is exceptional, far advanced amongst the world's working classes. We've seen great actions against oppression in Swaziland, Zimbabwe, Burma and now Palestine."[37]

While Durban dockers did not end Mugabe's rule, they demonstrated incredible commitment to pan-African struggles. Undeniably, they are the rightful heirs of Claude McKay's characters in his novel *Banjo*, who hailed from Senegal, the Southern United States, and the West Indies. These black maritime workers came together "on the beach" in 1920s Marseilles, where they discussed Garvey's Back-to-Africa movement and the mistreatment of blacks in both America's Mississippi and French West Africa.[38]

Today, Durban dockers discuss the troubles of people of color in places including Palestine, Swaziland, and Zimbabwe. SATAWU continues its involvement in South African, southern African, African, and global labor networks. As, perhaps, the most internationally connected and minded segment of the South African working class, marine transport workers, will continue to play a pivotal role in global struggles for social justice. Its membership in COSATU as well as the ITF allows Durban dockworkers to network with working-class organizations locally and globally.[39]

(Durban) dockworker power, rooted in appreciation of their strategic niche in global trade, exists even as the global logistics industry continues to be transformed and working-class port communities have largely disappeared. Social movement theorist Peter Waterman describes the early twenty-first century as a time of "globalized networked capitalism, in which production and services, work-for-capital and the working classes are undergoing the most de- and re-construction, and unions are being reduced in size and politically marginalized."[40]

What can be done to resist and overcome what, increasingly, is referred to as neoliberalism? Combining leftist and anti-racist ideologies, Durban dockworkers translated their beliefs in the need for and possibilities of solidarity into tangible action: boycotting ships. Such direct action, arguably, is more possible now than ever before, because of the links created by global trade and transnational labor organizations like the ITF. In the twenty-first century employers, governments, and global capital present tremendous challenges to workers. Despite containerization and other forces, dockworkers have held onto their unions better than many others. Too often and for myriad reasons, labor movements have become divorced from other social movements. Nevertheless, when workers do use their power—at the point of production, through direct action tactics—their centrality is once again revealed. Such is particularly the case for transport workers, as the global supply chain continues to operate using "just in time" production methods to keep inventory low (so as not tie up too much capital). While I do not suggest they represent the norm, the history of Durban dockers suggests what can be accomplished even as automation and powerful economic forces further threaten working people.

Notes

1   John Eppel, "Ghostly galleon," *South African Labour Bulletin* 32(3) (2008), p. 37. This research also forms the basis of part of Chapter 7 in Peter Cole, *Dockworker Power: Union Activism in Durban and the San Francisco Bay Area* (Urbana, Ill.: University of Illinois Press, forthcoming in 2018).

2   "New twist in Chinese arms shipment: union will refuse to handle cargo" and "SA Government says it can't interfere with China-Zim shipment," in *Ports and Ships*, April 18, 2008. Available at ports.co.za/news/article_2008_04_18_1308.html (accessed April 23, 2011). Peter Godwin, *The Fear: Robert Mugabe and the Martyrdom of Zimbabwe* (New York: Little, Brown, 2011). In some reports, the *An Yue Jiang* sometimes was spelled *Ai Yue Jiang*.

3   Marcel van der Linden, *Workers of the World: Essays Toward a Global Labour History* (Leiden, Netherlands: Brill, 2008), p. 259; Peter Cole, "An injury to one is an injury to all: San Francisco longshore workers and the fight against apartheid," *Journal of Civil and Human Rights* 1(2) (2015), pp. 158–81.

4   Peter Linebaugh and Marcus Rediker, *The Many Headed-Hydra: Sailors, Slaves, Commoners and the Hidden History of the Revolutionary Atlantic* (Boston, Mass.: Beacon, 2000), pp. 144–5.

5   Peter Cole and Lucien van der Walt, "Crossing the Color Lines, Crossing the Continents: Comparing the Racial Politics of the IWW in South Africa and the United States, 1905-1925," *Safundi* 12(1) (2011), pp. 88–90; Jonathan

Hyslop, *The Notorious Syndicalist: J. T. Bain: A Scottish Rebel in Colonial South Africa* (Auckland Park, South Africa: Jacana, 2004).

6 Peter Linebaugh, "All the Atlantic Mountains Shook," *Labour/Le Travail* 10 (Autumn 1982): 119.

7 Russell Rickford, *We Are an African People: Independent Education, Black Power, and the Radical Imagination* (New York: Oxford University Press, 2016).

8 Linebaugh and Rediker (2000), pp. 298–9.

9 Linebaugh and Rediker (2000), p. 319.

10 Risa Faussette, "Race, migration, and port-city radicalism: West Indian longshoremen and the politics of empire, 1880–1920," pp. 169–85 in Jerry H. Bentley, Renate Bridenthal, and Karen Wigen (eds.), *Seascapes: Maritime Histories, Littoral Cultures, and Transoceanic Exchanges* (Honolulu, Hawaii: University of Hawaii Press, 2007).

11 Robert Trent Vinson, *The Americans Are Coming! Dreams of African American Liberation in Segregationist South Africa* (Athens, Ohio: Ohio University Press, 2012), p. 65.

12 W. Jeffrey Bolster, *Black Jacks: African American Seamen in the Age of Sail* (Cambridge, Mass.: Harvard University Press, 1997); Peter Linebaugh, "All the Atlantic mountains shook," *Labour/Le Travail* 10 (Autumn 1982), p. 119.

13 Gopalan Balachandran, "South Asian seafarers and their worlds, c. 1870–1930s," pp. 186–204 in Bentley et al. (2007).

14 Holger Weiss, "The International of Seamen and Harbour Workers—a radical global labour union of the waterfront or a subversive world-wide web?" in Holger Weiss (ed.), *International Communism and Transnational Solidarity: Radical Networks, Mass Movements and Global Politics, 1919–1939* (Leiden, Netherlands: Brill, 2017); Joseph Fronczak, "Local people's global politics: a transnational history of the Hands Off Ethiopia Movement of 1935," *Diplomatic History* 39(2) (2015), pp. 245–74; Linebaugh (1982), p. 119.

15 Ralph Frans Callebert, "Livelihood strategies of dock workers in Durban, c. 1900–1959" (PhD thesis, Queen's University, Kingston, Canada, 2011), pp. 279–80.

16 *The Negro Worker* 5(9) (1935), pp. 3–6, quote on pp. 5–6.

17 *The Negro Worker* 5(9) (1935), pp. 3–6; Callebert, "Livelihood strategies," pp. 279–80.

18 Robinduth Toli, "The origins of the Durban strikes, 1973" (MA thesis, History, University of Durban-Westville, 1991), pp. 210–12.

19 L. Douwes Dekker, D. Hemson, J. S. Kane-Berman, J. Lever, and L. Schlemmer, "Case studies in African labour action in South Africa and Namibia (South West Africa)," p. 207 in R. Sandbrook and R. Cohen (eds.), *The Development of an African Working Class* (London: Longman, 1975), Also see Cole (2018), Chapter 4.

20 R. F. Drew to all divisional heads, "Rumoured strikes," File 1/12/9/1, June 19, 1975, and Port Natal Bantu Affairs Administration Board, "Minutes of the Special Meeting of the Sub-Committee on Labour and Transport held on

6th February, 1975 at 9.30 a.m.," both in Port Natal Administration Board, KCF 82 Roll 64, Killie Campbell Library, Durban.

21 Julian Brown, *The Road to Soweto: Resistance and the Uprising of 16 June 1976* (Auckland Park, South Africa: Jacana Media, 2016), ch. 6 (quote on p. 138); Alda Romão Saúte Saíde, "Mozambique's solidarity with the national liberation struggle in South Africa," in SADET, *The Road to Democracy in South Africa*, Vol. 5, Part 2: *African Solidarity* (Pretoria: Unisa Press, 2014), p. 746.

22 Patrick Bond and Ashwin Desai (eds.), "Foreign policy bottom up: South African civil society and the globalisation of popular solidarity," UKZN Centre for Civil Society, July 25, 2008. Available at: http://ccs.ukzn.ac.za/files/Bond_Desai_Foreign_Policy_Bottom_Up_July_2008.pdf (accessed June 2, 2016).

23 Human Rights Watch, "Zimbabwe: no justice for rampant killings, torture," March 8, 2011. Available at: www.hrw.org/news/2011/03/08/zimbabwe-no-justice-rampant-killings-tortureJames (accessed June 1, 2016); Hamill and John Hoffman, "'Quiet diplomacy' or appeasement? South African policy towards Zimbabwe," *The Round Table* 98(402) (2009), pp. 37–84; Brent Meersman, "The legacy of Thabo Mbeki," *Safundi* 13(3–4) (2012), pp. 425–32; Peter Godwin, "Day of the crocodile," *Vanity Fair*, September 2008. Available at: www.vanityfair.com/politics/features/2008/09/zimbabwe200809 (accessed April 23, 2011).

24 Bhekitemba Simon Gumede and Joseph V. Dube, interview with Peter Cole, Durban, July 29, 2010; "Boycott: Durban dockworkers block arms to Zimbabwe," *Maritime Workers' Journal* (Australia), July/August 2008, pp. 32–3 (Dube and SATAWU quotes); "Chinese ship carrying arms for Zimbabwe refused entry to Durban," *Ports and Ships*, April 17, 2008, available at: ports.co.za/news/article_2008_04_17_5052.html#one (accessed April 23, 2011); "Zimbabwe arms ship quits S Africa," BBC News, April 19, 2008, available at: http://news.bbc.co.uk/go/pr/fr/-/2/hi/africa/7354428.stm (accessed June 1, 2016; Masilela and Howard quotes).

25 Dube, interview with Cole; *Maritime Workers' Journal* (2008), p. 32.

26 Gumede and Dube, interview with Cole; *Maritime Workers' Journal* (2008), p. 32.

27 "Zimbabwe arms ship quits S Africa," BBC News; emails shared by Jane Barrett, who worked at SATAWU, May 2011; "SATAWU on campaign to stop weapons reaching Zim," *Politicsweb*, April 22, 2008, available at: www.politicsweb.co.za/politics/satawu-on-campaign-to-stop-weapons-reaching-zim (accessed June 2, 2016); Global Nonviolent Action Database, "Southern Africans block arms shipment for Zimbabwe, 2008", available at: https://nvdatabase.swarthmore.edu/content/southern-africans-block-arms-shipment-zimbabwe-2008 (accessed June 2, 2016); "A bishop's pursuit of justice for South Africa's shack dwellers," *Christian Today*, June 3, 2010, available at: www.christiantoday.com/article/a.bishops.pursuit.of.justice.for.south.africas.shack.dwellers/26028.htm (accessed June 2, 2016).

28 41st Congress of International Transport Workers' Federation, available

at: www.itfcongress2006.org/ (June 2, 2016); *Maritime Workers' Journal* (2008), pp. 32–3 (Cockcroft quote).

29 Geoffrey Wood, Pauline Dibben, and Gilton Klerck, "The limits of transnational solidarity: the Congress of South African Trade Unions and the Swaziland and Zimbabwean crises," *Labour History* 54(5) (2013), pp. 527–39.

30 Bernard Dubbeld, "Breaking the buffalo: the transformation of stevedoring work in Durban between 1970 and 1990," *International Review of Social History* 48 (2003), pp. 97–122.

31 Edward Webster, "Trade unions and the challenge of the informalisation of work," pp. 21–43 in Sakhela Buhlungu (ed.), *Trade Unions and Democracy: COSATU Workers' Political Attitudes in South Africa* (Pretoria: HSRC Press, 2006); Franco Barchiesi, *Precarious Liberation: Workers, the State, and Contested Social Citizenship in Postapartheid South Africa* (Scottsville, South Africa: UKZN Press, 2011).

32 Peter Cole, "'An irresistible force': longshore unions and the fight for freedom and justice in Palestine," *Briarpatch*, November/December 2013, available at: https://briarpatchmagazine.com/articles/view/an-irresistible-force (accessed November 24, 2017); "Swedish dockworkers block Israeli goods in boycott action," *IMEMC News*, June 24, 2010, available at: http://imemc.org/article/58994/ (accessed June 2, 2016); "Turkish dock workers union joins boycott against Israel," Labour for Palestine, June 25, 2010, available at: http://labourforpalestine.net/2010/06/25/turkish-dock-workers-union-joins-boycott-against-israel/ (accessed June 2, 2016).

33 COSATU and Palestine Solidarity Committee, "Victory for worker solidarity," February 6, 2009, available at: www.cosatu.org.za/docs/pr/2009/pro205c.htm (accessed July 29, 2013).

34 Azad Essa, "Opposition to Israeli cargo at Durban's dock: the significance of dockworkers' refusal to offload Israeli goods," *Pambazuka*, February 12, 2009, available at: pambazuka.org/en/category/comment/54031 (accessed April 8, 2011); Jon Soske and Sean Jacobs (eds.), *Apartheid Israel: The Politics of an Analogy* (Chicago, Ill.: Haymarket, 2015), Kathrada quote on back cover.

35 Azad Essa and Martin Jansen, "'What happens in Zimbabwe affects us': union hounds Chinese arms," *South African Labour Bulletin* 32(3) (2008), p. 37.

36 Essa (2009).

37 Essa (2009).

38 Claude McKay, *Banjo* (New York: Harper & Brothers, 1929).

39 Edna Bonacich and Jake Wilson, *Getting the Goods: Ports, Labor, and the Logistics Revolution* (Ithaca, N.Y.: Cornell University Press, 2008).

40 Peter Waterman, "Adventures of emancipatory labour strategy as the new global movement challenges international unionism," *Journal of World-Systems Research* 10(1) (2004), pp. 217–53 (quote on p. 221).

Part II

Disruptions: Logistics Workers Resisting Exploitation

4

Worker Militancy and Strikes in China's Docks

Bai Ruixue and Au Loong Yu

The rise of China's ports

Of the top 500 kinds of manufacturing goods produced globally, China is the leading producer of 221. China also now ranks number one globally in terms of net manufacturing exports. In 2013, China's global market share reached 30.6 percent for labor and resource-intensive goods, 17.8 percent for low-tech goods, and 17.1 percent for high tech goods.[1] China is both a dominant manufacturing country and an export-oriented country. Accompanying China's economic rise and the transformation of China into the "world's factory," China's ports have significantly expanded and become among the leading players globally. Its container throughput has come to rank among the highest in the world, and in 2015 China's port and harbor operations were estimated to have handled 11.5 billion tonnes of freight throughput. Seven of the world's top ten busiest container ports are now located in China (six in mainland China plus Hong Kong) (see Table 4.1).

Indeed the growth of China's ports has been both essential to and a strategic part of China's development plans globally, nationally, and locally. Since the country placed heavy emphasis on an export-led growth strategy, the expansion of its ports and logistics industry has been crucial to facilitating this, and container traffic has grown significantly. Significant investment is continuing to be made to expand the capacity of China's ports. In 2010 it had a total of 1,774 deep-water berths, and as part of the government's 12th Five Year Plan this was to be increased

Table 4.1 The world's top ten container ports by container volume (million TEU*) in 2015

Ranking	Location	Volume
1	Shanghai, China	36.54
2	Singapore	30.92
3	Shenzhen, China	24.20
4	Ningbo-Zhoushan, China	0.63
5	Hong Kong SAR, China	20.07
6	Busan, South Korea	19,45
7	Qingdao, China	17.47
8	Guangzhou Harbour, China	17.22
9	Jebel Ali, Dubai, United Arab Emirates	15.60
10	Tianjin, China	14.11

* TEU = twenty foot equivalent unit

Source: World Shipping Council, "Top 50 world container ports," www.worldshipping.org/about-the-industry/global-trade/top-50-world-container-ports

to 2,214 by 2015.[2] Currently the largest project in this respect is the construction of Yangshan deep-water port, close to Shanghai, with a planned 50 such berths by 2020 at a cost of more than US$10 billion.[3] China has also become a major investor in overseas ports, something which has only been given further strategic importance as it seeks to create a twenty-first-century Maritime Silk Road as part of Xi Jinping's "One Belt, One Road" development strategy.

Nevertheless, despite expansion and significant investment and although China's ports operate at a lower cost than those of most other countries, import and export procedures still take much longer. In 2012, for instance, while procedures typically took 21 days for exports and 24 days for imports in China, in the United States it took 6 days for exports and 5 days for imports, and in Brazil 13 days for export and 17 days for import procedures.[4] China has, however, been catching up very rapidly, and accompanying the growth and expansion, it has been keen to upgrade and modernize its port facilities and to introduce newer technological developments. Technologies and equipment that are in high demand include vessel traffic management information systems, laser docking systems, dredging equipment, terminal tractors, and security equipment.[5] In line with trends elsewhere, this also includes the increasing introduction of automation, something that might be expected to have significant impact on employment in the future.

In this respect China's introduction of Asia's first fully automated port terminal, the Qingdao New Qianwan Automatic Container Terminal, which began operating in May 2017, may mark a significant turning point. According to reports, operations at the terminal are controlled by artificial intelligence, something that has been viewed as advantageous by the terminal's management because it leads to a reduction in labor costs, as well as increased efficiency since operations can be carried out at night.[6] The speed at which the terminal was built (in only three years) has also been highlighted as an impetus for its design to be replicated across other ports in China.

As in many other industries, as rapid growth has occurred, workers have suffered from intense exploitation, and concerns about the adverse impacts on human health and environmental protection have been disregarded. The lack of regard for the safety of ordinary people was shown must brutally in the case of the Tianjin port explosions in August 2015, where collusion and blurred boundaries between private and state bureaucratic capital in the race to make a profit caused the safety and health of workers, local residents, and the environment to be endangered.[7] The explosions at a chemical storage warehouse resulted in at least 173 deaths and several hundred more people being injured.

Investment in and expansion of China's ports has also resulted in a growth in jobs related to the port industry, increasing the number of workers whose livelihoods and work conditions are affected by port operations and regulations. As is shown by the cases of the striking truck drivers from different locations (which we discuss below), this extends beyond workers directly employed by the port itself, and includes others upon whose labor port operations have also depended. As a result of poor pay and working conditions, strikes over port work are not an infrequent occurrence in China. The logistics workers in China occupy a very strategic position not only for China but also for the world, if they know how to make use of their power.

There are three main port regions in China connected to core economic coastal areas: around the Yangtze River delta (including Shanghai and Ningbo-Zhoushan), the Pearl River delta (including Hong Kong, Guangzhou, and Shenzhen) and the Yellow River and Bohai Sea (including Tianjin, Qingdao, and Dalian).[8] The focus of this chapter is recent cases of worker resistance to aspects of their exploitation in two of these port regions, the Yangtze River delta and the Pearl River delta, where cases from mainland China and the Hong Kong Special Administrative Region (SAR) are discussed.

The Yangtze River delta

Shanghai

In April 2011 a truck drivers' strike began in Shanghai and swept through the Yangtze ports of Shanghai and Ningbo, and at one point even extended to the northern port of Tianjin on Bohai Bay. On April 20, 1,000 truck drivers struck to demand the cancellation of unnecessary fees charged by the ports or related facilities owned by the Shanghai International Port (Group) Co., Ltd. Another grievance was police abuse of power in handing out penalties to drivers and sometimes even demanding bribes from them.[9]

The strike lasted three days and allegedly brought the whole port to a halt, with many container ships leaving the port half full. The striking drivers were self-employed and owned their own trucks. According to drivers who spoke to reporters, in 2005 they could make a profit of as much as 30–40 percent. In 2011, in addition to the burden of fees there was also the issue of rising oil prices. This was why the drivers also demanded that the oil price, which is controlled by the state, be cut. The combined effects of these factors cut the drivers' profits to 10–15 percent, and their income was eroded further when the police and other government departments made things difficult for them. The drivers complained that they needed to apply for more than 20 licenses, and this burdened them financially. The strike was only called off after the Shanghai mayor, Han Zheng, stepped in and announced that the port would cancel these unnecessary fees. At around the same time, drivers in the Ningbo and Tianjin ports also struck, and the latter strike allegedly cut in half the normal volume of transportation. There is only a little information available on these two strikes, however.[10]

Ningbo

Three years after the Shanghai strike, on August 21, 2014, more than 1,000 drivers at the Ningbo port in Zhejiang struck. Soon, 20–30,000 more drivers came out to join them and struck for four days. Around 60 percent of trucks at the port were involved. Conflict and arrests were also reported. These drivers were mainly self-employed, and owned and operated their own trucks. Their main demand was for the Ningbo International Freight Forwarders Association and the government to intervene to make the logistics companies raise the price of truck services.

The logistics companies had not raised the price for eight years, a period during which there had been an oil price hike. It is interesting that this was effectively a triangular struggle involving the drivers, the logistics companies, and the government, which controlled both the industry association and the association that was supposed to represent drivers.

In 1999 the then Ningbo Foreign Trade and Economic Cooperation Bureau had founded the Ningbo International Freight Forwarders Association to "represent" the logistic companies. "Representation" was also needed for the drivers, and so the Ningbo Traffic and Transport Committee, which is an arm of the municipal government, helped found the Ningbo Traffic and Transport Association, which it kept under its control. The truck drivers had to pay to join this association. However, one grievance of the drivers was that they felt this association was useless. According to the drivers, it was the arrogant attitude of the association and the government towards their demands that triggered the strike.[11] The strikers not only complained about the inaction of "their" association, but at one point demanded a new association which would be under their own control rather than controlled by the government.[12]

In 2006 the Ningbo Freight Forwarders Association set a "guide price" for transactions between logistics companies and truck drivers. In the midst of a 91.7 percent rise in the price of oil over eight years, the "guide price" was raised 12 percent in July 2014, after constant pressure from truck drivers. However the logistics companies refused to meet this rate, as they claimed that the "guide price" was not binding. This angered the truck drivers, who then struck against the logistics business.[13] Eventually, probably because they had been hard-pressed by the authorities, the logistics companies gave in and the Ningbo Freight Forwarders Association, "on behalf" of these logistic companies, signed an agreement accepting the 12 percent rise demanded by the truck drivers. The truck drivers, "represented" by the Ningbo Traffic and Transport Association, also signed the agreement.

The Pearl River delta

Yantian

On July 4, 2007, around 700 crane drivers at the Yantian International Container Terminals, Shenzhen, went on strike.[14] This was just the latest in a wave of strikes around Shenzhen ports in 2007. On March 24, more than 300 workers responsible for loading and unloading had gone on strike for three days over pay in Yantian. There was also a strike of 180 port crane drivers in Shekou, Shenzhen, over pay, and then on May Day 400 crane drivers from the Shenzhen Chiwan port went on strike to protest against low pay and their only having one or two days off each month.

According to one report, the Yantian Terminal workers went on strike because they were encouraged by the news that the Shekou port workers had received a wage raise after their strike.[15] Although the Yantian strike only lasted one day, this was long enough to leave more than 20 ships at the dock and 50,000 containers standing idle. This strike is significant because in addition to demanding a big pay rise, the workers demanded the founding of a workplace union, with officials elected by all frontline workers. When higher levels of the official union intervened and took over negotiation with the employer, it watered down the workers' demand for a pay rise of 5,000 yuan to 1,000 yuan.[16] Eventually the employer only agreed to a 3 percent pay rise (around 300 yuan) and the 500 yuan extra payment demanded by workers for working at a height. Although the employer also recognized the workers' demand for a union and collective bargaining, the deal between the company and the Shenzhen branch of the All-China Federation of Trade Unions (ACFTU) was that the employer was allowed "reasonable participation in the workplace union," which meant a promise of "a certain degree of dominant role for the employer" within the union.[17]

On May 8, 2013, the date a 40-day Hong Kong dockworkers strike ended, the pro-Beijing press in Hong Kong boasted how much better the working environment was at the Yantian port than at the Hong Kong port, and how Yantian workers only worked eight hours a day, while their Hong Kong counterparts worked 16–24-hour shifts. It also reported the words of Li Chuan, the vice bureau chief of the Shenzhen Bureau of Port Freight, who said that since the 2007 strike the Bureau had initiated reforms such as regular consultation between the employer and employees, and the launching of entertainment for workers, so as to "humanize" the management of labor. It further commented that for these reasons "there is comparatively low incentive [for the workers] to go on strike."[18]

It is ironic that just three months after this report, the Yantian port workers struck again. According to Mr. Chan, the former chairperson of the Hong Kong Dockworkers Union, Yim Lui-fai, managing director of Hongkong International Terminals (HIT), was moved by the company to head operations at the Yantian port.[19] Worried that Yim would pursue a hard-line policy, in addition to their existing grievances, 800 crane drivers went on strike on September 1, 2013, demanding a pay rise of 2–3,000 yuan and for the company to honor a promise to pay for the education of employees' children. The strike lasted for three days and brought the port's operations to a halt. It ended when the company agreed to raise a number of additional payments, which possibly amounted to a pay rise of 20 percent.[20] This was not the end of the story concerning Yantian port strikes. On December 29, 2009, hundreds of truck drivers blockaded the entrance of the terminal to protest against high entrance fees. This was followed by more radical actions, targeting not only the terminal operator but also the port authority and the local government.

Yantian International Container Terminals is chiefly owned by Li Ka Shing's company, but the whole port area is owned and managed by both the Yantian local government and the state-owned company Shenzhen Yantian Port Group, which are both responsible for providing necessary port facilities such as parking spaces for trucks and storage places for containers. Grievances accumulated as truck drivers became increasingly upset by the hiking of fees for parking spaces and entrance to storage places. On November 3, 2014, 1,000 truck drivers went on strike, which led to conflict with the police, who had fined many drivers for illegal parking. Some drivers had been fined ten times a month and had paid a total of 2,000 yuan. The drivers complained that this was not their fault, as the local government and the Yantian Port Group, in response to rises in the price of land and property, had demolished many parking spaces to make way for new residential housing and five-star hotels. The shortage of parking spaces had driven up the cost, and drivers were finding it hard to cope.

Most of these drivers were self-employed and owned their trucks. Some years earlier the local government had set up an association to represent them, but according to the drivers it was at most a channel for filing complaints and never really represented their interests. The association was entrusted by the local authorities with issuing permits for truck driving and for certifying that the holders had satisfied the customs department requirements. The drivers paid 300–500 yuan to sit the examination that was supposed to qualify them for a permit, but according to them it was very difficult to pass, and because of corruption in the association it was possible to pay 1,000 yuan to acquire a license without passing the exam. This had become common practice.[21] Probably because of the drivers' actions, between 2015 and 2016 the Yantian local government decided to provide four temporary parking areas and then to build a truck service center which provided 2,000 parking spaces.[22]

The 2013 Hong Kong dockworkers' strike

In response to falling wages, resulting in workers being paid less than they had been 18 years previously, and poor working conditions, in 2013 around 450 dockworkers at HIT went on strike for 40 days to demand a 23 percent wage rise. The strike is notable as one of the most significant and longest-running strikes in Hong Kong in recent years. The striking dockworkers initially occupied the container terminal but then after a court injunction set up camp outside the terminals. Later, the workers also set up another camp outside the Cheung Kong Centre, the headquarters of Li-Ka-shing, whose company is the largest shareholder in Hutchison Whampoa, the parent company of HIT. Workers also marched to the office of the labor secretary to express their frustration with the government's failure to help them.

The strike received a lot of solidarity from local Hong Kong students and activist groups. Hong Kong trade unions rarely have any strike funds as their union dues are astonishingly low compared with unions in the West. Fortunately, because of popular support for this strike, the union was able to raise HK$8 million, which helped to sustain the strike. In addition to collecting strike funds, supporters also organized a boycott of Park 'n' Shop (a supermarket chain owned by Li-Ka-shing) and participated in protest marches.

The strike and the degree of its success were, however, affected by two major related limiting factors, the lack of unified worker militancy and the political divisions and associated competition among labor organizations. Although Hong Kong had recently experienced the comparatively more militant bar benders' strike in 2007, labor militancy in the city has in recent decades generally been extremely low. Memories of the Chinese Communist Party 1967 ultra-leftist riots, one of the events unleashed by the unfolding Cultural Revolution at that time, negatively affected perceptions of militant labor action, and strategies pursued by the unions also had an impact. While the pro-Beijing Hong Kong Federation of Trade Unions (HKFTU) lost its militancy following the 1967 riots and in the post-handover period has been a part of the establishment, prior to Hong Kong's reuni-

Table 4.2 Other strike actions in the Pearl River delta

Place	Date	Event
Foshan New Port	March 22, 2011	All dockworkers struck
Huangpu Old Port	March 26, 2012	Workers struck to demand a pay rise and social security
Huangpu Wuchong Port	April 25, 2012	Hundreds of drivers blocked the main road to protest against mismanagement of the port
Shenzhen Shekou Port	September 17–27, 2013	400 workers struck to demand a pay rise
Zhuhai Jiuzhou Port	November 19, 2013	Dozens of workers struck to demand a pay rise

fication with China the strategy of the Hong Kong Confederation of Trade Unions relied on making appeals to the colonial government and was less concerned with consolidating organization in the workplace. In the post-1997 period it has been criticized for over-reliance on media publicity, although attempts to consolidate worker organization have slowly improved.

Worker organizing and representation has also been affected by competition between these two politically opposed main trade union bodies. This was also the case in the dockworkers' strike, where workers at the port belonged to different unions affiliated to different federations. Many striking dockworkers were members of the Union of Hong Kong Dockworkers (UHKD) and were represented by the HKCTU, to which it is affiliated. However during the negotiations between worker representatives in UHKD and HKCTU and their employers (the subcontractors of HIT), separate negotiations were also held with HKFTU (which represented other workers at the port, but none of those who had gone on strike). HKFTU put forward a demand for a 12 percent pay rise, far below what the striking workers were asking for. This division and the actions of HKFTU in undercutting the workers' demands therefore weakened the chances the striking workers and their union representatives had of winning their claim.

Another factor limiting the strike's impact was that it took place during a relatively low season, so its effect was weaker than it would have been at a busier time. This too reduced the workers' bargaining power. According to some of the workers, they had deliberately chosen to strike during the low season. One striking crane worker whom we interviewed at the time of the strike commented, "I think we need to tell them we are friendly. Let's talk when the season is low." According to him, workers had discussed going on strike six months earlier during a much busier period, but had rejected the idea out of goodwill. In a more recent interview Mr. Chan, the former president of UHKD, said that the strike nevertheless took place in a period of "good business" during the Easter season, although preparations for it had begun in 2012. He moreover noted that workers had first discussed going on strike in 2011, but then a subcontractor agreed to raise the wages of its employees by HK$200. Only some of the workers employed by this contractor joined the strike in 2013. Regardless, any notion of goodwill was not returned by the employers, which sought to vilify workers during the strike, and initial pay offers were very low.

While the strike clearly impacted on the operations of the port, for instance resulting in cargo having to be directed elsewhere, its impact was less than it could have been. Additionally, the striking workers only comprised 27 percent of the total workforce, and although they encouraged other workers to join in, this was largely unsuccessful. A lack of picket lines, different conditions for direct and subcontracted employees, and divided union representation did not help.

Despite this, the dockworkers' persistence and endurance in continuing their strike did result in a partial victory. In the end they received a 9.8 percent pay increase, far below what they had initially demanded. Since then workers' wages have been raised each year. The year after the strike they went up 10.1 percent, in 2015 5.5 percent, in 2016 4.5 percent, and then by 3 percent in 2017. Workers whose jobs were threatened when one of the subcontractors, Global Stevedoring Service, announced the closure of its operations during the strike,[23] were reportedly subsequently employed by two other contractors, and the company re-established itself under another name, suggesting that the initial threat could have been a trick to threaten the workers.

Important improvements to working conditions were also made following the strike. While previously workers had to sleep on the floor, leading many to suffer from rheumatism, bunk beds for workers were set up. Improved bathroom facilities were also installed, which provided access to hot water for the first time. The memory of the strike and the impact of worker action may also have acted to limit the former arrogance of the employers. According to Mr. Chan, before the strike the management "treated our workers like slaves," but after the strike they were unable to do this any more. When external contractors to HIT were threatened with further industrial action by UHKD in 2015 over pay, they eventually agreed to pay a 5.5 percent pay increase and avoid a strike.[24] While the outcome of the strikes might have been more successful if the workforce were fully united, and many improvements could still be made to pay and conditions today, the workers' actions can be said to have had a significant impact at the port.

Conclusion

When China became the world's sweatshop and number one exporter of cheap goods, this brought about a big leap forward for its ports and related industries. In mainland China, the Chinese government has been very capable in building a corporate state to mediate the interests of opposing classes through compelling all players to join its state-sponsored organizations. At times the corporate state does pacify class antagonism, but there are also times when it fails to function, and class conflicts erupt into a triangular struggle between the employers, employees, and the state.

In the 2007 Yantian crane drivers' strike, for instance, it was obvious that the official union was useless in conveying workers' grievances to the local authorities. This not only gave workers no other option but to go on strike, it also prompted them to target the official union and demand the right to set up an autonomous union. This was not successful, and the failure laid the ground for the 2013 strike. In the 2014 Ningbo truck drivers' strike the corporate state's role was even more obvious. Initially a tripartite arrangement between the local authorities and the two state-sponsored organizations (which were supposed to "represent" the drivers and the logistic companies respectively) was established to regulate the possible conflict of interests. The outbreak of the strike, however, proved that it was a complete failure. It was unsurprising when the drivers targeted the government, its police, and its sponsored organizations for their (failed) role in mediation, turning the strike into a three-way struggle between the drivers, the logistics companies, and the government. If these strikes remained economic it was because the authorities acted quickly to make concessions to the strikers. Although the corporate state within the export sector has often recovered its balance afterwards, it has been a new balance favorable to the workers because they won the battles, and they also gained the experience of struggle and emerged more confident.

In Hong Kong, where workers do not face the same restrictions on organizing as their mainland counterparts, the dockworkers' strike in 2013 reflects a case in which the collective action by workers resulted in an improvement to their situation and to a limited degree altered the balance of power between the workers and their employer. The union was not only able to win a pay rise, it also made the management improve working conditions and act more respectfully towards workers. However, the strike proved to be a one-off. Among the factors limiting the development of a strong workers' movement is the deep-rooted weakness of workers and unions in developing a class identity. That is also why Hong Kong's weak labor movement, despite comparative political freedom, has never been able to play a leading role in awakening Chinese worker activism. For the moment, the prospect of changing this relationship of forces in favor of the Hong Kong labor movement does not look good, because the Chinese government is now tightening control over Hong Kong.

There is still a long way to go before workers in both mainland China and Hong Kong can irreversibly shift the balance of power. Precisely because the strike actions are always very short-lived, they rarely expand to export processing zone workers. This weakness reflects the fact that they are unable to organize. With the help of the communication revolution we are now witnessing a new phenomenon where workers, even without the benefits of an organization, can coordinate actions through smart phones and the internet. This does not mean that organization has become obsolete, however. Organization is not just about sticking together, it is above all about trust, an element that is particularly lacking among Chinese workers because of decades-long atomization. This is why even if logistic workers can win concessions through spontaneous actions, they often return to the same kind of atomization after the actions. Actually the most advanced workers already understand the need for organization and have demanded this. Although they have been unsuccessful for the moment, we can say for sure that the long contest between workers, capital and the state within the export sector has only just begun.

Acknowledgment

The authors wish to thank Felix Fong for his help with research for this article.

Notes

1 Bao Zhicheng, 一帶一路戰略是國內國際政經大手筆 (The One Belt One Road strategy is a domestic and international grand plan), in Li Yining, Lin Yifu et al. (eds.), 讀懂一帶一路 (*Understanding the One Belt One Road*) (Beijing: Chung Hwa, 2017), p. 23.

2 Niels Van der Graaf and Bas Overtoom, *China Top Sector Ports: Opportunities for Dutch Companies* (Beijing: Netherlands Economic Network in China, 2013).

3 "China-marine industries," *Export.gov.*, May 31, 2016, www.export.gov/apex/article2?id=China-Marine-Industries (not publicly accessible).

4 Van der Graaf and Bas Overtoom (2013).

5 "China-marine industries" (2016).

6 Han Peng, "'Ghost port': Asia's first fully-automated port begins operations in Qingdao," *GCTN*, May 13 2017, https://news.cgtn.com/news/3d637a4e31677a4d/share_p.html

7 For details see Au Loong-Yu, "China: the Tianjin blast, 'connections', bureaucratic and private capital," *Europe Solidaire Sans Frontières*, August 20, 2015, www.europe-solidaire.org/spip.php?article35712 (accessed November 29, 2017).

8 Van der Graaf and Overtoom (2013).

9 *Apple Daily*, 司機罷工潮蔓延天津一半貨車停運 (Half of Tianjin trucks stop running when drivers struck), April 23, 2011, http://hk.apple.nextmedia.com/international/art/20110423/15193019 (accessed November 29, 2017).

10 *Apple Daily* (2011).

11 Xiong Bin and Li Yong, 宁波上万集卡司机大罢工 与警激战 30余人被抓 (10,000 Ningbo truck drivers struck and fought with police, more than 30 arrested), *NDTDV*, August 21, 2014, www.ntdtv.com/xtr/gb/2014/08/21/a1132025.html (accessed November 29, 2017).

12 宁波港集装箱车队罢工汇总 (Selected reports on Ningbo port truck drivers' strike), *Cnhuodai*, August 20, 2014, http://bbs.cnhuodai.com/thread-32925-1-1.html (accessed November 29, 2017).

13 宁波集卡罢工追踪：难破的集卡调价 (Tracing the Ningbo truck drivers' strike: the difficult issue of price regulation on truck transportation), *China Navigation Weekly*, issue 1071, September 10, 2014, http://news.hsdhw.com/170642 (accessed November 29, 2017).

14 Some reports claimed that the number of strikers was 280, although most said that it was 700.

15 深圳市盐田码头三百吊车司机停工 要求成立工会 (300 Shenzhen Yantian port crane drivers stop work and demand the founding of their union), *News Sohu*, July 7, 2007, http://news.sohu.com/20070407/n249274716.shtml (accessed November 29, 2017).

16 The workers' original monthly wages were around 10,000 yuan.

17 Xu Xiaojun and Ren Xiaoping, 从盐田国际罢工事件看中国工会维权路

径中的制度救济 (The Yantian international strike: an analysis on institutional remedies in relation to Chinese trade unions standing up for labor rights), May 24, 2016, http://study.ccln.gov.cn/fenke/shehuixue/shjpwz/shzzshx/309941.shtml (accessed November 29, 2017).

18 盐田港六年前爆工潮3天解决 劳资协商薪酬获双赢 (After a three-day strike at Yantian port a win-win agreement over pay is reached between employees and management), *Ta Kung Pao*, May 8, 2013, http://news.takungpao.com/hkol/politics/2013-05/1595447.html (accessed November 29, 2017).

19 Interview. See also the *Apple Daily* report by Guo Bojia, 碼頭風雲一周年　哀歌未完 (The anniversary of the dock drama, the sad song has not yet finished playing), March 28, 2014, http://hk.apple.nextmedia.com/news/art/20140328/18671621 (accessed November 29, 2017).

20 There are different reports on the scale of the pay rise. This is partly because the company offer was very complicated. It mainly consisted of increasing different kinds of extra payment. See 鹽田港罷工爭加薪 (Yantian port workers struck to get a pay rise), September 3, 2013, http://wknews.org/node/215 (accessed November 29, 2017).

21 深圳盐田港卡车司机罢工不仅仅是停车位短缺 "惹的祸 (It is not only the shortage of parking places which gave rise to the Shenzhen Yantian port drivers' strike), XGMYD.com, http://xgmyd.com/archives/9808 (accessed December 24, 2017).

22 盐田投43亿建拖车服务中心，可提供2000个拖车停车位 (Yantian invests 4.3 billion yuan to build a truck service center providing 2,000 parking spaces), *New Citizen Movement*, November 13, 2014, http://wap.ycwb.com/2016-12/21/content_23836098.htm (accessed November 29, 2017).

23 Phila Siu and Ada Lee, "Everyone a loser after Hong Kong dock strike ends," *South China Morning Post*, May 8, 2013, www.scmp.com/news/hong-kong/article/1232519/strike-end-sees-all-involved-losers (accessed November 29, 2017).

24 "Strike threat averted as dockworkers reach pay deal with HIT subcontractor," *JOC*, April 24, 2015, www.joc.com/port-news/longshoreman-labor/strike-threat-averted-dockworkers-reach-pay-deal-hit-subcontractors_20150424.html (accessed November 29, 2017).

5

"Work Hard, Make History": Oppression and Resistance in Inland Southern California's Warehouse and Distribution Industry

Ellen Reese and Jason Struna

The warehouse industry, seldom visible to the public, plays a critical role in the contemporary global "just in time" consumer economy. Before consumer goods appear on the shelves in retail stores, they are temporarily stored in warehouses. In addition to receiving and keeping track of these goods, and responding to retailers' or customers' orders for them, blue-collar warehouse workers also prepare these goods for sale. They often package goods and sometimes engage in the final stages of assembling them prior to purchase.[1]

The rise of e-commerce, which has recently outpaced the growth of traditional retail commerce, has further increased the economic role of warehouses by making them the main point of contact between retailers and consumers. Online retailers, such as Amazon, make it easier to shop, sometimes at the touch of a smartphone. Because they offer discount prices for various small items along with the consumer's original purchase, they also add to consumer demand in what has become known as the "Amazon effect."[2] In these ways, the rise of e-commerce has added to the demand for enormous warehouses, sometimes as large as 1 million square feet. Some of these mega-warehouses, such as the Amazon warehouse in Eastvale, California, employ hundreds of workers in an increasingly automated working environment.[3]

"Work hard, make history," Amazon tells its employees in an effort to make the company appear attractive and innovative. Yet for many of its warehouse workers, like those toiling for other companies, working conditions are terrible. Nevertheless, warehouse workers are making history through their innovative and courageous acts of resistance. This chapter provides a case study of blue-collar warehouse workers in Inland Southern California and their efforts to improve their working conditions since 2008. Inland SoCal, located about an hour's drive east of Los Angeles and within Riverside and San Bernardino counties, has quickly become one of the world's largest warehousing hubs. The warehouses in Inland SoCal, making up nearly 1 billion square feet of real estate, receive and store about 25 percent of all goods shipped through the Port of Los Angeles-Long Beach Harbor, the nation's largest port complex. Various retailers, suppliers, and logistics contractors have multiple facilities in the region because of the area's proximity to the ports, transport infrastructure, and relatively cheap labor markets.[4] Indeed, as of 2016, a total of six out of the nine Amazon fulfilment centers located in California were in Inland SoCal.[5]

We argue that warehouse workers' struggle for social justice in Inland SoCal illuminates some of the worst ills of precarious labor under neoliberal capitalism, the tremendous challenges for improving workers' rights in this context, and how innovative labor organizing can help to overcome them. We begin by describing the region's blue-collar warehouse workforce and its grievances. We then examine the efforts of Warehouse Workers United (wwu) and the Warehouse Workers Resource Center (wwrc) to organize and advocate for these workers through collective action and legal action respectively. Already, warehouse workers and their allies have won millions of dollars of back pay and new regulatory legislation to protect warehouse workers in California. We end by considering the future of this industry, particularly in the context of increased automation, and ongoing efforts to organize warehouse workers in this region.

Blue-collar warehouse workers and their discontents

Most blue-collar warehouse workers in Inland SoCal are "marginalized workers," mostly of color, who face multiple kinds of social and economic disadvantage.[6] Many are precarious workers who are subcontracted and/or employed through temporary agencies. In Riverside and San Bernardino counties, they are largely racial/ethnic minorities

(77 percent are Latino/a) while 40 percent are immigrants, mostly from Mexico or Central America. About 76 percent have high school education or less. About 66 percent are men and one-third are women. Most of these workers are also young adults: about 33 percent are 17–25 years old and another 38 percent are between 26 and 40.[7]

As we discuss more fully below, these workers face horrific working conditions.

First, most blue-collar warehouse workers earn poverty-level wages, and at least two-thirds lack employer-provided health insurance. A recent survey by University of California, Riverside (UCR) researchers found that, on average, they earn about $10.05 per hour.[8] This is well below the hourly wage that researchers suggest is needed to afford rent and other basic living expenses: $11.59 per hour for a single worker without dependants and $23.90 for one adult with a dependent child.[9] Temps tend to earn significantly lower wages and have less access to employer-provided health insurance than workers directly hired by warehouse employers and logistics companies. As one study found, only about one out of five temporary warehouse workers reported having employer-provided health insurance, compared with 54 percent of direct hires. On average, direct hires in the industry earned about $11.33 per hour and $21,444 per year. This compares with temps' average earnings of $9.42 per hour and $10,034 per year.[10] According to the 2009–13 American Community Survey (ACS), blue-collar warehouse workers earn an average annual income of only $16,800.[11]

In part, low incomes reflect the lack of year-round employment, and sometimes the lack of full-time employment. Serving "just-in-time" consumer markets, the warehouse industry is highly seasonal. Moreover, in order to respond effectively to the fluctuating market demand for consumer goods in the "just in time" retail economy while minimizing labor costs, many warehouse employers rely heavily on temporary agency workers (or temps).[12] Researchers find that between 46 and 63 percent of blue-collar warehouse workers are temps.[13]

As a result, unemployment and underemployment among warehouse workers is common. Indeed, about 28 percent of all blue-collar warehouse workers in the region were found to be unemployed in the 2009–13 ACS.[14] Unemployment is especially chronic among temps. Juan De Lara found that about 70 percent of all temporary blue collar warehouse workers in Inland SoCal were employed less than 10 months per year.[15]

Warehouse workers' wages and incomes do vary across this industry, with unionized workers typically earning more and having more benefits than non-union workers. For example, a review of sample Teamsters Union contracts covering warehouse workers in the region show that they provide employer-provided health insurance and good wages (ranging from about $17.60 to $31.93 per hour, depending on the employer and workers' seniority). Some contracts also restrict the percentage of workers who can be employed as temps and part-time, and provide other employee benefits, including paid vacations and paid leave for illness, jury duty, and bereavement.[16]

Some employers also treat their workers better than others. Amazon warehouses are considered among the best in the industry relative to wages for both direct hire and temporary agency workers. A job ad posted by Amazon in 2017 for a full-time warehouse worker or "fulfilment associate" position in Rialto offered $12.25 per hour, somewhat better than the regional average wage rate cited above.[17] Yet this wage is still below a living wage for the region, and no higher than the starting rate Amazon paid such workers four years earlier.

Warehouse work is highly strenuous, and it takes a toll on workers' bodies. Workers are often required to repeatedly lift heavy materials, move items quickly from one end of gigantic warehouses to the other, and engage in repetitive motion with fast-paced machinery. Workers are often expected to work 12 hours per day and wear heavy "wearable computers" and printers strapped to their arms or hips. Those who unload trucks must frequently work in triple-digit heat during the summer months, sometimes without adequate work breaks or sufficient access to drinking water. While some warehouses have good climate control, not all do.[18]

Working conditions are often stressful and dangerous. Warehouses commonly compete for work by minimizing labor and other production costs as much as possible. Thus, they pressure workers to work as quickly as possible, and often fail to provide workers, particularly temps, with proper safety equipment and training. Cost-cutting pressures also contribute to neglected machinery and the failure to keep warehouses free from egress obstructions, clutter, and spills.[19]

Even according to official statistics, the warehouse industry had among the highest rates of reported workplace-related injuries among employees nationwide. Yet official statistics rely on employers' reports and so often underestimate the actual incidence of workplace-related injuries. A survey of 103 warehouse workers in Inland SoCal, carried out by University of California Los Angeles (UCLA) researchers and a team of WWU members, suggested that workplace-related injuries and illnesses are commonplace. Nearly 65 percent of surveyed workers reported that they had personally experienced at least one workplace injury in the past year, while 83 percent of workers reported that they had witnessed at least one workplace injury in the past year. About 81 percent of surveyed workers attributed workplace injuries or illnesses to dangerous machinery, while 55 percent attributed them to substances, such as dust or chemicals. Nearly 40 percent claimed that pressure from management to work quickly contributed to workplace-related injuries among warehouse workers.[20] Indeed, because workplace injuries are so frequent some warehouses, including Amazon, even employ on-site emergency medical staff.[21]

Managers following ubiquitous "continuous improvement" models or other forms of total quality management schemes also frequently engage in "management by stress," putting pressure on workers to work as quickly as they can, or intentionally under-staffing particular work tasks to see if they can reduce staffing going forward.[22] As under-staffed workers work frenetically to meet their required work quotas and avoid penalties, they experience workplace accidents and hazards: slips and falls, dropped materials, forklift collisions, failures to keep work stations clean, unsafely stacked materials, and obstructed fire exits.[23]

The implementation of "management by stress" is facilitated by the trackability of labor in warehouses. Wearable computers in many facilities tell workers what goods need to be picked, packed, moved, or stowed, as well as where to find and move them—through either "voice command headsets" or arm-mounted scanners and displays—all the while tracking the number of tasks, time to completion, and number of mistakes in the process. The technology can be used to direct and evaluate workers in order to see if they can meet or exceed predetermined output goals or quotas, as well as discipline workers who are unable to meet demanded output in time. As is common in other industries, warehouse employers rely upon various forms of coordination and control of workers, often in combinations, including piecework, simple hourly quotas, or points systems in which workers lose their jobs for failure to meet the output quotas over a certain amount of time.[24]

Cost-cutting pressures and heavy reliance on "management by stress" contribute to labor law violations in the industry, including violations of health and safety regulations and wage theft. Blue-collar warehouse workers are especially vulnerable to such workplace abuses because they are highly disposable and/or, as undocumented immigrants, vulnerable to deportation. Despite recent legal rulings to the contrary, many warehouse employers also feel less obligated, morally or legally, to ensure safe and legal working conditions for temps, because they employ these workers indirectly and/or for short time periods.[25]

In sum, blue-collar warehouse jobs tend to be low-wage and precarious "brown collar" jobs which are most commonly filled by young Latino/as with high school education or less.[26] Because warehouse jobs are often temporary and/or seasonal, warehouse workers chronically suffer from unemployment or under-employment, and most lack access to employer-provided health insurance. The work is often physically taxing and dangerous. Workplace accidents and labor law violations are fairly common in the industry. Such working conditions have made many warehouse workers ripe for organizing.

Challenging industry leaders in Inland SoCal

In 2008, the Change to Win federation established WWU with the goal of organizing warehouse workers in Inland SoCal and improving their working conditions through collective action. In 2011, in order to provide additional resources and legal assistance to warehouse workers in Southern California, WWU staff and their allies formed WWRC, a nonprofit workers' center.

WWU did not pursue a traditional unionization campaign for several reasons. First, temps are highly vulnerable to employer retaliation, while undocumented immigrant workers face the further threat of deportation. Organizing temps into unions is not only practically challenging given their high turnover, but also legally complicated, as their employer of record and right to collective bargaining are complex and decided on a case by case basis. In light of this, WWU sought to improve warehouse workers' employment conditions mainly through a combination of coalition building and collective action, while WWRC helped workers to file formal complaints against labor law violations.[27]

Rather than targeting warehouse employers or temporary agencies, WWU targeted retailers, which have the most power and resources in the goods movement industry. WWU organizers chose to target Walmart for several reasons, besides its being a highly visible transnational corporation popularly known for its cheap goods and questionable labor practices.[28]

First, in 2010 the Change to Win union federation and other organizations like UniGlobal, a global union representing workers from over 150 countries, had begun a coordinated, transnational campaign targeting Walmart throughout its supply chain from producers to retail outlets. The broader Making Change at Walmart campaign included the United Food and Commercial Workers Union (UFCW) campaign organizing Walmart employees, as well as various labor organizations that represented workers employed by Walmart's subcontractors. These included WWU as well as several other groups organizing warehouse workers in the United States, namely Warehouse Workers for Justice in Chicago and New Labor in New Jersey. It also involved the Teamsters, who were organizing port truckers, the National Guestworkers Alliance, and other organizations engaged in labor-organizing drives at other goods movement and production facilities domestically and globally, from Bangladesh to Chile, across Walmart's global supply chain.[29] The transnational supply chain strategy sought to build workers' power against Walmart, a target that has effectively used capital mobility to undermine worker power amongst its employees and contractors.[30]

Second, by engaging in the transnational supply chain campaign, WWU could use the coalitional power and media attention that the Making Change at Walmart campaign generated to gain public and political support for its own specific policy goals.[31] Given the difficulties of seeking change from local policy-makers in Inland SoCal, where Republicans had long dominated, WWU and WWRC sought to "scale up" and target state policy-makers, namely state regulatory agencies and California legislators.[32] Through their participation in the anti-Walmart campaign and a series of well-publicized legal and administrative cases, WWU and WWRC gained media and political attention to health and safety problems, wage and hour violations, and other systemic problems in the warehouse industry.

WWRC helped workers file legal or administrative complaints about labor law violations by Walmart warehouse contractors and their temporary agency. WWU, meanwhile, protected the workers involved in these complaints and other organizing efforts against employer retaliation through Unfair Labor Practice [ULP] strikes, online petitions, and other collective actions. Such ULPs frequently served as focal points to mobilize workers and allies for public demonstrations, and helped show the commonality of bad working conditions in Walmart's supply chain.

Together, WWU and WWRC gained greater state oversight over working conditions in the industry, and won a series of legal and administrative cases involving warehouse workers. Organized warehouse workers' collective actions and workers' complaints about illegal working conditions generated media and public attention.[33]

To gain even more publicity, WWU and its allies organized a 50-mile, United Farm Workers-style march from WWU offices in Ontario to City Hall in Los Angeles. "Walmarch," as organizers called it, coincided with a 15-day ULP strike aimed at Walmart cross-dock contractor Swift Transportation, and Warestaff, the temp agency used as one of the employers of record for the massive facility. Health and safety violations that eventually resulted in fines and other corrective sanctions included faulty equipment and dock safety protocols, as well as lack of access to clean, potable water: workers had been instructed to drink from an outdoor garden hose adjacent to rat traps, and were provided with powdered Gatorade to mask the unpalatability of the water. The conditions at the facility—operating on a more or less 24-hour basis for the world's largest retailer, and serving one of its largest markets— were bad enough to provoke roughly ten workers to spontaneously join the strike and Walmarch for its entire duration after having refused to cross the picket line.[34]

Hundreds of supporters from various union and community organizations joined the Walmarchers at various strategic rally points like Walmart parking lots, East LA Community College, and LA City Hall, generating considerable media coverage. The Walmarch demonstrated public support for organized warehouse workers, and put additional political pressure on state legislators to improve regulation of the industry. At the culmination of the march, the Brown administration announced that the governor would sign a WWU-sponsored bill that required firms and temp agencies to guarantee that they had sufficient funds for workers' wages and to comply with existing labor law. Additionally, shortly after the march Walmart announced its intention to execute random inspections of its contractors' facilities to enhance their compliance with safety standards.[35]

The campaign thus demonstrated the effectiveness of symbolic power and coalitional power for increasing the influence of marginalized workers.[36] Symbolic power refers to the power of naming to draw broader public and political support for a cause by appealing to social justice ideals and legal norms. Coalitional power refers to the power organized workers gain through expanding the scope of conflict and building alliances with non-labor groups in order to increase their visibility and leverage.

The organization also amassed an impressive record with its legal and regulatory strategy. Focusing on warehouse firms and temporary agencies contracted or subcontracted with Walmart, warehouse workers, with help from WWRC, won a series of administrative cases involving wage theft or health and safety violations through the California Occupational Health and Safety Administration (CalOSHA) and the California Labor Commission. Further, in 2013, warehouse workers supported by WWRC secured a $4.7 million legal settlement from Schneider Logistics, a Walmart contractor, for nearly 600 workers.

In another case involving Schneider, the organization also succeeded in naming Walmart as a codefendant. While the case settled before adjudication, the US District Court's allowance that Walmart could be considered as possibly responsible for the working conditions in its contract firms' facilities served as a warning to the industry that the blurry legal boundaries of retailers, warehouses, and temp agencies might not protect them from legal liability up the chain. Indeed, the class action suit initiated by workers affiliated with WWRC settled for $21 million in 2014.[37]

Altogether, through the anti-Walmart campaign, Inland SoCal warehouse workers won an impressive series of legal/administrative victories, new state regulations for the warehouse industry, and improvement in Walmart's policies towards worker safety. Even so, the campaign did not succeed in unionizing workers, and UFCW, the major funder for the WWU campaign at the time, pulled most of its funding in 2014. Since 2014, education, advocacy, and organizing among warehouse workers has been sustained through WWRC, which has been financed through grants and donations.

Since 2014, WWRC has helped warehouse workers to pursue successful legal claims against labor law violations, with other cases still pending. One such case awarded more than $80,000 in back wages to 10 warehouse workers employed by Waitex who experienced various forms of wage and hours violations, including not being paid overtime or given their work breaks.[38] Another legal case contributed support for SB1167, signed into law in 2016, which requires CalOSHA to propose new regulations by 2019 to better protect indoor workers from heat illness and injuries. In that case, the California Occupational Safety and

Health Appeals Board ruled in favor of a worker's complaints that a warehouse operator and temporary staffing agency failed to adequately protect him against injury and illness. The worker, Domingo Blancas, was hospitalized for heat stroke and required emergency surgery after working in a warehouse in the heat of summer in 2011.[39] Other cases, some successful and others still pending, involve warehouse workers who handle goods for California Cartage. Along with Teamsters-affiliated port-truckers, these workers have organized a series of strikes in protest against employer retaliation and other labor law violations by this company.[40]

The specter of automation

Automation threatens to eliminate hundreds of thousands of blue-collar warehouse jobs. Currently, various labor-intensive tasks involved in moving goods within warehouses, formerly carried out by hand by blue-collar workers, are being supplemented or replaced by robotics and artificial intelligence. Research is also under way to further automate forklifts and picking tasks.[41]

Amazon, seeking to take over more logistics functions globally, has been a driving force for logistics automation.[42] Since 2012, it has used orange Kiva robots to bring goods from robot-organized product shelves to warehouse workers at packing stations—allowing for roughly double the productivity of conventional hand-picking methods.[43] Amazon announced that by January 2017 it had 45,000 Kiva automated guided vehicles in its distribution centers worldwide.[44] As other firms vie to keep up with the robotic revolution by deploying their own systems, pressures on employment, and ever-increasing scales of real estate demand, will grow as well.

The counter-pressures of increasing size of facilities—the "World Logistics Center" in Riverside County, California will comprise a single campus with 40 million square feet of warehousing space alone[45]—and increasing automation are likely to have massive environmental and employment impacts on local communities. The promise that the facility will create "20,000 jobs" must be tempered with the realities of automation in a future where 47 percent of all jobs in the United States have the potential of being automated in the next decade.[46] Indeed, warehousing and distribution appear to be leading sectors for automation alongside the trucking industry, with Amazon actively funding research towards that effort.[47] Much organizing will be needed to help blue-collar warehouse workers facing this automation threat to remain employed and/or to obtain severance pay and job training.

Conclusion

The logistics sector has become a key choke point for global consumer capitalism, particularly its under-paid workforce. Our case study of the warehouse industry in Inland SoCal suggests that there are many grievances among blue-collar warehouse workers that make them ripe for organizing: poverty-level wages and incomes, temporary employment, the lack of employer-provided health insurance, unsafe working conditions, wage theft, and chronic unemployment.

The stark contrast between the wages and benefits of unionized and non-unionized warehouse workers demonstrates the continued importance of "worksite-based organizing, where workers are aided by skilled organizers, but not replaced by them."[48]

Yet unionization in the United States, as elsewhere, remains extremely challenging under neoliberal global capitalism. When workers organize and seek to form unions, they increasingly face the threat of capital flight and other forms of employer retaliation, while undocumented immigrant workers frequently face the threat of deportation.[49]

Organizing low-wage logistics workers into unions is especially challenging because so many of them are temps and/or employed through subcontractors. Despite recent legal victories for temps' rights to collective bargaining, temporary agency employment continues to present serious legal as well as practical complications for unionization. As WWU's organizing efforts illustrate, employers readily retaliate against organizing workers, sometimes by failing to renew their contracts with temporary agencies.[50]

In this context, we must continue to press for labor law reforms and enforcement to protect workers' rights to organize, but we should also think "outside the box" in terms of labor organizing and advocacy strategies. As the warehouse workers' anti-Walmart campaign demonstrated, it is possible to win victories for non-unionized workers through a combination of legal advocacy and social justice organizing for policy gains, and to do so in alliance with other workers linked through a global supply chain.

Since 2014, WWRC has continued to mobilize warehouse workers in

Inland SoCal and Los Angeles, seeking political and legal redress for their grievances at state and local levels. WWRC is currently working with other unions and community organizations to improve the region's economic development policies and to shift the balance of regional political power. In doing so, it is building new community–labor alliances around shared concerns regarding working conditions, traffic congestion, access to green space, and air pollution. WWRC is also at the forefront of the struggle to expand workers' legal rights, continuing to promote improved heat regulations for indoor workers in California, and working in alliance with others to pursue new state laws for temporary workers' rights.

Warehouse workers have the capacity to make history, but not as they please—the circumstances inherited require innovation and novel forms of organizing and resistance.[51] The obstacles to organizing posed by capital mobility, automation, political/legal uncertainty and the sheer structural power of capital requires multi-site, coordinated campaigns throughout the global supply chain and across the boundaries of firms. Workers face the daunting task of overcoming the tension between local demands and the demands of workers in other nodes of supply chain networks. Yet these impediments are not insurmountable. Just as capital has adapted new organizational forms to overcome the power of workers in the past, warehouse workers and other workers can and will adapt novel organizational forms in their struggle against neoliberalism and global capitalist hegemony.

Acknowledgments

The authors wish to thank the members and staff of the Warehouse Workers Resource Center and Warehouse Workers United campaign without whom this research would have been possible. UCR surveys of warehouse workers were carried out with the assistance of undergraduate student researchers and funded by the UC-Institute for Research on Labor and Employment, the UC Humanities Research Institute, and the UC Center for Collaborative Research for an Equitable California.

Notes

1   Edna Bonacich and Jake B. Wilson, *Getting the Goods: Ports, Labor, and the Logistics Revolution* (New York: Cornell University Press, 2008);

Jason Struna, Kevin Curwin, Edwin Elias, Ellen Reese, Tony Roberts, and Elizabeth Bingle, "Unsafe and unfair: labor conditions in the warehouse industry," *Policy Matters* (University of California, Riverside) 5(2) (2012), pp. 1–11, http://policymatters.ucr.edu/wp-content/uploads/2014/10/pmatters-vol5-2-warehouse.pdf (accessed May 2017).

2   Shorr.com, "The Amazon effect: impacts on shipping and retail," 2015, www.shorr.com/packaging-news/2015-06/amazon-effect-impacts-shipping-and-retail (accessed May 2017).

3   Fielding Buck, "Logistics: what Amazon means to Eastvale," *The Press Enterprise*, May 26, 2016, www.pe.com/2016/05/26/logistics-what-amazon-means-to-eastvale/ (accessed May 2017); Nick Heath, "Amazon, robots, and the near-future rise of the automated warehouse," *TechRepublic*, January 26, 2016, www.techrepublic.com/article/amazon-robots-and-the-near-future-rise-of-the-automated-warehouse/ (accessed May 2017).

4   Bonacich and Wilson (2008); Struna et al. (2012).

5   Buck (2016).

6   Jennifer Chun, *Organizing at the Margins: The Symbolic Politics of Labor in South Korea and the United States* (Ithaca, N.Y.: Cornell University Press, 2009).

7   Juliann Allison, Joel Herrera, and Ellen Reese, "Why the City of Ontario needs to raise the minimum wage: earnings among warehouse workers in Inland Southern California," UCLA Institute for Research on Labor and Employment, Research & Policy Brief, 36 (2015), pp. 1–10, www.irle.ucla.edu/publications/documents/ResearchBrief_Reese36.pdf (accessed May 2017).

8   Juliann Allison, Joel Herrera, Mila Huston, and Ellen Reese, "Health care needs and access among warehouse workers in Southern California," UCLA Institute for Research on Labor and Employment, Research & Policy Brief, 35 (2015), pp. 1–10. www.irle.ucla.edu/publications/documents/ResearchBrief_Reese35.pdf (accessed May 2017).

9   A. Glasmeir, Living wage calculation for Riverside, California, 2015, http://livingwage.mit.edu/counties/06065 (accessed May 2017).

10   Allison et al. (2015).

11   Allison et al. (2015).

12   Bonacich and Wilson (2008); Juan De Lara, "Warehouse work: path to the middle class or road to economic insecurity?" USC Program for Environmental and Regional Equity (PERE), September 2013, https://dornsifecms.usc.edu/assets/sites/242/docs/WarehouseWorkerPay_web.pdf (accessed May 2017).

13   Because "staffing services" is considered a distinct industry in government statistics, estimates of the percentage of blue-collar warehouse workers who are employed as temps vary somewhat: Allison et al. (2015).

14   Allison et al. (2015).

15   De Lara (2013).

16   Personal communication with Teamsters International staff, May 31, 2017.

17 See https://search.amazondelivers.jobs/job/rialto/full-time-fulfill ment-associate/3413/4500245 (accessed May 2017).

18 Jason Struna, *Handling Globalization: Labor, Capital, and Class in the Globalized Warehouse and Distribution Center*, PhD dissertation, UCR (2015).

19 Struna et al. (2012).

20 Struna et al. (2012).

21 The Amazon Jobs site has several ads for "onsite medical representative" (see www.amazon.jobs/en/jobs/528374). Minimum qualifications for the Nevada ad include "Valid State EMT-Basic Certification from the Department of Health from the state you are working in and/or valid National Registry of Emergency Medical Technicians (NREMT) certification."

22 Mike Parker and Jane Slaughter, "Management-by-stress: management's ideal," in M. Parker and J. Slaughter (eds.), *Working Smart: A Union Guide to Participation Programs and Reengineering* (Detroit, Mich.: Labor Notes, 1994), pp. 24–38.

23 Struna (2015); Struna et al. (2012).

24 Richard Edwards, *Contested Terrain: The Transformation of the Workplace in the Twentieth Century* (New York: Basic Books, 1979); Struna (2015).

25 Struna et al. (2012); Juan De Lara, Ellen Reese, and Jason Struna, "Organizing temporary, subcontracted, and immigrant workers, " *Labor Studies Journal* 41(4) (2016), pp. 1–23.

26 Lisa Catanzarite, "Brown-collar jobs: occupational segregation and earnings of recent-immigrant Latinos," *Sociological Perspectives* 43(1) (2000), pp. 45–75.

27 De Lara et al. (2016).

28 Gary Gereffi and M. Christian, "The impacts of Wal-Mart: the rise and consequences of the world's dominant retailer," *Annual Review of Sociology* 35 (2009), pp. 573–91.

29 De Lara et al. (2016).

30 Marissa Brookes, "Varieties of power in transnational labor campaigns: understanding workers' structural, institutional, and coalitional power in the global economy," *Labor Studies Journal* 38(3) (2013), pp.181–200; Gereffi and Christian (2009); Stephanie Luce, *Labor Movements: Global Perspective* (Cambridge: Polity Press, 2014).

31 Brookes (2013) defines "coalitional power" as "the capacity of workers to expand the scope of conflict by involving other, nonlabor actors willing and able to influence an employer's behavior" (p. 192).

32 Luce (2014).

33 De Lara et al. (2016).

34 De Lara et al. (2016); Luce (2014); Struna (2015).

35 De Lara et al. (2016); Struna (2015).

36 Chun (2009); Brookes (2017).

37 De Lara et al. (2016).

38 WWRC, "Waitex warehouse workers win $80,000 in back wages," 2017, www.warehouseworkers.org/waitexdlse/ (accessed May 2017).

39 Atkinson, Andelson, Loya, Ruud, & Romo, "New California law protects workers from indoor heat exposure," *Lexology*, October 20, 2016, www.lexology.com/library/detail.aspx?g=079a7316-11be-4119-b896-296a7e27c915 (accessed May 2017); WWRC (2017).

40 Teamsters.org, "Warehouse workers protest retaliation with strike," *Teamsters News*, April 6, 2016, https://teamster.org/news/2016/04/warehouse-workers-protest-retaliation-strike (accessed May 2017).

41 Heath (2016).

42 Patrick Clark and Kim Bhasin, "Amazon's robot war is spreading," *Bloomberg Technology*, April 5, 2017, www.bloomberg.com/news/articles/2017-04-05/robots-enlist-humans-to-win-the-warehouse-war-amazon-started (accessed May 2017).

43 S. Wingo, "An inside perspective on Amazon's purchase of Kiva Systems (or Domo Arigato, Mr. Roboto)," *ChannelAdvisor*, March 20, 2012, www.channeladvisor.com/blog/scot/an-inside-perspective-on-amazons-purchase-of-kiva-systems-or-domo-arigato-mr-roboto/ (accessed May 2017).

44 Sam Shead, "Amazon now has 45,000 robots in its warehouses," *Business Insider*, January 3, 2017, www.businessinsider.com/amazons-robot-army-has-grown-by-50-2017-1 (accessed May 2017).

45 Imran Ghori, "All you need to know about the World Logistics Center," *Press Enteprise*, August 19, 2016 (updated May 3, 2017), www.pe.com/2016/08/19/all-you-need-to-know-about-the-world-logistics-center/ (accessed May 2017).

46 Carl B. Frey and Michael A. Osborne, "The future of employment: how susceptible are jobs to computerisation?" Technological Forecasting and Social Change, 114 (2013), pp. 254–80.

47 Jonathan Camhi and Stephanie Pandolph, "Amazon looks to further logistics automation," *Business Insider*, April 26, 2017, www.businessinsider.com/amazon-looks-to-further-logistics-automation-2017-4 (accessed May 2017).

48 Jane McAlevey, "The crisis of new labor and Alinsky's legacy: revisiting the role of the organic grassroots leaders in building powerful organizations and movement," *Politics and Society* 43(3) (2015), p. 437.

49 Luce (2014); Kate Bronfenbrenner, "No holds barred: the intensification of employer opposition to organizing," Briefing Paper No. 235, Economic Policy Institute, Washington DC (2009), www.epi.org/publication/bp235/ (accessed July 28, 2016).

50 De Lara et al.(2016).

51 Paraphrasing Karl Marx, "The Eighteenth Brumaire of Louis Bonaparte," in K. Marx and F. Engels, *Basic Writings on Politics and Philosophy*, ed. L. S. Feuer (New York: Anchor, 1959 [1852]).

6

"Stop Treating Us Like Dogs!" Workers Organizing Resistance at Amazon in Poland

Amazon workers and supporters

In the first part of this chapter we present the conditions at work in Amazon warehouses in Poland, the technology used, and the effects on workers' health: in other words, the daily experience of exploitation in one of the largest global logistics enterprises. This constitutes the background of our experience of organizing and resistance described in the second part: our attempts to build up workers' power—something that has to happen at the workplace and by workers themselves (and not, as some propose, by "customers" from the outside). In the third part we turn to some of the challenges we are facing and to our attempts to build a solidarity network that we want to develop further.

Amazon goes to Poland

Amazon was founded in 1994 as an online bookstore but since then has grown into a conglomerate active in online sales, global logistics, IT services, cloud computing, TV productions, book publishing, and more. Amazon's online sales platform sells all kinds of goods, which are delivered to customers through Amazon's own warehouses. The company operates more than 400 delivery, distribution, and sorting warehouses in the Americas, Europe, and Asia. In early 2017, it employed more than 340,000 people, and the number is still rising.[1]

In 2014, Amazon set up its first warehouses in Poland, one close to Poznań and two close to Wroclaw. Two more will open in the fall of 2017 near Szczecin and in Sosnowiec (close to Katowice), and there are rumours that one more is planned for 2018 close to Łódź.[2] Amazon's Polish warehouses service customers in neighbouring Germany, not in Poland.[3] What make Eastern European countries like Poland attractive for logistics and industrial capital are not the local consumers but labor costs that are significantly lower than in Western Europe, capital-friendly labor laws, cheap land, and tax bonuses offered by the state. Eastern European regions adjacent to Germany and Austria especially are well connected to Western European consumer markets, with a growing network of airports and motorways. So it is not surprising that Amazon did not just choose Poland to expand its distribution network, but has also invested in the Czech Republic and will open a facility in Slovakia soon.

Dual employment strategy

Amazon Poland relies on a dual employment strategy, hiring permanent workers directly and adding large numbers of temporary agency workers. While there is some seasonal change in the demand or number of orders—for instance, in the pre-Christmas period—Amazon also exaggerates these seasonal changes and uses them as an excuse for the employment of large numbers of temporary agency workers it can hire and fire. In May 2017, Amazon Poland employed about 6,800 warehouse workers directly and 4,000 workers through temporary agencies like Adecco and Randstad. Before the last peak season (Christmas 2016), Amazon announced it would hire an additional 16,000 temporary agency workers.[4]

Lousy conditions

In the cities close to the existing warehouses, Poznań and Wrocław, the unemployment rate is low, and regarding terms of employment, wages, and promotion opportunities, working at Amazon is not particularly attractive—especially for urban workers with other job opportunities.[5] As a result, Amazon has to rely on hiring a large part of its labor force from villages within a 120 kilometre radius around its warehouses, and organizing their transport with buses. For the workers this means long hours of commuting: most spend more than 12 hours—some up to 17 hours—per day away from home.

Like other logistics warehouses, Amazon's are made up of two main departments, "inbound" divided into dock (unloading), receive (unpacking and registering) and stow (storage and shelving), and the larger "outbound" divided into pick (taking down from shelves), pack and AFE (Amazon Fulfillment Engine, or packaging), ICQA (quality control), and ship (shipment). Different warehouse departments are connected by conveyor lines that move goods destined for storage, packaging, or shipment, while few departments use transport robots, for instance for moving shelves.

Most workers use scanners and computers connected to Amazon's (global) IT network, which processes all information on the location of goods, orders, and so on. Despite the use of this technology, the operation of the warehouse mainly relies on physical work. Most employees have to work standing or walking (some for several miles during one shift), and many jobs involve highly repetitive movements, lifting heavy goods and boxes, or pushing heavy carts. Amazon wants the warehouses running day and night. Therefore workers in Poland have to work four 10-hour shifts per week, with an additional unpaid 30 minutes break. The shifts schedule changes every month from day shift (6:30 a.m. to 5:00 p.m.) to night shift (6:00 p.m. to 4:30 a.m.). Such a shift system and shift rotation disturbs workers' sleeping rhythm and leads to serious health problems. In addition, it makes it difficult to organize a private life.

Work as hell

Amazon allows workers to log into a system that monitors each worker's performance, and the data is used to set their obligatory work rates, such as the demanded number of products scanned per hour. As long as they do not do anything that can be registered in the system (like "scanning goods") the system records "time off task." That means that even if they work—doing something that is not registered—this time is recorded as taking a break. Such periods are added up and calculated as illegitimate "extra breaks." If workers do not meet the rates (that is, they work "too slowly") or have too many "extra breaks," they get negative "feedback," and after several "feedbacks" they can get a warning and eventually be sacked.

Trying to reach the rates is stressful enough, but even worse are days when Amazon tries to set "records," like 1 million orders processed in one warehouse within 24 hours. Warehouses compete with each other, and Amazon uses those days to push workers to the limit, ordering obligatory overtime and cancelling breaks before midnight.

If workers reach the demanded "record," managers get an extra bonus and workers get T-shirts.[6]

Amazon's search for maximum labor intensity is also illustrated by the way the AFE department is organized. AFE is a special department in "pack." Ordered goods are "picked" from storage before entering the AFE process, where they are scanned, sorted, and put into bins, which are put on a special conveyor belt. So-called rebinners take the goods out of the bins and put them on shelves. On the other side of the same shelves, workers take goods out and put them into a box, close it, paste on a barcode and throw the box onto another belt that leads to "ship."

AFE is more computerized and automated than the regular "pack" department. For the workers that means the work is even harder. Along the shelves lights indicate which goods have to be packed first. If the shelves are full of red lights it means packers are working too slowly. In their attempt to prevent the flashing of too many red lights, workers start hurrying and checking the work speed of colleagues too. The result is a competitive atmosphere, a permanent state of emergency as rebinners and packers rush to make the flashing lights disappear while team leaders and so-called process guides at their back yell what workers should do.[7]

Amazon makes workers sick

The continuous stress, noise, physical exhaustion, and lack of time to rest between shifts affect workers' health. The heavy workload, running, and lifting particularly place stress on joints, feet, and backs. No wonder the sickness rate among permanent workers is high.[8] For workers, going on sick leave is a way to get a rest and "repair" their health, but for Amazon it is a cost factor. To bring down the sickness rate, Amazon Poland hired a company in spring 2017 which checks whether workers are at home during sick leave. A worker who was dismissed because of a sick leave wrote: "At Amazon we hear about safety every day, about health, but the reality is different. Not everyone can keep up the race at Amazon. People are treated like machines. But even machines fail and stand still. We are not allowed to do that."[9]

Organizing and struggle

In late 2014, a few months after the warehouse opened, a group of Amazon workers in Poznań set up a section of the grassroots union

Inicjatywa Pracownicza (IP, or Workers' Initiative), a union without paid staff, based on self-organizing and self-empowerment of workers.[10] At the time, rank-and-file workers and team leaders were involved, but since then the union section has been primarily made up of rank-and-file workers. Currently it has a membership of about 400.

The issues the workers raised were higher wages, bonuses, benefits, longer breaks, long-term work schedules, and more. The union started leafleting and organized several petitions, for instance on work schedules and on rates, which hundreds of workers signed. The management of Amazon Poland had to allow the setting-up of the union section (in compliance with Polish union law) but tried to limit union activity on company premises, and ignored or rejected all workers' demands voiced in early 2015. During the same period, IP activists made first contact with workers from Amazon in Germany. They met for several grassroots "cross-border" meetings in Germany and in Poland, attended by a handful to a few dozen workers. The first result of these meetings was that workers in both Poland and Germany learned about each other's wages and working conditions as well as their experiences of struggle. Workers in Poland heard, for instance, that in Germany, the mainstream union Ver.di had started an organizing drive at Amazon a few years earlier. Since 2013 it has been calling for short, usually local strikes to force Amazon to sign a bargaining contract—so far without success. The strikes have mostly relied on rank-and-file activists, with those in the warehouses in Bad Hersfeld and Leipzig being the most active and militant.[11]

The slowdown(s)

Before a strike in Germany in June 2015, the management the Poznań warehouse announced one hour of overtime during the upcoming strike day across the border. Workers in Poznań were already aware that Amazon tried to bypass and undermine strikes in Germany by shifting orders between warehouses (in this case to Poland). Growing local tensions in the Poznań warehouse and the prospect of being used as scabs led to vivid discussions among workers on how to resist. Eventually, during the night shift on June 24–25, 2015, a few dozen workers improvised a slowdown in one department, taking advantage of a bottleneck in the processing of orders and disturbing operations in other parts of the warehouse. They showed a collective will to resist, their solidarity with workers on strike in Germany, and a keen knowledge of the work process and how to disrupt it.

Afterwards, workers were summoned by managers for questioning. Some declared they deliberately slowed down their work and would do it again. Several people were suspended and sacked, and some signed a contract termination agreement and left. Currently, some cases are still pending in the labor courts.[12] Soon afterwards Amazon raised the hourly wage by 1 zloty (about 8 percent), but it denied that the raise had anything to do with workers' organizing and the slowdown.[13] Another smaller spontaneous slowdown happened before Christmas 2016, when some workers in the AFE department significantly slowed down the packing process for a few hours, citing safety regulations. Team leaders tried to replace the workers but were not trained enough to do so efficiently.

Both slowdowns were not just responses to low wages and work intensification but also protests against management strategies which force workers to compete, demand complete subordination, and undermine workers' dignity. After the slowdown in AFE, one of the workers shouted at the pre-shift stand-up meeting: "Stop treating us like dogs!"

The strike ballot

After the first slowdown in June 2015, IP started an official collective bargaining process demanding, besides other things, a wage increase to 16 zlotys (20 to 25 percent more) and a different calculation of breaks (as workers lost a lot of break time walking to the canteens). When negotiations and mandatory mediation ended without agreement, IP could not call for a strike although more than 97 percent of those participating in the strike ballot voted for strike. Polish labor law, one of the most restrictive in Europe, requires a ballot with a turnout of at least 50 percent of the entire workforce and a majority vote. At Amazon Poland, only 30 percent of the workforce participated in the ballot.[14] Still, more than 2,000 workers—directly employed and temporary agency workers—voted for strike, a clear sign of the discontent among Amazon's workforce.[15]

The strike ballot was lost, but it made IP's organizing drive, the conflict about working conditions, and the resistance more visible to all Amazon workers in Poland. Amazon Poland raised the hourly wages again by 1 zloty (to 15 zlotys, plus an extra zloty for senior workers), offered higher bonuses, and made more concessions, which can again be seen as a result of the workers' pressure and the continuing labor shortage.

The survey

With Amazon not willing to negotiate and Polish labor law putting up high obstacles against a strike, IP's Amazon section decided to ask the workers what to do next. In April and May 2017, it conducted a survey among workers, with questionnaires available in the canteen and online, to learn more about their expectations and demands, and plan further steps.[16]

According to the survey, the most important demand is an increase in the basic wage by another 30 percent (chosen by nearly 70 percent of participants), and many workers also demanded wages and bonuses similar to those at Amazon in France and Germany (chosen by more than 40 percent).[17] More than 20 percent of the participating workers demanded long-term work schedules (not just monthly schedules), to have more control over the shift schedule in general, like the ability to chose certain shifts, and the end of arbitrary transfers of workers between departments. Amazon has previously rejected such changes, claiming that the company needs to remain flexible to serve customers, but this clearly contradicts workers' interest.

In the questionnaires workers also mentioned the lack of time during breaks. This problem persists, and workers keep losing a big part of their break time walking to the canteen (for instance, the Poznań warehouse is as big as 13 soccer fields). And they mention recurrent conflicts about work rates. In other words, the evaluation of workers' performance is seen as arbitrary and unjust, and insecurity is produced by short-term temporary agency contracts. Regarding labor actions, more than 40 percent favored more petitions and other protests, and slightly fewer proposed that trade union officials and shop stewards should be more visible at the workplace, with more leaflets and a trade union newspaper. These demands show the desire for more "open" organizing, but that clashes with Amazon's strategy of limiting, silencing, and downplaying workers' activity and protest.

Daily struggle against subordination

This points to another level of struggle, the daily confrontations at the workplaces as Amazon continuously refines its control mechanisms.

Workers usually do not react with collectively organized protests, but with multiple (minor) acts of disobedience like starting breaks early, working slowly, rejecting tasks, using gaps in the system, challenging decisions of superiors, regularly visiting the toilet or otherwise leaving the workplace, and simulating accidents. Amazon is unable to completely subordinate the workers' activities to the rhythm of the warehouse machine.

Challenges and solidarity

The organizing drive has encountered a series of problems. Following the slowdown and the strike ballot, Amazon increased the pressure on activist workers. While initially, workers were allowed to speak during the pre-shift meetings and general assemblies called "all hands," this was limited after workers had used them to voice complains and demands. Amazon also tried to prevent regular leafleting outside the warehouses. It assigned IP activists to the most boring and tedious positions, and frequently transfers them so they do not form closer relations to colleagues. Amazon also tries to get rid of union activists and senior workers in general, and to replace them with temporary agency workers without experience (and without the opportunity to take sick leave).

Workers from temporary agencies are in a more precarious situation. They are under pressure to work hard (should they want to "qualify" for permanent employment) and can be sacked easily. Some of them have been active in the union, and IP has tried to get them involved by addressing their specific situation, organizing rallies in front of agency offices, starting collective bargaining processes in the agencies, and including them in the strike ballot—but it remains difficult to bridge the gap created by the dual employment structure.

The high labor turnover at Amazon is because of not only temporary agency work but also the fact that often permanent workers quit the job because they are tired and fed up with the conditions. This represents a challenge for IP, too. Quitting can be seen as a sign of discontent and resistance, but also weakens the union as members leave and drop out of union activities. To keep its strength and numbers, the union constantly has to recruit new members, which absorbs a lot of resources. So far IP has not managed to include the many other logistics workers in the region in the organizing effort, especially as many former Amazon workers who were part of IP have switched jobs and found other employment in the region—a good chance to get involved in workers' struggles there as well. The organizing experiences at Amazon Poland also show the limits of "official" or "formal" union activity, meaning the limits imposed by labor laws and the "representative" form of a union, for instance during collective bargaining processes and strike ballots. The Amazon section of IP has organized a number of less formal activities, often with the help of supporters, such as rallies, and it has got involved in activity organized autonomously, such as debates on social media where workers share experiences with others, and spread information to the press. And of course, workers have become active themselves outside the legal framework, as during the slowdowns and other acts of defiance at work.

No Solidarity from Solidarność

Solidarity has been organized to connect permanent workers and temporary agency workers at Amazon, and in some cases workers from other sectors organized in IP supported the Amazon section, for example theatre workers from Poznań who demanded that their theatre stop sponsorship relations with Amazon, referring to the latter's work practices. Meanwhile, a particularly annoying conflict was provoked by the mainstream Polish union *Solidarność*, which has far more members in general in Poland but a weaker stance in Amazon warehouses. While IP has its strongest presence in the Poznań warehouse, *Solidarność* is mainly present in the warehouses close to Wrocław, but has not managed to organize as many workers as IP. *Solidarność* tries to sell itself to Amazon as a collaborative and "reasonable" union, while publicly attacking IP for being too "radical" and irresponsible.

Besides its union activity, *Solidarność* focuses on culturally conservative and religious issues, and actively supports the current right-wing Polish government run by the party PiS. This has not prevented nominally left-leaning mainstream unions in other European countries from building organizational ties with *Solidarność*, for example including them in the "international" federation UNI Global Union.[18] In recent years, German Ver.di has been trying to build a campaign around Amazon through UNI Global Union. As part of that, *Solidarność* has received financial support for hiring professional organisers at Amazon Poland. So far these attempts have been rather unsuccessful. Rather than fighting Amazon, *Solidarność* seems to focus more on attacking IP, undermining both workers' solidarity and IP's drive to increase pressure on Amazon.[19]

Cross-border Amazon workers' meetings

Workers' struggles at Amazon need to be coordinated beyond one country if they are to be efficient. Amazon warehouses in Europe are part of one distribution network, and—as warehouses in different regions store the same items—orders can be shifted from one warehouse to another if problems arise, such as bad weather, traffic jams or worker protests. However, UNI Global Union, Ver.di and *Solidarność* stand for social partnership and business unionism as well as leadership control (top-down) where union bureaucrats (hired by other union bureaucrats and beyond the control of workers) decide on union strategies.[20] As a critique and alternative, and to allow workers to directly discuss strategies of resistance, Amazon workers from Poland and supporters initiated cross-border meetings of Amazon workers which have been attended by workers from Poland and Germany and later from France too.[21]

Five such cross-border Amazon workers' meetings have taken place so far in Poland, Germany, and France, and more are planned. The meetings are organized "beyond" union memberships and hierarchies. In other words all Amazon workers and supporters are welcome, as the goal is to build workers' power and solidarity beyond the competition of union organizations. Only a few dozen workers have so far actively attended, but the cross-border meetings proved valuable for exchanging information on wages, bonuses, labor contracts, and labor court cases, and the information has been used in leaflets and statements, and found its way into workers' discussions at the workplace and demands to local managements.

The self-organized cooperation changed the perspective of many workers, who had previously seen colleagues "across the border" rather as competitors with higher/lower wages, but now see them as potential allies against a common enemy. The slowdown in the Poznań warehouse in June 2015 was partly a solidarity action for striking Amazon workers in Germany, and a practical expression of such "cross-border" reference and practical support. After the first meetings, which mainly offered space for information exchange on work processes, conditions, management strategies, and so on, the last meeting in Poznań in April 2017 focused on a common campaign. Since wage levels differ grossly between countries but all Amazon warehouse workers share similar working conditions, the campaign will focus on those conditions, and especially health problems as a result of the tedious work.

Conclusion

The grassroots organizing and "formal" union activity at Amazon had some success, in maintaining a group of worker activists, the documentation of experiences of struggle, the continued involvement of new workers, and so on. Amazon's dual employment strategy, its attacks on worker activists, the high rate of labor turnover, the obstacles presented by Polish labor laws, and the activists' exhaustion as a result of the shift system are among the problems the union faces. "Informal" forms of struggle have been tested, and might offer an alternative way to increase workers' power at the workplace in the future. Rather than mere organization-building, the confrontation with the company hierarchy in the warehouses and the collective experience of creating change through formal and informal means remain the main focus.

The Amazon workers' cross-border meetings are still at an embryonic stage. A core of worker activists are willing to take on the challenges in Poland, Germany, and France. They are driven by the fact that "cross-border" organizing helps workers involved to see the potential power of collective struggles as they learn that they are not isolated and others are willing to support them. They understand that it is vital to document and analyze workers' experiences in different countries, and present them to new workers at Amazon and others in logistics companies elsewhere. However, the impact of the cross-border activity will remain limited unless more Amazon warehouse workers (and supporters) from more countries get involved. This article is also meant as a call to everyone working at Amazon or connected in some way to logistics workers' struggles to get in contact and join in the organizing.[22]

Amazon has been fairly successful in limiting the effects of struggles and strikes (as in its warehouses in Germany), and empty union bureaucrats' meetings like those of UNI Global Union do not help in building up of workers' power (but rather undermine it). So there is no alternative to further grassroots organizing attempts—locally in each warehouse as well as across borders. And this is not limited to Amazon workers and temporary workers working for Amazon. We have taken part in meetings with logistics workers from other warehouses and other logistics sectors in several countries, and such meetings are important to learn from other experiences and to form alliances for a broader struggle against capitalist exploitation.

Acknowledgment

This is a collectively written text based on our experience as workers in Amazon warehouses in Poland, as activists of a grassroots union, and as co-organizers of Amazon workers' meetings with participants from several European countries.

Notes

1 From its beginning in the 1990s, Amazon concentrated its warehouses in the largest consumer markets, first in North America and later in Western Europe and East Asia, but the company has tried to gain access to markets elsewhere in recent years, like India. See "Amazon Global Fulfillment Center Network," www.mwpvl.com/html/amazon_com.html. On the number of employees, see Todd Bishop, "Amazon soars to more than 341K employees—adding more than 110K people in a single year," GeekWire, February 2, 2017, www.geekwire.com/2017/amazon-soars-340k-employees-adding-110k-people-single-year (accessed November 30, 2017).

2 Since moving to Poland, Amazon has opened more warehouses in Germany too, so this is no typical case of relocation but rather an expansion with a partial relocation of work processes. Amazon announced it will open 15 more warehouses in Europe in 2017 and create 15,000 new jobs (information given by Amazon managers in Poland, May 2017).

3 "Cheap" labor means that workers in Poland earn about one-third of what workers in Germany get: Amazon's hourly wages (before tax) for warehouse workers start at 15 zlotys (around €3.50) in Poland and about 45 zlotys (€11) in Germany. Amazon Poland pays warehouse workers the same hourly wage on weekdays, weekends, and public holidays. Overtime is paid slightly higher, and Amazon pays performance bonuses.

4 Information provided by Amazon managers in Poland. Currently, Amazon Poland hires all new workers through agencies, which usually give them contracts for one month. These can be renewed several times up to six months. Permanent workers are recruited exclusively from among the temporary agency workers.

5 According to the Polish central statistical office (Główny Urząd Statystyczny) at the end of April 2017 unemployment in Poznań stood at 1.8 percent, and in Wrocław at 2.7 percent. The unemployment rate in Poland is the lowest in 26 years at 7.7 percent: (http://stat.gov.pl/obszary-tematyczne/rynek-pracy/bezrobocie-rejestrowane/liczba-bezrobotnych-zarejestrowanych-oraz-stopa-bezrobocia-wedlug-wojewodztw-podregionow-i-powiatow-stan-w-koncu-kwietnia-2017-r-,2,56.html (accessed November 30, 2017).

6 See, for instance, the report "Amazon: Milion przyjęć czy milion rozczarowań," IP website, November 20, 2015: www.ozzip.pl/teksty/informacje/

pilne-akcje/item/1999-amazon-milion-przyjec-czy-milion-rozczarowan (accessed November 30, 2017).

7 For another description of AFE by a worker in an Amazon warehouse in the United States see the blog entry on Amazon Emancipatory: http://amazonemancipatory.com/afe-amazon-fulfillment-engine (accessed November 30, 2017).

8 Not just at Amazon in Poland: the average sickness rate in all Amazon warehouses in Germany is around 20 percent while the rate for all workers in Germany is about 5 percent. See "Geld fürs Gesundbleiben," *Zeit online*, April 1, 2017, www.zeit.de/karriere/beruf/2017-04/amazon-betriebsvereinbarung-fehltage-gewerkschaft-krankschreibung-online-versandhaendler (accessed November 30, 2017).

9 See "'Amazon zatrudnia? Amazon zwalnia!'—akcja ulotkowa," IP website, August 2, 2016, http://ozzip.pl/teksty/informacje/wielkopolskie/item/2152-amazon-zatrudnia-amazon-zwalnia-akcja-ulotkowa (accessed November 30, 2017).

10 For more information on IP see its website: http://www.ozzip.pl (some texts in English).

11 These more militant workers in Bad Hersfeld and Leipzig were first contacted by IP activists when outreaching to get information.

12 Other pending labor court cases against Amazon Poland are about workers being sacked for not reaching the rates or for going on sick leave.

13 See "W Amazonie: strajk w Niemczech, niezadowolenie w Poznaniu," IP website, June 24, 2015, www.ozzip.pl/teksty/informacje/wielkopolskie/item/1948-w-amazonie-strajk-w-niemczech-niezadowolenie-w-poznaniu; and "Wybuch konfliktu w Amazonie," IP website, June 29, 2015, www.ozzip.pl/teksty/informacje/pilne-akcje/item/1950-wybuch-konfliktu-spor-zbiorowy-i-represje-w-amazonie. For more information on the slowdown and its background see Ralf Ruckus, "Confronting Amazon: through creative actions and cross-border solidarity, Polish workers are undermining Amazon's anti-union playbook," *Jacobin*, March 31, 2016, www.jacobinmag.com/2016/03/amazon-poland-poznan-strikes-workers (all sites accessed November 30, 2017).

14 The support was bigger than in the Amazon warehouses in Germany where strikes could go ahead because German labor law stipulates strike ballots among union members only.

15 Amazon did not allow temporary agency workers to participate in the strike ballot at Amazon premises. So IP started collective disputes with the temporary agencies in order that the 4,000 temporary agency workers could be balloted too. For a report on the strike ballot see "Wyniki referendum w Amazonie: Ponad 2 tys. pracowników za strajkiem!" IP website, June 23, 2016, http://ozzip.pl/teksty/informacje/ogolnopolskie/item/2134-wyniki-referendum-w-amazonie-ponad-2-tys-pracownikow-za-strajkiem; and Ralf Ruckus and Jan Podróżny, "Amazon Poland: over 2,000 People want to go on strike but restrictive Polish labor laws prohibit it," English trans-

lation from German Telepolis, July 27, 2016, https://angryworkersworld. wordpress.com/2016/07/27/amazon-poland-over-2000-people-want-to-go-on-strike-but-restrictive-polish-labor-laws-prohibit-it/ (all sites accessed November 30, 2017).

16 The multiple-choice questionnaire includes 4 questions and lets respondents choose 3 out of 8 to 12 options. These notes are based on about 450 questionnaires returned up to May 2017.

17 Extra payments offered by Amazon in other countries include a 13th monthly wage (as in France), but also a share scheme which workers see as an additional source of income—while it is, in fact, meant to give workers the illusion of "owning" part of the company—and payments according to seniority as some workers think it is "unfair" for new workers to get the same wage as senior workers. That is also problematic as payments according to seniority (or skill) divide the workers even more and weaken their collective power.

18 See its official website: www.uniglobalunion.org.

19 Solidarność not only publicly condemned IP's activities and "autonomous" struggles like the slowdown described in June 2015, but recently even tried to claim that any wage rises at Amazon were a success of its own clever negotiation tactics. See "Solidarność układa się z Amazonem – to nie jest sukces na światową skalę," IP website, February 9, 2017, http://ozzip.pl/teksty/informacje/ogolnopolskie/item/2221-solidarnosc-uklada-sie-z-amazonem-to-nie-jest-sukces-na-swiatowa-skale (accessed November 30, 2017).

20 This is what Ver.di in Germany does too, when coordinating "its" strike actions, and the decision-making process leads to frequent conflicts between rank-and-file activists in Amazon warehouses who want to have more control over their own strikes and Ver.di bureaucrats who are interested in not self-organized militancy but centrally controlled strike actions.

21 For more on the cross-border meetings see https://amworkers.wordpress.com/

22 See the blog mentioned in note 7 or write directly to: amaworkers@open-mailbox.org

7

Decolonizing Logistics: Palestinian Truckers on the Occupied Supply Chain

Jake Alimahomed-Wilson and
Spencer Louis Potiker

In recent decades, the global capitalist system has been transformed by the logistics revolution.[1] As the neoliberal global capitalist economy became driven by the technocratic principles of supply chain management, the Palestinian economy has been subjected to the complete inversion of such principles. Instead of a logistics-powered economic system that emphasizes the smooth and efficient circulation of goods, the occupied Palestinian supply chain became structured by a complex system of Israeli-imposed inefficiencies, disruptions, and violence. The combination of Israeli state violence and the targeted military destruction of Palestine's key logistical nodes, such as the Gazan seaport construction site and international airport, coupled with Israel's devastating immobility programs and the Israeli supply chain security apparatus, systematically disrupt and undermine the flow of Palestinian goods through a matrix of checkpoints, closures, militarized border crossings, and myriad other physical obstacles.[2] These forces amount to a totalizing Israeli assault on the Palestinian supply chain logistics infrastructure, a process we describe as the *logistics of occupation.*[3]

The driving force behind the movement restrictions imposed on Palestinian goods and workers is the Israeli supply chain security apparatus, which has created one of the most inefficient supply chains in modern times. Israel's systematic disruption of the flow of goods in Palestine has created severe consequences for Palestine's economy and workers. It has also undermined Palestine's manufacturing base by eroding its ability to access critical inputs and participate in global commodity trade.[4] While there is an established body of literature documenting the broader economic conditions related to Israel's colonial occupation of the Palestinian economy,[5] far less research has been conducted on the labor and working conditions of Palestine's primary group of logistics workers: Palestinian truck drivers. Because of the Israeli military assault on Palestine's logistical infrastructure, Palestine lacks an airport, seaport, and viable rail system, thereby undermining its ability to directly exchange goods with the global economy.[6] This means that the trucking sector remains Palestine's primary transportation industry. In light of the central role that truck drivers play in Palestine's economy, this chapter analyzes the structural forces shaping the labor conditions of Palestinian truckers working in the occupied supply chain.

This chapter is organized in three major parts. First, we examine the labor conditions of Palestinian truckers who work under a hyper-securitized racialized supply chain. Next, we analyze some of the ways that Palestinian truckers have resisted Israel's dehumanizing security policies and exploitive working conditions by focusing on some of the wildcat strikes that have occurred at checkpoints in recent years. Finally, we look at the role of global labor solidarity in supporting Palestinian labor's call to boycott Israeli goods in support of the broader anti-colonial Palestinian freedom struggle.

Working conditions in the occupied supply chain

The working conditions of Palestinian truckers are directly shaped by the imposition of racialized Israeli security checkpoints. In order to maintain public approval in Israel and the West, these checkpoints rely on "long-standing Orientalist tropes portraying the non-Westerner as a barbaric, exotic Other."[7] As of 2017, there were 59 internal checkpoints scattered across the West Bank.[8] This, however, does not include the matrix of bottlenecks created by Israeli settlements, the Israeli-only apartheid road system, and other physical impediments that Palestinian truckers are forced to navigate while driving their daily transport routes.[9] Laleh Khalili argues that Israel "uses roads to isolate Palestinian communities from neighboring countries and the global market. In Palestine, Israeli-constructed bypass roads physically block Palestinians from accessing regional trade networks."[10] Currently there are approximately 540 internal obstacles prohibiting free movement within occupied Palestine.[11] In addition to these physical obstacles, a recent report by the United Nations Office for the Coordination of Humanitarian Affairs documented the regular and ongoing imposition of Israeli military "flyover checkpoints."[12] These are a part of myriad population control techniques used around the world in what Stephen Graham calls the vertical axes of surveillance.[13]

Adding to the internal disarticulation of trucking routes that Palestinian truckers face, they are also forced to navigate a complicated and highly inefficient non-intermodal transport system—known as the back-to-back system—at all Israeli border crossings and checkpoints. In contrast to a global logistics system that relies upon intermodal transportation,[14] the Palestinian economy is forced to use a cargo system that harkens back to the old "break-bulk" era method, which preceded containerized shipping. The back-to-back system is an outcome of the Israeli-imposed hypersecuritization of the Palestinian supply chain.

The back-to-back system works as follows. On arrival at a crossing, Palestinian truck drivers are required to register their names at the entrance. After registration, the Palestinian trucker must then wait until an Israeli driver becomes available on the other side of the crossing. The goods are unloaded by a group of intermediary workers to be picked up by a trucker on the other side; Israeli and Palestinian truckers never meet face to face. In the process of moving the goods from truck to truck, the cargo is subject to further security and customs inspections, creating more delays.[15] Recently representatives from Unifor, Canada's largest private sector union, sent a delegation to Palestine in order to better understand the working conditions of Palestinian truckers. Unifor's secretary-treasurer, Peter Kennedy, commented on the working conditions of Palestinian truckers: "They could be held up for one hour, two hours, eight hours, only to be told to come back the next day .... It's all arbitrary."[16]

Israel's colonial domination of Palestine's logistics system has also made it difficult for any large or medium-sized logistical enterprise to be profitable. Therefore Palestinian truckers are often sole proprietors, operate in a small enterprise, or work directly for local retailers or manufacturers.[17] The truckers working as owner-operators, or those that are partners in or working for small firms, are typically paid on a per-haul basis. This also means that the temporal inconsistencies—a direct outcome of the structural conditions on the occupied supply chain—created by delays at checkpoints directly and severely undermine Palestinian truckers' incomes. According to David Jaffee and David Bensman, "For owner-operators, who are paid by the trip, wait time is one of the most significant factors impacting compensation, contributing to extended hours of the workday, and generating health-draining levels of stress."[18] For those truckers that work directly for a larger merchant, producer, or fleet, the inefficiencies created by the Israeli security state have deleterious consequences for the Palestinian economy at large. Depending on the nature of the truckers' contracts they are often paid on a per-haul basis, resulting in a similar loss of overall income to that of owner-operators.

Deborah Cowen connects the role of supply chain security with labor control.[19] We contend that supply chain security is further grounded within a racial logic. Andy Clarno connects neoliberalism with racial capitalism by emphasizing the role of securitization in settler colonial regimes.[20] On the occupied supply chain, the Israeli security state subjects Palestinian truckers to a host of other non-economic forms of racialized labor control. In other words, the Israeli supply chain security apparatus actively relies on a racialized form of worker surveillance, as the racial profiling of Palestinian truckers at checkpoints regularly includes physical searches. That is, Palestinian truckers are subject to searches of their persons when registering at the crossing, including strip searches.[21] Checkpoints combine a racialized form of surveillance and anti-Arab racism in the everyday working conditions for Palestinian truckers. For Palestinian truck drivers, checkpoints serve to normalize and actively embed these oppressive racist conditions in the labor process itself. In fact, it has been documented that the dehumanizing and humiliating treatment experienced by Palestinian truckers at checkpoints is a deterrent for Palestinian drivers from using the ever-shrinking amount of roads open to their use.[22]

Wildcat strikes

Israel holds discretionary power to close down commercial crossings on the Israel–Palestine border. Sometimes crossings are temporarily closed, and in other instances they have been permanently shut down. In March 2011, Israel announced the permanent closure of Karni crossing, which at the time was the primary commercial crossing between Gaza and Israel because of its capacity to process a large volume of goods.[23] For Gazan truckers, this also meant that the Karni crossing was, relatively speaking, the "most efficient" crossing in limiting delays during exchanges. Additionally, it was located closer to the major urban hub in Gaza City than the alternative Karem Shalom crossing. After the permanent closure of the Karni crossing, Gazan truckers were forced to rely on the Karem Shalom crossing, the only remaining commercial crossing. Not only does Karem Shalom lack the capacity to handle large volumes of goods, it is located approximately 18.6 miles (30 kilometers) from Gaza City.[24] The closure of the Karni crossing not only had direct negative consequences for the Gazan economy, it also harmed the Gazan trucking sector. The truckers had to absorb additional costs incurred by increases in fuel consumption brought on by the longer routes, coupled with more delays owing to the increased idle time from the longer queues at the Karem Shalom crossing. Additionally, the customs expenses which are assessed per truckload were also far more costly at the Karem Shalom crossing.[25]

Israel's closure of the Karni commercial crossing was not an isolated incident, but was part of a broader series of economic measures aimed at further isolating Gaza. The Israeli closure of Karni followed the closure of two other commercial crossings in Gaza, bringing the total closures to three of the four major commercial crossings—an action that amplified the economic siege and Israeli blockade on Gaza, further isolating Gazans from both the West Bank and the rest of the world. The Israeli-imposed closures of the commercial crossings in Gaza were not only a form of collective economic punishment, but also a direct violation of international law.[26]

The closure of the Karni crossing was also the catalyst that sparked a wave of resistance by Palestinian truck drivers. Following the closure truck drivers organized a wildcat strike at the Karni crossing in protest at the increased costs they were forced to incur. One of the striking truckers and spokesperson for the protesters, Nahed Shehaibar, provided further insight into the reasons behind the strike: "Customs fees at Karni were approximately $100 per truckload, but at Karem Shalom they are approximately $500.... That's why we will keep striking."[27]

Despite the principled resistance exhibited by truckers during the wildcat strike, it could not last very long because of the ongoing crisis in Gaza and the urgent need for Palestinian civil society to receive outside goods in order to survive. The broader context of Israel's economic siege on Gaza implicitly limited the effectiveness and long-term impact that trucking strikes might have. However, the Karni crossing wildcat strike did achieve some modest success. About a week after the start of the strike, Israel temporarily reopened the Sufa crossing in order to allow cement into Gaza to rebuild homes destroyed in Israel's 2008–09 attack on Gaza. The Gazan truckers heroically made the decision to pick up and haul the much-needed humanitarian supplies into Gaza, despite weakening their own bargaining position during the strike, ultimately putting the needs of the Palestinian people ahead of their own class struggle. "According to the Private Courier Companies Association, only ten truckloads were allowed in."[28] Through the economic siege on Gaza, Israel was effectively able to break the strike and continue the exploitation of Palestinian people, who remain a captive consumer market for Israeli products, by playing on the humanitarian spirit of the Palestinian truck drivers.

Palestinian truckers have also resisted Israel's apartheid economic system throughout the West Bank. In April 2014, Palestinian truckers in the city of Jenin, located in the northern canton of the West Bank, went on strike. The reason was a legislative decision that permitted Israeli truckers to make trips into the West Bank, while simultaneously prohibiting Palestinian truckers from making the entire trip to their destination. This gave Israeli truckers an unfair advantage in the competitive haulage market, ultimately undercutting the Palestinian trucking sector in the West Bank.[29]

Union member Kayid Awwad stated, "Our demand is clear. If Israel allows Israeli trucks into Palestinian territory, then Palestinian trucks must be allowed into Israeli territory."[30] This legislative decision concerning trucking mirrors the fundamental disparity in granting free movement for Israelis in contrast to the devastating immobilization program imposed on Palestinian people and goods. Both Israeli citizens and its goods have far more uninhibited and direct access to Palestine and its consumer markets, whereas Palestinian people, including truckers, must obtain special permits in order to access Israel for either work or travel.[31] As a result, Palestinian goods remain largely noncompetitive in Israel because of the colonial domination of Palestine's logistics system and the subsequent de-development of the Palestinian economy.[32]

Gaza's tunnels and the underground supply chain

Thus far we have discussed some of the ways Palestinian truck drivers have used their labor position in the occupied supply chain to resist

Israel's exploitive and dehumanizing economic policies. Israel's suppression of Palestine's logistics sector has led to other forms of resistance, particularly with the rapid growth of the underground logistics tunnel systems in Gaza. The Israeli siege and blockade on Gaza following the democratic election of Hamas in 2006 drastically slowed the flow of goods into Gaza, leading to a shortage in basic commodities for Gaza's population of approximately 1.8 million. As the movement of goods came to a halt at the commercial crossings into Gaza, the number of trucking hauls also dropped substantially. This led to other forms of underground resistance, most notably a sharp increase in Gaza's underground supply chain tunnel system.

The tunnel system served as a mechanism for limited logistical discretion for the Palestinian supply chain, partly subverting surveillance by using spaces below ground out of the sight of drones, helicopters, satellites and other vertical axes of the Israeli security apparatus.[33] The Gazan tunnel economy connected Gaza to Egypt and Israel through a complex network of underground goods movement tunnels.[34] In 1997 only about 1 percent of Gazan imports arrived through the tunnels. However, by 2010, imports through Gaza's underground tunnels had soared to 68 percent of the total.[35] One trader described the tunnel economy as "the lungs through which Gaza breathes."[36]

Gaza's informal underground logistics workers faced perilous working conditions, and labored under constant danger, as the tunnel infrastructure was under the continuous threat of military destruction by either Egyptian or Israeli aggression. At the behest of Israel, the Egyptian army successfully flooded over 30 underground tunnels entering Egyptian territory; in some cases, Egypt even flooded the tunnels with raw sewage.[37] In 2016 four Palestinian tunnel workers were killed when the Egyptian army flooded a tunnel, causing it to collapse.

In many ways, the underground tunnel economy was more efficient than the formal Israeli-controlled commercial crossings. It was not only a primary way for Gazans to receive basic goods and commodities, it was also a source of employment. According to Nicholas Pelham, Gaza's underground logistics industry became Gaza's largest non-government employer for a period of time. The tunnels also led to an overall economic stimulus for the Gazan economy, as merchants and manufacturers were able to secure critical economic inputs.[38] The added income for consumers created a multiplier effect, spurring more business growth and more jobs, cutting into the crisis levels of unemployment found throughout Gaza. The tunnel economy was eventually brought to an end by military force. Most of the remaining tunnels that the Egyptian army did not flood, Israeli armed forces managed to attack and destroy using drones and fighter jets.[39]

General strikes

In 2012, Palestinian government workers held a general strike because of the lack of payment for their services. This crisis was aggravated when Israel withheld customs payments from the Palestinian Authority (PA).[40] The Paris economic protocol of 1994 established a one-sided customs union, which meant that Israel controlled the customs collection on behalf of the PA.[41] This in effect is used as a political mechanism to exercise authority over the occupied territories. The Israeli government has used this mechanism recently, for example, by withholding customs payments to the PA following the PA's decision to join the International Criminal Court in 2015.[42]

In 2017, Palestinian workers called for a general strike, which resulted in a complete shutdown of schools, banks, and business throughout the West Bank. Buses, taxis, and trucks also came to a halt. Major cities across the West Bank, along with towns and refugee camps, became ghost towns; the scene was reminiscent of the 1987 Palestinian general strike, which infamously became the catalyst for the First Intifada.[43] The 2017 general strike was in solidarity with the more than 1,500 Palestinian prisoners in Israel who were on hunger strike.[44] The next month, following the general strike for prisoner solidarity, another general strike was organized. Once again, stores and government offices were shut down in protest at US President Donald Trump's visit to Israel. Protesters blocked roads throughout the West Bank.[45] In sum, Palestinian workers continue to resist in numerous ways on the occupied supply chain.

Palestinian labor's resistance to occupation

Palestinian labor represents a crucial component in the broader struggle for Palestinian freedom and self-determination. Palestine's labor movement includes several unions and workers' organizations, such as the Palestine General Federation of Trade Unions (PGFTU), the General Union of Palestinian Workers, and the Palestinian

Federation of Independent Trade Unions, along with a plethora of other labor organizations with connections to other international unions, including transportation unions. Palestine's unions have also played a key role in galvanizing a growing international labor solidarity movement by workers and unions around the world. Logistics and transportation unions, in particular, have played a notable role in the growing Boycott, Divestment, and Sanctions (BDS) movement. The overwhelming majority of Palestinian labor unions support BDS and labor's unique role in boycotting Israeli goods.

In 2011, the first Palestinian trade union conference on BDS was held in Ramallah. The conference also marked the formation of the Palestinian Trade Union Coalition for BDS (PTUC-BDS).[46] PTUC-BDS represents a broad coalition of Palestinian trade unions that support the global BDS movement. The formation of PTUC-BDS received immediate support from a number of unions around the world, including Brazil's *Central Unica dos Trabalhadores*, the International Federation of Arab Trade Unions, the Congress of South African Trade Unions, the Irish Congress of Trade Unions, along with a diverse array of other unions from Canada, the United States, Scotland, Italy, Sweden, France, Turkey, Spain, and Australia, among other nations. In 2015, the Gazan-based local of the PGFTU issued an official statement reiterating their support of Palestinian civil society and the BDS movement.[47]

As BDS specifically relates to logistics unions, PTUC-BDS explicitly called on international dockworkers to boycott Zim Shipping—Israel's largest shipping company—and all other Israeli cargo ships. A similar direct action tactic was used by dockworkers in resisting apartheid in South Africa.[48]

BDS, international labor, and the global picket line for Palestinian justice

Logistics workers around the world occupy a strategic site of potential resistance, not only to capitalist exploitation, but also in the broader struggle for social justice. It should be no surprise then that dockworkers' unions around the world have played a key role in supporting global anti-colonial and anti-racist struggles by refusing to unload cargo ships complicit in or connected to racist and/or colonial regimes.[49] Peter Cole provides a rich historical analysis of the longstanding role of dockworkers around the world supporting anti-colonial and anti-racist struggle in South Africa and on the US West Coast.[50]

In 1984, the San Francisco Bay Area's Local 10 chapter of the International Longshore and Warehouse Union (ILWU) refused to offload a South African ship for 11 days in solidarity with the anti-apartheid freedom struggle.[51] In fact, during Nelson Mandela's first tour of the United States in 1990 he made a point of visiting members of ILWU Local 10, in recognition of their contributions to ending apartheid.[52] ILWU has also showed its support for Palestine's anti-colonial struggle by drawing out connections between the apartheid colonial regimes of South Africa and Palestine. During the 1988 ILWU convention, the union took an official stance on Palestinian apartheid, proclaiming that Israel was guilty of state-sponsored terrorism.[53] According to Cole, "The resolution also noted that: 'The work day for a Palestinian in Israel is 12 to 13 hours including travel (as is the case with Black workers in South Africa).'"[54] Moreover, "In 2002 [the ILWU's] Local 10 officers signed a statement 'For International Labor Solidarity to Stop Zionist Repression and Build a Just Peace' to protest the Zionist bombing of the headquarters of the Palestinian General Federation of Trade Unions in the West Bank city of Nablus."[55]

Along with these showings of solidarity, the Transport Salaried Staffs' Association (TSSA) sent a delegation to learn more about the struggles experienced by Palestinian workers. The delegation reported upon return, "Driving through Israel itself alongside the West Bank border ... the land is cut apart. Much of the landscape, certainly on the Palestinian side, looks stony and barren, even bleak looking .... And everywhere is the ever oppressing wall."[56] The International Transport Workers' Federation (ITF) and Unifor (Canada's largest private sector union) have also demonstrated solidarity with Palestinian truckers, especially relating to the oppressive conditions at the crossings. For example, ITF has been working on a support project at the Ertah crossing, which Unifor is helping fund.[57] "The project was launched to provide Palestinian drivers with access to refreshments, toilet facilities, shade and union meeting space when they experienced long delays at the crossing."[58] AUSPalestine (Australian Unionists Supporting Palestine) has called upon Australian transport unions to contact the Israeli ambassador to condemn the exploitive working conditions that Palestinian truck drivers face.[59] This was, in part, a response to ITF's demand for "the opening of facilities to provide land, air, and sea points of entry and exit for trade for the Palestinian people free from interference by the Israeli occupying power."[60]

Block the boat

In 2010, community activists in the San Francisco Bay area of Northern California created a picket line blocking the entrance at the port of Oakland in order to prevent the unloading of cargo on an Israeli Zim cargo ship. They were joined in their protest by members of ILWU Local 10, who refused to cross the picket line, citing a potential health and safety provision in their contract. This marked the first time Zim shipping had been prevented from unloading goods at a North American port.[61] Inspired by this action, in 2014 the US Palestinian Solidarity Movement organized more port actions in a mobilization called "Block the Boat." The Block the Boat actions were organized by a coalition of social justice organizations with the explicit intent of preventing Zim shipping from unloading goods in major US ports. Community activists successfully created a picket line, which ILWU members once again honored, in order to delay and prevent the Zim shipping line from unloading its cargo.

Following the Bay Area's Block the Boat action, which succeeded for four days in preventing the *Zim Piraeus* from unloading, actions in the port of Tacoma, Washington state, followed. This action prevented the unloading of a Zim ship for five days. It is estimated that this showing of solidarity cost Zim US$0.5 million in lost revenue.[62] Later, the Zim shipping cargo ship *Haifa* was targeted by Block the Boat protestors in the port of Long Beach. Protesters created a picket line which resulted in the morning shift of longshore workers being sent home.[63] Finally, once again at the port of Oakland later that year, another Zim cargo ship was picketed by "protesters mobilized by the Stop Zim Action Committee and the Transport Workers Solidarity Committee. Three of the organizers were Local 10 retirees, veterans of ILWU's 1984 anti-apartheid action in San Fransisco."[64]

The South African Transport and Allied Workers Union (SATAWU) has also been instrumental in resisting on behalf of their comrades in Palestine. The year before the 2010 port protests in Oakland targeting the Zim cargo ship, the Durban branch of SATAWU announced that its members would not unload Zim shipments following Israel's Operation Cast Lead military assault on Gaza.[65]

The Workers Advice Center (WAC-MAAN) is an independent workers' organization headquartered in Israel which seeks to organize workers, including Arab-Israeli and Palestinian workers, who remain largely unorganized following the neoliberal restructuring of Israel's economy beginning in the 1990s. WAC-MAAN points to the shifts that occurred in the trucking industry following the neoliberalization of Israel's transportation sector. Truckers in Israel used to be largely unionized. However, the privatization of the trucking sector all but destroyed union density throughout the sector.[66] WAC-MAAN explicitly opposes Israel's occupation, and "demands equal rights for all workers—Israeli, migrant, and Palestinian."[67]

Conclusion

Israel's colonial domination of Palestine's logistics infrastructure undermines Palestine's capacity to participate in global trade in the neoliberalized, logistics-driven global capitalist economy. Moreover, it simultaneously contributes to the de-development of Palestine's economy by undermining its manufacturing base.[68] These dynamics have also created severe consequences and organizational challenges for Palestinian (and Israeli) workers. For Palestinian truckers, Israel's supply chain security apparatus has further entrenched a racialized form of labor control and surveillance, immobilization, and exploitation across the occupied supply chain. Palestinian truck drivers face a systematic form of colonial exploitation, racism, and dehumanizing working conditions across the numerous checkpoints and commercial crossings in the Occupied Territories.

The inefficiencies related to the back-to-back trucking system lead to a direct loss of income for Palestinian logistics workers, but there are also a number of other non-economic consequences. The back-to-back system, grounded in the hypersecuritization of the logistical supply chain, also structurally weakens potential efforts at building solidarity between the Israeli and Palestinian working classes by preventing contact between each group of truckers. John Dewey famously wrote, "Green and red lines, making out political boundaries, are on the maps and affect legislation and jurisdiction ... but railways, mails and telegraph-wires disregard them ... [and] influence more profoundly those living within the legal local units than do boundary lines."[69] However, Israel has been able to reinforce their boundary lines and thus the

Zionist[70] project by colonizing Palestine's logistics system, adding layers of difficulty to organizing across the "Green Line."

Today, the Israeli neoliberalized trucking sector remains a largely exploited and unorganized group of workers, many of whom are Arab-Israeli workers and migrants. This logistical choke point, divided by an apartheid system of economic relations, remains a key potential site of future organizing. In addition, building capacity within international workers' movements and unions across the global logistics and transportation sectors remains a crucial component in labor's role in supporting the broader Palestinian freedom struggle.

Notes

1 Edna Bonacich and Jake B. Wilson, *Getting the Goods: Ports, Labor, and the Logistics Revolution* (Ithaca, N.Y.: Cornell University Press, 2008).

2 Jeff Halper, "The 94 percent solution: a matrix of control," *Middle East Report* 216 (2000), pp. 14–19; Jake Alimahomed-Wilson and Spencer Louis Potiker, "The logistics of occupation: Israel's colonial suppression of Palestine's goods movement infrastructure," *Journal of Labor and Society* 20(4) (2017).

3 Alimahomed-Wilson and Potiker (2017).

4 Shir Hever, *The Political Economy of Israel's Occupation: Repression Beyond Exploitation* (New York: Pluto Press, 2010); Sara Roy, *The Gaza Strip: Political Economy of De-development* (Washington DC: Institute for Palestinian Studies, 2016).

5 Leila Farsakh, "The political economy of Israeli occupation: what is colonial about it?" *Electronic Journal of Middle East Studies* 8 (2008); Hever (2010); Roy (2016); Mandy Turner and Omar Shweiki, *Decolonizing Palestinian Political Economy: De-Development and Beyond* (New York: Palgrave Macmillan, 2014).

6 "Much less reported has been a systematic and continuous programme by Israeli forces which adds a new twist to the geographic and politics of contemporary siege warfare against urban civilians: the targeting and destruction of modern infrastructure systems. In May 2001, for example, Ben Azri, then Israel's minister of labor, called for the dismantling of Palestinian roads, utilities and cultural institutions as a way of 'making the Palestinians' lives hell.'" Steven Graham, *Cities Under Siege: The New Military Urbanism* (Brooklyn, N.Y.: Verso, 2011), p. 284.

7 Graham (2011), p. 55.

8 B'Tselem, "Restriction of movement: checkpoints, physical obstructions, and forbidden roads," (2011, updated February 2017), www.btselem.org/freedom_of_movement/checkpoints_and_forbidden_roads (accessed November 30, 2017).

9 MA'AN Development Center, "Apartheid roads: promoting settlements, punishing Palestinians" (2008); Mutasim Elagraa, Randa Jamal, and Mamoud

Elkhafif, "Trade facilitation in the Occupied Palestinian Territory: restrictions and limitations" (Geneva: UNCTAD, 2014).

10 Laleh Khalili, "The roads to power: the infrastructure of counter-insurgency," *World Policy Journal* 34(1) (2017), p. 97.

11 Elagraa et al. (2014), p. 9.

12 The report tallied 256 military flyover checkpoints in December 2013, 456 in December 2014, and 361 in April 2015 (B'Tselem, 2017).

13 Stephen Graham, *Vertical: The City from Satellites to Bunkers* (Brooklyn, N.Y.: Verso, 2016), p. 340.

14 Bonacich and Wilson (2008).

15 Paltrade, "Internal commercial crossings," n.d., www.paltrade.org/en_us/page/internal-commercial-crossings (accessed January 12, 2017); Alimahomed-Wilson and Potiker (2017).

16 Unifor, "Unifor helps Palestinian truckers," www.unifor.org/en/whats-new/news/unifor-helps-palestinian-truckers (accessed September 30, 2017).

17 Samir Abdullah, "Palestine economy," www.palestineeconomy.ps/files/server/20152501101729-1.pdf, pp. 29–30 (accessed January 20, 2017).

18 David Jaffee and David Bensman, "Draying and picking: precarious work and labor action in the logistics sector," *Journal of Labor and Society* 19(1) (2016), p. 61.

19 Deborah Cowen, *The Deadly Life of Logistics: Mapping Violence in Global Trade* (Minneapolis, Minn.: University of Minnesota Press, 2014).

20 Andy Clarno, *Neoliberal Apartheid: Palestine/Israel and South Africa after 1994* (Chicago, Ill.: University of Chicago Press, 2017), p. 13.

21 Alimahomed-Wilson and Potiker (2017); Paltrade (n.d.).

22 B'Tselem (2017).

23 Rami Almeghari, "Gaza truckers protest Israel's closure of commercial crossing," *Electronic Intifada*, March 11, 2011, https://electronicintifada.net/content/gaza-truckers-protest-israels-closure-commercial-crossing/9263 (accessed November 30, 2017).

24 Almeghari (2011).

25 Almeghari (2011).

26 AUSPalestine, "Boycott call 'doing a good job,'" March 15, 2011, https://auspalestine.org/2011/03/15/boycott-call-doing-a-good-job/ (accessed November 30, 2017).

27 Almeghari (2011).

28 Almeghari (2011).

29 Ma'an News Agency, "Jenin truckers strike against new Israeli delivery rules," April 6, 2014, www.maannews.com/Content.aspx?id=687758 (accessed November 30, 2017).

30 Ma'an News Agency (2014).

31 Ma'an News Agency (2014).

32 Sara Roy, "The Gaza Strip: a case of economic de-development," *Journal of Palestine Studies* 17(1) (1987); Sara Roy, "De-development revisited:

Palestinian economy and society since Oslo," *Journal of Palestine Studies* 28(3) (1999); Roy (2016).

33 Graham (2016), p. 340.

34 Nicolas Pelham, "The role of the tunnel economy in redeveloping Gaza," in Mandy Turner and Omar Shweiki (eds.), *Decolonizing Palestinian Political Economy: De-development and Beyond* (New York: Palgrave Macmillan, 2014), p. 202.

35 Pelham (2014), p. 204.

36 Pelham (2014), p. 204.

37 Ruth Margalit, "The tunnels of Gaza's next war," *New Yorker*, February 27, 2016, www.newyorker.com/news/news-desk/the-tunnels-under-gaza; Fares Akram and David D. Kirkpatrick, "To block Gaza tunnels, Egypt lets sewage flow," *New York Times*, February 20, 2013, www.nytimes. com/2013/02/21/world/middleeast/egypts-floods-smuggling-tunnels-to-gaza-with-sewage.html (both accessed November 30, 2017).

38 Pelham (2014), p. 209.

39 Pelham (2014), p. 210.

40 *Aljazeera*, "West Bank workers strike over unpaid salaries: public sector staff strike as some 50,000 employees have not got paid due to Israeli financial sanctions," December 19, 2012, www.aljazeera.com/news/middle east/2012/12/201212191245697775.html (accessed November 30, 2017).

41 Alimahomed-Wilson and Potiker (2017).

42 UNCTAD, "Report on UNCTAD assistance to the Palestinian people: developments in the economy of the Occupied Palestinian Territory" (2016), p. 5.

43 Ma'an News Agency, "In photos: Palestinians launch general strike in support of imprisoned hunger strikers," April 27, 2017, https://maannews. com/Content.aspx?id=776707 (accessed November 30, 2017).

44 *Aljazeera*, "Palestinians on strike in solidarity with prisoners: general strike held in solidarity with hunger striking prisoners as Fatah party calls for 'day of rage' on Friday," April 27, 2017, www.aljazeera.com/news/2017/04/palestinians-strike-solidarity-prisoners-170427041901617.html (accessed November 30, 2017).

45 *Deutsche Welle*, "Palestinians greet Trump with West Bank general strike," May 22, 2017, www.dw.com/en/palestinians-greet-trump-with-west-bank-general-strike/a-38933064(accessed November 30, 2017).; *Aljazeera*, (2017).

46 BDS Movement, "Palestinian trade union coalition for BDS (PTUC-BDS) formed at historic conference," May 5, 2011, https://bdsmovement.net/news/palestinian-trade-union-coalition-bds-ptuc-bds-formed-historic-conference-o (accessed November 30, 2017).

47 Ali Abunimah, " Connecticut labor federation backs Israel boycott," *Electronic Intifada*, November 11, 2015, https://electronicintifada.net/blogs/ali-abunimah/connecticut-labor-federation-backs-israel-boycott; Ryan Rodrick Beiler, "Defying leaders, Norway trade unionists endorse Israel boycott," *Electronic Intifada*, May 18, 2017, https://electronicintifada. net/blogs/ryan-rodrick-beiler/defying-leaders-norway-trade-unionists-

endorse-israel-boycott; BDS Movement, "May Day: Palestinian trade unions call for intensifying BDS," April 28, 2017, https://bdsmovement.net/news/may-day-palestinian-trade-unions-call-intensifying-bds (all accessed November 30, 2017).

48 See Peter Cole's excellent work on this subject: Peter Cole and Lucien van der Walt, "Crossing the color lines, crossing the continents: comparing the racial politics of the IWW in South Africa and the United States, 1905–1925," *Safundi* 12 (2009); Peter Cole, "'An injury to one is an injury to all: ILWU Local 10 and the fight against apartheid," *Journal of Civil and Human Rights* 1(2) (2015); Peter Cole, "Hooks down! Anti-apartheid activism and solidarity among maritime unions in Australia and the United States," *Labor History* 58(3) (2017). PTUC-BDS is also calling upon unions to examine wage theft from Palestinians by the Histadrut (General Federation of Laborers in the Land of Israel) of approximately $2.43 billion over decades of occupation, and to subsequently sever their ties to the corrupt organization: BDS Movement (2017).

49 Cole and van der Walt (2009); Cole (2015, 2017).

50 Cole (2017).

51 Cole (2015), p. 158.

52 Cole (2015), p. 174; Jake Alimahomed-Wilson and Dana Williams, "State violence, social control, and resistance," *Journal of Social Justice* 6 (2016).

53 Peter Cole, "'An irresistible force': longshore unions and the fight for freedom and justice in Palestine," *Briarpatch*, November 1, 2013, https://briarpatchmagazine.com/articles/view/an-irresistible-force (accessed November 30, 2017).

54 Cole (2013).

55 Transport Workers Solidarity Committee, "Transport Workers Solidarity Committee's response to ILWU International's Statement on ZIM Protests," October 8, 2014, www.transportworkers.org/node/1554 (accessed November 30, 2017).

56 TSSA, "Rail union delegation to Palestine," September 22, 2015, www.tssa.org.uk/en/whats-new/news/index.cfm/rail-union-delegation-to-palestine-in-conjunction-with-the-palestine-solidarity-campaign-a-report-by-mick-carney-tssa-president (accessed November 30, 2017).

57 International Transport Workers' Federation, "Union mission to Palestine and Israel promotes justice and rights for workers," September 14, 2015, www.itfglobal.org/en/news-events/press-releases/2015/september/union-mission-to-palestine-and-israel-promotes-justice-and-rights-for-workers/ (accessed November 30, 2017).

58 International Transport Workers' Union, "Advance notice to press – invite to join ITF youth mission on Palestinian truck drivers project visit," May 8, 2016, www.itfglobal.org/en/news-events/press-releases/2016/may/advance-notice-to-press-invite-to-join-itf-youth-mission-on-palestinian-truck-drivers-project-visit/ (accessed November 30, 2017).

59 AUSPalestine (2011).

60 AUSPalestine (2011).

61 Cole (2013).

62 Charlotte Silver, "Protestors block and delay Israeli ships up and down US West Coast," *Electronic Intifada*, August 28, 2014, https://electronicintifada.net/blogs/charlotte-silver/protestors-block-and-delay-israeli-ships-and-down-us-west-coast (accessed November 30, 2017).

63 Silver (2014).

64 Transport Workers Solidarity Committee (2014).

65 Cole (2013).

66 Benjamin Balthaser, "Labor organizing across Israel's apartheid line: an interview with Israeli labor activist Yoav Tamir," *In These Times*, July 5, 2016, http://inthesetimes.com/working/entry/19262/organizing_across_the_apartheid_line_interview_with_israeli_labor_activist (accessed November 30, 2017).

67 WAC-MAAN has not formally supported boycotting Israeli goods: WAC-MAAN, "About us," www.wac-maan.org.il/en/about (accessed August 1, 2017).

68 Alimahomed-Wilson and Potiker (2017).

69 John Dewey, *The Public and its Problems* (Athens, Oh.: Ohio University Press, 1927), p. 107; cited from Stephen J. Collier, James Christopher Mizes, and Antina von Shnitzler, "Preface: public infrastructures/infrastructural publics," *Limn* 7 (2016).

70 "The analysis of Zionism as a settler colonial project is part of a broader reorientation of scholarship and activism away from a narrow focus on the occupied territories toward a more comprehensive focus on Israeli practices toward Palestinians inside Israel, the occupied territories, and in Diaspora": Clarno (2017), p. 6.

Part III

Neoliberalism and the Global Transformation of Ports

8

Decoding the Transition in the Ports of Mumbai

Johnson Abhishek Minz

Introduction

Global value chains (GVCs) have reconfigured production processes over numerous geographies of the globe, leading to an international division of the labor process. This division has been congruent to the plot of the expansion of transnational corporations, posited within the logic of capitalism, which continuously seeks to traverse to greenfield avenues. This process has been aided on one side by capital becoming increasingly mobile, and on the other by the financialization of markets. However, these transitions in the world economy have been made possible by the coming-in of a supranational state embedded in the international bodies that govern world trade, finances and credit structures in our present times.[1]

In all of these processes, an important factor has been the "locking in" of economies to maintain their competitive advantage. The shift of global capital from the developed to the developing world has been made possible by the extraction of relatively cheap labor, flouting basic regulatory mechanisms, and an expanded market opportunity. The logic of global capital would be to maintain the status quo of the developing countries by retaining their competitive advantage. Thereby, what has been witnessed is that even after changes in the world economy from the early 1980s onwards, production processes have been delineated in specific pockets of developing countries that promise a higher output–input ratio. Moreover, any attempts to rectify this arrangement through the countervailing force of worker organizations or trade unions have been met by the heavy hand of the state.

World trade has received a major fillip in this process of the expansion of the GVC. Trade has increased not only between the developed and developing world, but also between developing countries. Currently, trade forms 22.4 percent of the gross domestic product (GDP) of India, and the foreign value-added component of gross exports has risen from a meager 9.3 per cent in 1995 to 24 per cent in 2011.[2] This explains the extent of the trade and the integration process initiated by the GVCs. Since the 1990s developing economies have been rallying for a greater share in world trade, and this is been made possible not only by making products more competitive but also by rearranging the organizational structures that aid this competitiveness. A decentralized governance system that vouches for the grabbing of these rearrangements in organizational structures is initiated at the very touch points of trade between countries. One important touch point of global trade is through the ports, and these are the subject of discussion in this chapter.

The Indian port sector is also witnessing transition, and while there has been much discussion on the important role of trade and hence the role of ports in the economy, this examination tends to ignore labor as a subject of analysis. It becomes especially relevant for country like India, which has a huge supply of labor. The Indian port sector comprises 12 major ports, of which half are located on the east coast and half on the west. Most of the major ports are owned by the Government of India (GOI), except Ennore port which is a corporate port. This chapter concentrates specifically on the ports of Mumbai.

Background to the port workers of Bombay

The port of Mumbai (formerly known as Bombay) lying on the west coast of India is one of the oldest and most important ports in the country.[3] The Mumbai port is owned by GOI and overseen by the Ministry of Shipping (formerly the Ministry of Surface Transport). It is administered by the local port authority, the Mumbai Port Trust (MBPT), which is an autonomous body formed by law under the Major Port Trust Act, 1963.[4] Although the makings of the port were initiated at the beginning of the seventeenth century, it was only in 1873 that a port trust similar to the present structure came into existence. Owing to its long history, it has been one of the premier ports of India and also served as a gateway to India during colonial times. The history of the port of Bombay has been intrinsically linked with the history of the city itself. People working in the port of Bombay formed a considerable chunk of the city population. Since loading and unloading cargo to and from ships is a labor-intensive activity, the port attracted a lot of workers from outside Bombay, and was responsible for large in-migration to the city.

During the colonial era, the Bombay port proved to be an important avenue for trade. Ships regularly visited the harbor to load and unload pepper, precious stones, silk and cotton goods. The East India Company also made Bombay its first port of call, which ensured that ships came there not only for trade but also for servicing. The first dry dock in Bombay was constructed between 1748 and 1750, and a couple more followed later.[5] For a large part of its existence under the British rule, the port and dock workers of Bombay were unorganized and worked in the *tolli* system. In this the companies responsible for loading and unloading cargo to and from the ships, known as stevedore companies, employed contractors who in turn provided the necessary labor. The contractors or *tolliwallas/serangs* were intermediaries who supplied workers.[6] Cases of *serangs* demanding remuneration for a full gang of workers even when not all the workers had been present were not uncommon.[7]

Within the milieu of colonial times, the port and dock workers in Bombay started to unionize in the 1920s under the leadership of F. J. Ginwalla, N. M. Joshi, E. M. Bahadury, and S. N. Jhabvala. One unique aspect of the growth of unionism in the Mumbai ports is based on the craft distinctions that are prevalent in the ports. There were unions that catered specifically to the cargo-handling workers (that is, the dockworkers), and others that only represented port workers. Among the unions for dockworkers, the Bombay Port Trust Dock Staff Union (BPTDSU) was the first, founded in 1926. The Bombay Dock Workers' Union (BDWU) started in 1931, and catered exclusively for stevedores. Many unions were established in the following year. In 1954, five different unions with different focuses and with members from different categories of workers in the docks merged into the Transport and Dock Workers' Union (TDWUB).

There was a wide variety of jobs in the broad category of general port workers, including engineering, marine, stores, railways, crane drivers, sweepers, and watchmen, which initially all had separate unions. The Bombay Port Trust Employees' Union (BPTEU) was the first, started in the year 1920. A few months later the Bombay Port Trust Railway Men's Union (BPTRMU) was started, and a third union, the Bombay Port Trust General Workers' Union (BPTGWU), was established in 1944. Disagreements between these unions were counterproductive to the cause of the workers. The veteran trade union leader Placid D'Mello provided some unification for the dockworkers, which benefited the workers in periods of crisis, but there was little unification among the port workers' bodies.[8]

The sheer size of the port and the number of workers in Bombay meant they were seen as a force to be strategically utilized by the nationalists. During the pre-independence era, trade union formation and the articulation of class consciousness and solidarity gained momentum, ably led by Mahatma Gandhi. The formation of trade unions was considered little short of treason by the British. The push for *swadeshi* (domestically produced) goods led to a demand that the dock workers boycott all foreign goods. The BDWU heralded the resistance and dumped bales of cotton from Britain in the sea. Further boycotting of foreign goods took place, and during the ensuing unrest a few workers were killed. The British administrators took various measures to stifle the strike, and eventually succeeded in destroying the union.[9]

During the early twentieth century (and particularly in the 1930s and 1940s) the intermittent nature of work in the docks meant that employment tended to be on a casual basis. The work available depended on a variety of factors such as the volume of shipping traffic, traders' discretion, and ships being held up at sea because of bad weather. For the Bombay docks one other feature was the monsoons. During this season it was important to take the minimum time to load and unload ships. Because of all these factors, the demand for labor was not fixed, but varied considerably.

Working conditions were deplorable. Issues related to health and safety were not properly addressed. Child labor was also prevalent for certain activities. Those workers who were not Port Trust employees, but were employed via the stevedoring companies, typically had no written contracts, and the work was largely agreed by word of mouth.[10] As a result there was widespread corruption, and a large part of the payment for dock work was retained by the *serangs* themselves. The

Indian Dock Labour Act was passed in 1934, and specified health and safety measures for dock workers, but it was not implemented until Independence. There were increasingly hostile conditions for the huge bulk of dockworkers.

The trade unions, particularly BDWU, went on strike, as a result of which the *tolliwala* system was abolished and the Dock Workers (Regulation of Employment) Act 1948 was passed. This was the first step towards the decasualization of the workers. This Act came into force in Bombay in 1952. A tripartite Bombay Dock Labour Board (BDLB) was established under this Act, with equal numbers of members representing the government, the employers, and the workers. This was a major victory for the workers and the trade unions, as it paved way for registration and regularization of the dockworkers. It also helped the workers get social security and regularity of employment during slack times. On the other side, this Act guaranteed a steady supply of labor for dock work.

Apart from the stevedores, there were also attempts to regularize the status of other workers in the docks. The Bombay C&P Workers (Regulation of Employment) Scheme 1969, Bombay Foodgrains Handling Workers (Regulation of Employment) Scheme 1975, and Bombay Dock Clearing and Forwarding Workers (Regulation of Employment) Scheme 1983 were steps in this direction.[11]

However, these provisions were slowly being challenged by the mid-1980s, when welfarism as a concept was increasingly fading out of favor. The BDLB found it increasingly difficult to maintain a regular pool of workers for the docks. In 1983 all hiring was stopped, which tilted the employment figure downwards. This period also saw a reversion to the use of workers who were not registered with the BDLB. Another important marker during this time was the setting-up of the Jawaharlal Nehru Port (JNP), also located in Bombay, which specialized in handling container traffic.[12] Initially Jawaharlal Nehru Port was conceptualized as a satellite port to the Mumbai Port and its Trust, but later it came to be managed separately, by the Jawaharlal Nehru Port Trust (JNPT). Cargo was increasingly being traded in containers, and this led to a sizeable reduction in the number of workers required to handle it.[13] Further, the system of using workers came increasingly to be through private contractors and third parties, where the Dock Labour Board (DLB) was not involved. Jawaharlal Nehru Port slowly emerged as a popular port for container traffic. These factors had a vitiating effect on the BDLB, which eventually saw a slow dismantling of the protective schemes for workers.

Mumbai ports: a glance

Amid increases in the size and importance of trade ushered in by the GVCs, the currently held view favors major reforms in the Indian ports, which would alter their very character. The impetus for the corporatization of the major ports of India was provided in the early 1990s, when India's economy underwent a liberalization process.[14] In 1996 GOI invited private-sector participation in major ports of the country through joint ventures. In 2010 it set up a National Transport Development Policy Committee (NTDPC) to overhaul the country's transport policy.[15] Among other things, the committee recommended changes to the port sector. It looked at various aspects of port development including the creation of megaports, shifts in the port governance pattern, usage of port land, the impetus to coastal shipping, new stevedoring and shore handling policy, and benchmarking of best practices from across the globe.[16] It has cited recommendations from the World Bank for such a transformation at regular intervals.

This makes it essential to look at the current statistics regarding the ports of Mumbai. The cargo that is handled in the major ports of the country mostly comprises POL (petroleum, oils and lubricants), coal, containerized cargo, and iron ore and other raw materials for the country's manufacturing industries. Table 8.1 summarizes the traffic handled by Mumbai Port and JNPT from 2011–16. It is instructive to compare Mumbai Port and the JNP, since both are located in Mumbai, albeit JNP is considered to be a modern container port while Mumbai Port is nicknamed the "ailing giant." The figures show however that there has been a consistent rise in the traffic handled by Mumbai Port, while JNPT has experienced more or less constant traffic figures.

Some performance indicators for these ports are given in Table 8.2. The average pre-berthing detention period in port for Mumbai is less than for JNPT. However, the average turnaround time for Mumbai is higher than for JNPT. The capacity utilization for Mumbai appears to be the highest among all the major ports of India, and the average output per ship berth day is greater for JNPT than Mumbai.

The Ministry of Shipping is also trying to augment trade and business through various mechanisms such as one-time trading licenses, a web-based port community system, and standardized bidding documents. The Sagarmala project, initiated by GOI on recommendations of the National Transport Development Policy Committee (NTDPC), undertakes various

Table 8.1 Traffic handled in two major ports of Mumbai (India) (in million tonnes)

Port	Year				
	2011–12	2012–13	2013–14	2014–15	2015–16
Mumbai	56.18	58.03	59.18	61.66	61.11
JNPT	65.73	64.48	62.3	63.8	64.03

Source: Ministry of Shipping, *Annual Report 2016–17* and *Update on Indian Port Sector* (2016).

aspects of transformation of ports in the country through initiatives that look into port modernization, connectivity enhancement, port-linked industrialization, and coastal community development. A key aspect is that all these recommendations of the government invariably ignore any discussions on the labor aspects of the change process.

A look at the employment figures in the ports of Mumbai could be helpful at this point. The employment data from 2001–14 (see Figure 8.1) show a stark contrast in the levels of employment of MBPT and JNPT. Mumbai Port, being an old port, employs a large number of workers to handle the cargo on the docks. JNPT in contrast was established quite recently, with the latest state-of-the-art technology, and is able to handle container traffic. The Mumbai ports present a case of a declining work force where modernization plans are associated with a constant trimming of the workforce. However, employment at JNPT has been more or less constant over the years. The Mumbai Port had a total employee strength of 10,166 in 2015–16, with a total wage bill of 774.23 crore.[17]

The employees working in the ports have been classified into four

Table 8.2 Performance indicators for two major Indian ports (2015–16)

Port	Average pre-berthing detention on port/account (in hours)	Average turnround time (in days)	Capacity utilization (%)	Average output per ship berth day (in tonnes)
Mumbai	7.41	2.90	123.9	7922
JNPT	8.53	1.60	71.6	21287

Sources: Ministry of Shipping, *Annual Report 2016–17* and *Update on Indian Port Sector* (2016).

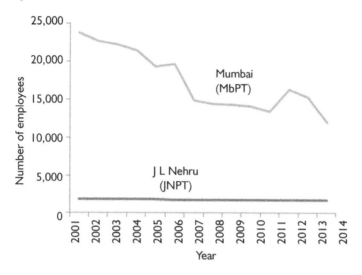

Figure 8.1 Employment in the major ports of Mumbai, 2001–14

Source: Government of India, "Employment in ports," https://data.gov.in/catalog/
employments-ports (accessed November 30, 2017).

different categories, Classes I–IV. Statistics for each port are not available, but the overall strength of employment at the major ports of India is presented in Figure 8.2.

GOI intends that all these changes designed to modernize the ports will be channeled through a bill put forward in 2016 and approved in July 2017, the New Major Ports Authority Bill. Its aim was to replace the Major Port Trusts Act, 1963, and make the governance of port lands and port operations autonomous. In the current system, although the port trusts are empowered to make operational decisions, expenditure of more than 100 crore requires the approval of the Ministry, which is seen as an additional bureaucratic hurdle.[18] This bill encapsulates all the provisions outlined above, but more importantly it marks an institutional shift in the character of the ports. Among the changes proposed are:[19]

- Decentralizing the decision-making process to the level of the newly created Ports Authority, which will have full power to control the operations of the port. This includes deciding on the kind of project undertaken, leasing port land to outsiders, fixing tariffs to ease the bidding process for public–private partnerships (PPP), infrastructure development, and corporate social responsibility (CSR) activities.[20]
- Reducing the membership of the Board of the Port Authority from

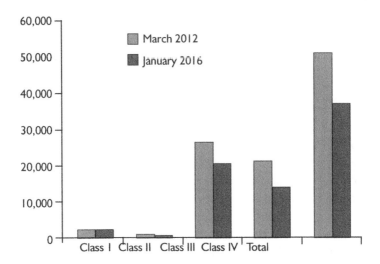

Figure 8.2 Employee numbers for the major ports of India, 2012 and 2016

Source: Indian Ports Association E-Magazine (http://ipa.nic.in/WriteReadData/Links/
e-magazine-Mar16b89187b6-480e-4674-a652-97bd409d44ea.pdf), March 2016.

17–19 to 11, to include representatives of the state government and the Ministries of Railways, Customs, Defense, and Revenue.

- Shifting the governance model of the major ports from the current hybrid model (a mixture of the service and landlord port models) to a landlord port model, with a continual push towards disinvestment and eventual privatization of public terminal operators.[21]
- Setting up an independent review board to look into the projects and services provided by the ports.

The role of the state would no longer be primary. In many ways, the proposed amendments represent a continuation of the ongoing drive to capture port lands and privatizing them. This is justified by arguments that it will lead to optimality and greater efficiency of port operations.

Resisting port reforms

Given the narrative of changes planned for the Indian ports, there has obviously been resistance. At the helm of the resistance efforts have been the trade unions, which have a long history. Today the Indian port sector is represented by a combination of six national trade union federations which have time and again expressed their displeasure about such moves by the government. There are various unions at the ports which have affiliations to these national federations which are HMS (Hind Mazdoor Sabha), CITU (Centre of Indian Trade Unions), AITUC (All India Trade Union Congress), BMS (Bharatiya Mazdoor Sangh) and INTUC (Indian National Trade Union Congress), so they represent the entire national political spectrum.

Given the shift in the institutional character of the port trusts and the ports themselves, we now need to look at the ways in which the trade unions have resisted these changes. This section of the chapter draws on data gathered from the field, in the form of interviews with the major stakeholders in the port reform process. These include trade union leaders, government officials, and the director of a labor institute in Mumbai. For my purposes here, I shall cover those aspects of the proposed changes in the ports that have implications for workers.

Regarding the changes that have been taking place in the port sector, one veteran trade unionist recalls from his experience of interacting with international delegates of port authorities:

> During the heydays, the ports of the UK and Mumbai were considered to be the best ports in the globe. Nowadays, there is no port in the UK, Thatcher had completely transformed it. The Mumbai port still survives however in the process of tremendous transformation [sic].

The implications for labor are focused on two areas, as shown in Figure 8.3:

- Shift in governance: the change from a hybrid service port model to a landlord port model is claimed to infuse a professional approach into the handling of ports. The drive to privatization is seen as an efficiency-enhancing measure in the long run.
- Containerization: Containerization is now well established and its share of port traffic is expected to increase further in the future.

These two areas are not mutually exclusive, and there are intersecting reasons for the decision to move towards these proposed arrangements. However, the reason that they have been taken separately, as we shall see, is the implications that each has for the workers.

Different stakeholders in the ports appear to conceptualize the pro-

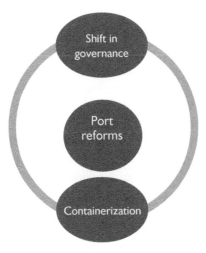

Figure 8.3 Classification of port reforms

posed port reforms in a variety of ways. As one official in the MbPT remarked, "Regarding the proposed amendments there is no change in the new bill with respect to labor. This is all done to modernize the Indian ports so that it is competitive with the global ports of the world."

Meanwhile trade union officials claim that "This bill, if implemented, is going to change the entire work as we know it [in the ports]."

Perceptions of the bill itself also differ between the classes of stakeholder. Let us now look at the main aspects in greater detail.

Shift in governance

The bill relegates the role of port trusts to one of regulator or landlord than decision-maker in terms of operations. The Mumbai Port, which had been an important source of employment, is changing now. As G. S. Dwarakish and Akhil Muhammad Salim point out, the method of port governance, and hence of organizing work, had an economic impact in terms of employment, wages, output and tax revenues.[22] However, the steady reduction in the number of jobs in the port sector points to the changing character of the ports. The Mumbai ports are no longer the key employer in Mumbai. The socio-economic ramifications of such a change, in a country like India which has a huge supply of labor, are immense.

The increasing push towards port reforms has been justified by the claim that they will enhance efficiency. The current neoliberal environment has prompted the backtracking of the state and the introduction of privatization in many other sectors as well as in ports. Public management of ports, like such management elsewhere, has been seen as synonymous with inefficiency and liability, notwithstanding the social benefits of a strong public sector. However, this view of state inefficiency is more of a theoretical doctrine than a proven fact.

Mumbai Port has been called an "ailing giant" among the Indian ports because of its year-on-year cargo handling metrics. They do indeed indicate a sorry state of affairs, given the prime location of the port. However, it is questionable whether a wish to improve these statistics is the main push behind the proposed reforms. The All India Port and Dock Workers' Federation, a major union with members in all the 12 major ports of the country, alleges that the intent behind the proposed changes is to involve multinational companies in running the ports.[23] The MBPT owns a considerable stretch of land—as much as 1,800 acres, from Ballad Pier to Wadala—and the union in Mumbai believes the government wants to sell much of it to private players, who might create for example a multi-specialty hospital, hotels, and restaurants. These developments would indeed generate revenue for the port. A 2014 GOI document, "Land policy guidelines for major ports," proposes the licensing or lease of port lands.[24] The Federation has suggested that instead of repealing the Major Port Trusts Act, the government could amend it and retain the public structure of the port trusts.

GOI has also emphasized the problem of the ageing workforce, which it has argued is incapable of retraining. It is important to note that there has been a freeze on hiring in Mumbai Port since 1992. Almost all the employees are now in their 50s, which could indeed make it relatively difficult to retrain them for other occupations or prepare them to cope with changes in technology. MBPT is on record lamenting that an elderly workforce is incapable of adjusting to the new work organization. One trade unionist claimed that the underlying agenda is that "the port authorities want to get rid of the unions." The Port Authorities Bill initially proposed a reduction in the number of labor representatives on the board from two to one. After union protests GOI finally agreed to retain two positions, on condition that those appointed to them should not be outsiders to the ports.

According to a report by BRIEF, the major inefficiencies that haunt

Mumbai Port are congestion at the port gate, which is largely to do with traffic handling in the city as a whole, storage space on port land, the low draft of vessels, and a tendency for part-offloading of cargo. All these issues have pointed to operational inefficiency and mishandling by MBPT.[25] The report also mentions that "despite such reduction in manpower, there has been no substantial mechanization of the port, and it lacks [an] adequate number of cranes to handle both general and container cargo."[26] Further, the report brings to the light another aspect: that "despite the availability of [a] scanner at MBPT, physical inspection of import cargo is also conducted at the CFS [container freight station] by customs officials. This delays the cargo evacuation process in addition to increasing transaction costs incurred by traders by way of CFS charges."[27] In short, the government's plan to privatize the ports in order to improve their operational efficiency is not targeting the required areas.

Containerization

JNPT was created solely for the purpose of handling container traffic. However, its operational efficiency is restricting it from achieving optimal levels of throughput. Although JNPT as a port uses much less labor than Mumbai Port, still it has not been able to achieve optimal levels either. Mumbai Port has consistently been ranked as having the highest capacity utilization in the country.[28] It outranks both the modern port of JNPT and the corporate port of Ennore. One reason is its strategic location: Mumbai continues to be the focus of India's international trade. However, JNPT shares this advantage, and nearly 90 percent of the shipments it handles are containerized.[29] JNPT also ranks at number 33 of the top 50 container ports (by volume of traffic) in the world.[30] The pre-berthing time at Mumbai Port is less than for JNPT. Given such stark differences between the two ports of Mumbai, the operational efficiency of Mumbai Port seems to be better than that of JNPT.

One union leader pointed out the "fact that the way JNPT has not been able to reach optimal levels speaks a lot about the government initiative. It reflects the lack of planning from the part of the government. There has been a lack of political vision."

However, union officials claim that the major thrust amongst all the new initiatives has always been to reduce the demand for labor. The union official also stated that "We are not opposing modernization of ports. We are only telling the government to consider us also before making any such new provisions."

Another union official remarked that "there should be a national maritime policy along with the new bill for the ports. If the government wants to streamline the ports and makes provisions for the same, labor should also be appropriately dealt with." However, the government has stayed silent on these aspects, and its proposals for changes in the port sector make little or no mention of the workers employed in the ports.

Mumbai Port does have the ability to handle containers, albeit at a lesser capacity than JNPT. The fact is that handling containerized cargo means a smaller labor demand, and that is why Mumbai Port is slowly trimming down its workforce. Apart from facing operational inefficiencies in handling container traffic, the decision to shift to structures that employ less labor in a country with abundant supplies of labor might not be fruitful in the long run. Better alternatives could be to take advantage of India's long coastline by creating newer ports, or augmenting the capacities of minor ports.

Conclusion

This chapter has looked into the dimensions of the changes proposed in the port sector of India. This has included the ways in which this transformation is comprehended and dealt with by the ports' stakeholders. An important aspect of this chapter was to look at these changes from an institutional perspective. Specific themes that affect labor, particularly the governance model of the ports and the recent trend of containerization, have been considered. The response of workers through their unions has been crucial in this.

An important departure from the past has been the collective nature of labor's response to these changes. It has transcended the political affiliations of the unions. It is notable however that the unions have not been able to voice clearly any alternatives to the ongoing changes. Certain suggestions, such as a national maritime policy, have been noteworthy, but a much more concerted effort needs to be put in place if the sector is to develop in a way that benefits its workers. A more coherent union response is also needed to the issue of privatization. When private operators come into the picture, such as JNPT which employs workers on a contractual basis, the response of the unions is something that needs to be seen.

Appendix: models of port management

Table 8.3   Models of port management

Model	Infrastructure ownership	Service and operations provider	Labor employed	Examples of countries
Service port	Public	Public	By port authority	India, Sri Lanka
Tool port	Public	Private (cargo-handling operations)	Private	France
Landlord port	Public	Leased to private (port operations)	Predominantly private	Rotterdam, Antwerp, New York
Fully privatized port or private service port	Private	Private	Private	UK, New Zealand

Source: World Bank, *Port Reform Toolkit* (Washington DC: World Bank, 2007).

Notes

1   Surendra Pratap, *Emerging Trends in Factory Asia: International Capital Mobility, Global Value Chains, and the Labour Movement* (Hong Kong: Asia Monitor Resource Centre, 2014).

2   World Trade Organization, "Trade profiles: India," http://stat.wto.org/CountryProfile/wsDBcountryPFview.aspx?Language=E&Country=IN; and "Trade in value added and global value chains: India," www.wto.org/english/res_e/statis_e/miwi_e/IN_e.pdf) (both accessed June 12, 2017).

3   The other important port was Kolkata (formerly known as Calcutta).

4   Mumbai Port Trust, *Administration Report 2015–16* (Mumbai, India: Mumbai Port Trust, 2016).

5   A dry dock is useful for repair and maintenance of a ship: the area or basin used to anchor ships can be flooded or drained as necessary. A wet dock, on the other hand, has a body of water maintained regularly.

6   M. V. Kamath, *Of Time: History of Mumbai Port* (Mumbai, India: Mumbai Port Trust, 2000).

7   The number of workers in a gang varied depending on the kind of cargo that was being handled. See Ernesto Noronha, "Bombay Dock Labour Board 1948–1994: From insecurity to security to insecurity?" *Economic and Political Weekly* 36(52) (2001–02), pp. 4851–8.

8 Michael Bogaert, *Trade Unionism in Indian Ports: A Case study at Calcutta and Bombay* (New Delhi: Shri Ram Centre for Industrial Relations, 1970).

9 Shubhankita Ojha, "Dock workers in Bombay," *Economic and Political Weekly* 30 (July 25, 2015).

10 Kamath (2000).

11 Noronha (2001–02).

12 Containerization is a modern method of transportation in which the cargo is packed into standard containers which can be reused. It eases the handling of cargo and is also cost-effective.

13 Refer to Figure 8.1 for a comparison of the employment figures for MBPT and JNPT.

14 World Bank, *Reforming the Indian Ports Sector* (Washington DC: World Bank, 2013).

15 Also known as the Rakesh Mohan Committee owing to the name of its chairman.

16 Ministry of Shipping, Annual Report (2016).

17 Mumbai Port Trust, *Administration Report, 2015–16*. As of November 2017, 1 crore rupees = approx. US$160,000.

18 See Amit S. Ray, "Managing port reforms in India: Case Study of Jawaharlal Nehru Port Trust (JNPT) Mumbai. Background paper prepared for the *World Development Report 2005*." (2004).

19 GOI, *Annual Report 2016–17* (New Delhi: GOI Ministry of Shipping, 2017).

20 This work is currently being undertaken by the TAMP (Tariff Authority for Major Ports).

21 See Table 8.3 in the Appendix for a summary of the different port models.

22 G. S. Dwarakish and Akhil Muhammad Salim, "Review on the role of ports in the development of a nation," *Aquatic Procedia* (2015), pp. 295–301.

23 Hindu BusinessLine, "Port union reiterates opposition to new bill", March 9, 2017, www.thehindubusinessline.com/economy/logistics/port-union-reiterates-opposition-to-new-bill/article9578072.ece. (accessed July 23, 2017).

24 "Amended Land Policy Guidelines, Major Ports, 2014 issued by the Ministry of Shipping," www.tariffauthority.gov.in/writereaddata/UploadFile/LandPolicy%20Guid2014_1672.pdf (accessed January 2, 2018).

25 Bureau of Research on Industry and Economic Fundamentals (BRIEF), *Bridging Infrastructural Deficits at Select Trade Ports in India* (New Delhi: BRIEF, 2016).

26 BRIEF (2016), p. 93.

27 BRIEF (2016), p. 93.

28 Refer to Table 8.2.

29 See BRIEF (2016).

30 GOI, "Basic port statistics of India 2014–15" (New Delhi: Transport Research Wing, Ministry of Road Transport and Highways, 2016); GOI, "Update on Indian port sector" (New Delhi: Transport Research Wing, Ministry of Shipping, 2016).

9

Back to Piraeus: Precarity for All!

Dimitris Parsanoglou and Carolin Philipp

Introduction: crises!

Crisis has become the defining term when it comes to describe any development in Greece during the last few years. Since 2010, when the Greek government appealed to the International Monetary Fund (IMF) for financial aid and inaugurated a long and ongoing period of consecutive structural adjustment programs, the country has been a stage for intensive and extensive crisis. From sovereign debt to bank bailouts and from austerity packages to persistent economic stagnation, dismantling of social security and labor rights, and an explosion of unemployment, Greece has been transformed to an arena where any economic and political institution has been questioned, while any prior certainty has been challenged. Formerly marginal parties gained popularity: in 2012 the neo-fascist party Golden Dawn entered the national parliament, and in 2015 the allegedly radical-left Syriza party was elected to the government.

Without any doubt, the "Greek crisis" is part of a broader European sovereign debt crisis, which has affected several EU countries, particularly Greece, Portugal, Ireland, Spain, and Cyprus, since the end of 2009. Bailout programs launched by European institutions and the IMF were implemented in one way or another in all these countries, generating austerity and social unrest. Greece, however, has been the laboratory of ground-breaking experiments elaborated from both above and below.[1] In a very short period of time Greek society at large has experienced a massive amount of violent change and uprising. All the above took the form of emergency measures through the ratification and implementation of three consecutive memoranda of understanding (MOU) between the Greek state and its major creditors, the European Commission (EC), European Central Bank (ECB), and IMF. The austerity measures that have been implemented only on the grounds of the first 2010 MOU have been described as the "harshest fiscal policies" ever applied in a Western country in peacetime.[2] The second (2012) and the third MOU (2015) only consolidated and deepened the measures.

The results of the austerity, however, have not been as promised by the Troika institutions, as the economy of the country is still struggling. The sharp fall in gross domestic product (GDP) by over 45 percent (from US$356,140 million in 2008 to US$194,248 million in 2016), combined with a cut in workers' income in both the public and private sectors, have created a completely new economic environment. Further, the high public indebtedness, which was cited as one of the causes of the crisis, has increased from 109.4 percent of GDP in 2008 to 179 percent in 2016.

Greek officials have repeatedly claimed that the creditors have far too often misjudged the current state, as they have either over-estimated or under-estimated the impact of recessionary policies on Greece. A common criticism is that wrong assessments are used to justify austerity measures.[3] Moreover, while the IMF has repeatedly corrected its analyses and admits misjudgment on its part,[4] the European institutions have not revised their strategy. Internal devaluation policies continue to be accompanied by a massive privatization program affecting all public economic activities and even the national infrastructure. But while the "Greek case" can be used to demonstrate the hopelessness of resistance to neoliberal hegemony and to re-establish the doctrine that there is no alternative (TINA) as a hegemonic narrative, people in Greece have tried to resist austerity via mass mobilizations, occupation of squares, empty houses and public buildings, extensive strikes, and creating grassroots solidarity networks.[5]

"You idiot, get back in there at once and Sell! Sell! Sell!"[6]

A study by the Transnational Institute examined privatizations in seven European countries, and came to the conclusion that "state companies are consistently undersold and even end up costing governments extra money. Particularly in Greece, state assets have often been sold for prices far below their true market value."[7] This points to a general strategy of sell-offs in Greece that the economist Vladimiro Giacché equates to the selling-off of East German industries after the reunification of Germany.

In fact, privatizations in crisis-ridden Greece are a prerequisite in order to ensure funding from the creditors. The Hellenic Republic Asset Development Fund (HRDF/TAIPED) was established on July 1, 2011 in order to "promote the implementation of privatizations in the country, having full responsibility for the application of the respective policy in close cooperation with the Greek government."[8] Under these conditions, valuable and often profitable assets are sold under-priced. The former airport property of Elliniko, worth €1.25 billion, was finally acquired by a private investor for €915 million.[9] Hadjimichalis claims that the airport was sold for €75/m² to a company belonging to the influential Latsis shipowning family while neighboring plots are worth €1.100/m².[10] Aris Chatzistefanou and Katerina Kitidi's film *Catastroka* shows a worker from the public electricity company DEH claiming that while the stock market price of the company is €750–800 billion, it was planned to be sold for €16–17 billion.[11] A further example is the selling of the state's 33 percent stake of OPAP, one of Europe's biggest betting companies with an annual turnover of €4 billion, for €652 million.[12]

The selling-off of more than 14 regional airports in 2016 also attracted criticism. Initially, the package of airports to be sold also included unprofitable enterprises in order that they too would attract investment. However the original package was unpacked and repacked by HRDF/TAIPED, and only highly profitable objects were included. The 14 assets were sold for €1,230 million, even though they were making an annual profit of €150 million.[13] The technical advisor to the HRDF/TAIPED privatization fund in this deal was Lufthansa Consulting, a company that is directly involved (with a share of 8.45 percent) in the public German FRAPORT company which was the purchaser.[14]

While profitable companies are sold under market value, unprofitable assets are sold without their debts. When the state-owned Olympic Airways went to Aegean Airlines, the Greek state spared the investor its debts. The highly indebted railway company TRENOSE/EESTY went debt-free to the Italian investor Ferrovie.[15] In other words, while the Greek state concedes prospects for profit to the private sector—both Greek and international private firms—or to the foreign public sector, it keeps for itself the cost of debts.

The anti-corruption prosecutor has filed charges over the sale of

state-owned properties by the Greek privatization fund.[16] But HRDF/
TAIPED board members have immunity, as was requested by the creditors. During a May 2016 Eurogroup meeting, Greek Finance Minister
Euclid Tsakalotos wanted to make privatization fund officials account-
able for under-value deals that had already been concluded. He was
unsuccessful in his demand and at the end of the meeting, a paragraph
protecting HRDF/TAIPED experts was added to the Eurogroup statement. According to the Greek daily *Kathimerini*, the paragraph was
not included in the official document, but leaked from documents
summarizing the conversations.[17]

Similarly, the port of Piraeus, one of the most significant ports of the
Mediterranean, was sold as prescribed by the EU and IMF creditors. The
Chinese Cosco company purchased a concession until 2051 of 67 percent of the state-owned harbor. The entire port was sold for €280.5
million when its estimated worth is over €1,630 million.[18] The deal was
approved on March 8, 2016. While the Greek Minister of Merchant
Marine was trying to stop the deal, HRDF/TAIPED was speculating that
there would be profits of €1,500 million, for instance through the investment of €350 million (the calculation includes €115 million subsidies
by the European Union that would have been provided to Piraeus even
if it had remained state owned).[19] Additionally it assumed that 125,000
jobs would be created in the process.[20]

In this chapter, we use as our focal point this emblematic case of
the privatization of Piraeus port. The first phase of its privatization
was initiated and completed before the Greek debt crisis, as a significant part of Piraeus's transformation into a global logistical hub. The
"Piraeus-Cosco" project is considered the cornerstone of the national
strategy regarding trade and logistics, and as emblematic for the transformation of labor politics. It theoretically ensures that Piraeus has a
privileged position in the supply chain of Chinese products to Europe,
and is accompanied by the enhancement of relevant infrastructure—
railways, freight centers and so on—and privatization of other major
ports (notably Greece's second biggest port of Thessaloniki, which
has been purchased by a German-led consortium).[21] Even if the case of
Piraeus seems to have definitively closed now that the majority of the
Piraeus Port Authority (OLP) stock will be in the hands of Cosco until
2051, these processes have not been linear or unhindered.

Captain Fu, Cosco's top official in Greece, was asserting before the
take-over of Piraeus, "No other country in Europe offers such potential.

... We believe that Piraeus can be the biggest port in the Mediterranean and one of the most important distribution centers because it is the gateway to the Balkans and southern Europe."[22] With over 18 million passengers per year, it is already the busiest passenger port in Europe, and the third largest container port in the Mediterranean Sea.[23]

Until a decade ago, the port was mainly owned by the state. Pavlos Kambouri and colleagues explain that in Europe "during most of the 20th century, much of the infrastructure was owned and maintained by national governments: postal and telecommunications services, seaports, airports, roads and railways, giving national governments the power to set standards, charges and terms of use and to monitor traffic across frontiers."[24] While this changed in most European countries from the 1980s, in Greece there was no privatization until Kostas Simitis was elected prime minister in 1996 with the Socialist Party. He was welcomed by the rest of Europe as a truly "European"— meaning "neoliberal"—leader.[25] Still, according to Karl-Heinz Roth, the attempts of Simitis and the demands by the European Union for neoliberalization—such as privatizations, financialization, withdrawal of government from major economic activities, flexibilization of labor conditions, and deregulation of the public sector—were hindered by strong union resistance in Greece.[26]

Moreover, in the port area of Piraeus, in Perama and in Elefsina local business structures were a highly intertwined "string of pearls," a collection of labor for logistics as Mithilesh Kumar calls it, of labor structures surrounding the actual labor site.[27] Starting at the Gulf of Elefsina west of Piraeus, the economic fabric consisted of steel factories, ship repair yards, and scrap metal yards. The port and the metal factories employed a large and strongly unionized workforce, while the self-employed truck drivers and the various semi-legal scrap seekers worked in individualized or atomized precarity. These workers came from all over Greece and beyond, migrating to the capital city and its port.

Since the economic crisis and despite it, the economic performance of all piers in Piraeus was increasing, in terms of both net profit and turnover.[28] As a dockworker we interviewed admitted, "in a port, there is ALWAYS work!" The container-handling Piers II and III were privatized in 2009. They are the only container terminals in Cosco's global portfolio that it owns 100 percent.[29] They are mainly used for transhipment, while Pier I, which was privatized in 2016, is mainly used for "storage" of cars.

Resistances

Deregulation policies and privatizations are not entirely successful, as examples of labor resistance in Greece show. Greece hosted 44 percent of Europe's general strikes from 1980 to 2008.[30] In the port, the harbor workers went on strike repeatedly, and in 2016 for a whole month.[31] But as one of the dockworkers explained to us, "postponing the process of privatization was the maximum that we could achieve."

As this dockworker unionist and other grassroots unionists explained to us, the established large trade unions have failed to renew their strategies and to create alternative narratives. They claimed that many unions which want to be acknowledged as workers' representatives have become "bureaucratic and consensual," and activism in unions has declined significantly. A labor lawyer stressed in an interview that at the same time, public institutions built to ensure workers' rights are practically "inactive." For example the:

> Labour Inspectorate Body (SEPE) that is responsible for assuring that e.g. health and security rules are implemented at a workplace, that the workers are insured etc., could play a crucial role in workers' rights, but they don't. This problem of inactivity and corruption, also applies to the public social insurance institute IKA that is supposed to monitor and control workers' insurance conditions. There are cases of employers bribing IKA inspectors not to control workplaces.

Lefteris Kretsos asserts that the renewal of unions is connected to general social movement cycles of protest.[32] The December riots of 2008 which boosted many facets of social movement organization seemed to prove him right, as he counted 35 newly established unions from 2008 to 2011 in Greek urban areas.[33] While the labor lawyer we interviewed stated that "workers that are my clients have become less demanding concerning their rights," she also underlined the importance of the newly established grassroots unions: "Based on my experience, workers who are organized in grassroots unions have the best support. Grassroots unions have a different character from other unions. They are functioning based on direct democracy, they try to involve workers in every decision, they have no representatives or professional members."

At the same time, migrants and young people are increasingly attracted to newly formed, often grassroots unions.[34] New grassroots unions, which started from the early 1990s and increased during the 2000s and especially during the crisis, cover sectors where precarity is the dominant form of labor, such as couriers, delivery workers, call-center agents, engineers who work under a supposedly freelance scheme, and workers in the tourism industry. These unions, which are based on horizontal and direct-democratic organization, seem to be able to tackle many difficulties of the deregulated labor market in a much more effective way than the traditional unions.[35]

Since the emergence of precarity as "the central organising platform for a series of social struggles that spread across the space of Europe,"[36] there has been an effort, particularly by precarious activists, to build a subject that could be considered as the dominant form of the contemporary (post-Fordist) working class:

> The precariat is to postfordism what proletariat was to fordism: flexible, temporary, part-time, and self-employed workers are the new social group which is required and reproduced by the neoliberal and post-industrial economic transformation. It is the critical mass that emerges from globalization, while demolished factories and neighborhoods are being substituted by offices and commercial areas. They are service workers in supermarkets and chains, cognitive workers operating in the information industry.[37]

Nevertheless, it seems that the experiences of precarious workers cannot be accommodated in a unified subjectivity in analogy with previous patterns of class-based collective identities. Precarious labor exists only in the plural, as a multiplicity of experiences variously positioned, exploited, and lived within contemporary capitalism, and not as a unified subjectivity or "precariat."[38] Precarity is a multifaceted and ambivalent condition, including vulnerability, insecurity, and possibly poverty, but also ambivalences such as flexibility and mobility, as well as a strange kind of freedom. Independence can be valuable for some precarious workers, such as the postdoc researcher cum scrap collector whom we interviewed for our research in Piraeus, who stressed, "I don't have a boss. I work whenever I want."[39] Maybe this is the strong point of the concept: that it offers a theoretical and empirical framework of/for new forms of subjectivities and agencies that largely shape contemporary labor.

Seen from this perspective, we can have a better understanding of the social struggles that emerged in crisis-and-austerity Greece during the last few years: labor struggles around precarious labor in the margins of formal unionism; social struggles targeting issues linked directly or indirectly to a social wage through alternative forms of solidarity networks. Characteristic of these emerging resistances is this summary by an activist in a social clinic in Athens, who paradigmatically described the clinic's organizational and networking approach and its ethics:

> We are a non-hierarchical organization, all are equal, no matter if doctor or volunteer. We try to implement the non-hierarchical characteristic also in our relationships with the patients who come here. It is not about charity, it is political activism. We don't accept moneys donation from anyone in order to stay independent and we have a problem with NGOs who do that. We cooperate with the other 50 social clinics in Greece, in the network of solidarity economy and we work together with refugees who are in camps or in squats.

These characteristics are also found in refugee housing squats and other solidarity networks. The new resistances and solidarities are rather displaced from or go beyond the working space, as—not always successfully—they do not only want to ensure good working conditions. In the same vein, grassroots unions go beyond claims for good working conditions (without abandoning collective bargaining) as they also intervene in broader issues such as urban inequalities, repression, and gender issues.

Back to Piraeus: "The 'Chinaman' [sic] is not the issue here, Dude"

In the center of Athens there is a frequent graffiti stencil saying "Resistance to the Chinification." In the port region, the graffiti is more precise: "Never the port to the Chinaman" ("Ποτε λιμανι στον Κινεζο"). The bulk of criticism of economic policies during the Memoranda years, stemming either from trade unions or from political forces on both the left and right that stand against them, focuses on two interrelated issues: deregulation and Chinification. Both of these positions imply a lost paradise, described above as the "string of pearls"; a world of a regulated labor regime—defined explicitly or implicitly in Fordist terms—which entails stable working relations with all the elements of labor protection that the Fordist regime of accumulation made us believe existed, at least for some decades within and beyond the *Trente Glorieuses*. (This supposed regime ensured mass production while guaranteeing specific rights to unions like collective bargaining.) On the other hand, "Chinafication," a term often accompanied or replaced by "balkanization" and/or "africanization," is usually lined up as a synonym for the degradation of the country to an allegedly lower status in the international pecking order. A common denominator of these signifiers is independent of the strong racist connotations: the allusion is specifically to that labor regime. That is, it is to the labor regime that the creditors of the country want to impose on Greek workers.

Piraeus, and more specifically the port of Piraeus, is one of the few places which can so clearly resemble a Purgatory of the crisis, because it has suffered two major losses: of the old labor regime and national sovereignty. Piraeus is a hub where the old Paradise and the new Hell collide in a paradigmatic way. This process of alienation has been long, and has only been completed very recently. Whatever could be thought of as Fordism in terms of organization, processes, and relations can exemplarily be found in the Piraeus Port Authority SA (OLP).

At the end of 2012, the OLP was employing 1,206 workers, mostly dockers.[40] Most of them are unionized along the lines of the Dockworkers' Union – Port of Piraeus, founding member of the International Dockworkers Council (IDC), which is an international association formed by 92 organizations from 41 countries with more than 100,000 affiliated members.[41] Even some years before the concession agreement between OLP, Piraeus Container Terminal (PCT), and Cosco Pacific, signed on November 25, 2008, governments and conservative media were insisting on the "outrageous privileges of OLP dockworkers."[42] This allegedly unjustified Paradise was replaced by a new regime, at least in Piers II and III (which were constructed and equipped mainly by Cosco).

The PCT labor regime, however, could be described for the moment more as a "black hole" than a clear-cut hell. Working conditions and labor relations inside the PCT do not easily become public, while even entering the PCT's facilities is from difficult to impossible. Even the worker recruitment process, which is mainly monitored by the Diakinisis Port & SIA E.E., subsidiary of ELGEKA S.A., the largest Greek commercial company in the food sector, is kept as a sealed secret, a fact that raises questions regarding recruitment pathways and working rights. As an employee and unionist in OLP put it, "we do not have any formal contact with the company, because the company is theoretically a subcontractor of Cosco. With the people of Diakinisis who are in the recruitment team, whenever we have gone inside, in any case you confront them, you know who they are, you know names, but there is no discussion on [recruitment process and labor issues]." This silence hinders any effort to politicize labor relations and negotiate better conditions for the workers, who remain individualized without any possibility of collective representation. Similar silence exists in the PCT, according to the same unionist:

> In the beginning, they were talking; they had the [director] of Human Resources to speak, who was trembling like a leaf every time, because we went with Alavanos [former leader of Syriza], when he was a candidate for head of the region of Attica, and they gave us this little lady. And there were two guys from Diakinisis who were pretending to be indifferent passers-by, but they were following us everywhere. We were in front of the whole recruitment team, and she was trembling like a leaf, she couldn't look us in the eye. She was a 50–55-year-old woman in this condition. Now, they have changed policy, they have stopped talking entirely. For example, they were not responding to IDC or after, they were giving some vague answers. Then [even] the IDC [demands had to be] addressed to the headquarters in Antwerp. They were not yet moved to Piraeus, because now the headquarters have moved to Piraeus.

Little information exists on the everyday working conditions of laborers. Just a glimpse of the deteriorating conditions has been provided by workers who complained about the company after being fired. More precisely, they pressed charges against the subcontractor for which they worked in the PCT pier, because they were fired when they tried to form a union inside PCT. The working conditions and work arrangements could best be described as extreme flexibility: "You were receiving an SMS to be at work in three hours. Nobody knew in which shift he would work the next day. Me, for nine months, I never worked on the basis of a work schedule. There was no schedule at all."[43] The question that is logically posed from the descriptions provided here is what margins for resistance exist, particularly after the sale of Pier 1 and the rest of the port to Cosco.

The general structures increasing the precarization of work come from the heart of Europe, as is exemplified by two-thirds of the Troika, the European Commission and the European Central Bank, as well as by the Eurogroup. The framework of labor in Greece is set by the creditors. This is hidden by the fact that the European institutions want to blame China for the poor working conditions. European Commission officials raised objections about the sale based on unfair competition and monopolization, and considered a screening for investments by state-owned Chinese companies.[44] Yet these claims of "improper privatization" have to be seen in the framework of German and Dutch harbor companies' fearing a loss of their monopoly on the European market to the Chinese.[45]

While labor protection laws in Greece used to be (at least considered) strong compared with other OECD countries, their erosion is undisputed.[46]

A dockworker explained to us that after privatization they have been struggling to implement International Labour Organization (ILO) conventions dedicated to dockwork (numbers 137 & 152), but these rights were actually included in their now expiring CBA (collective bargaining agreement). Chrisos Boukalas and Julian Müller describe a process of structural adjustments of the labor market that were demanded by the EU and IMF creditors.[47] The all-over logic of labor market policies is characterized by individualizing workers and demoralizing them to discourage from organizing into trade unions or engaging in other forms of collective action. The weakening of workers' organizations is achieved by weakening collective agreements even more. For instance, firm-level agreements are given precedence over sectoral agreements even if they include worse terms for the workers. An estimated 80 percent of Greek private-sector workers are not covered by any sectoral or firm-level agreement. This situation is worsened by creditors' instructions to facilitate redundancies in both the public and private sectors. In addition, there is a growing tendency to implement the "active labor market policies" (ALMPS) launched by the Public Employment Service (PES), through which unemployed persons work temporarily, without the same rights and labor law provisions as a formally employed worker.[48]

An employment lawyer pointed out the total failure of the labor policies launched in the MOU in both creating and keeping existing employment:

> The logic of memorandum politics is that when the salary is low, the employer would more easily employ a new worker and also the black market is tackled. Practically this did not happen. It has not really affected the

employment for all ages, nor the black market. I assume it was just an excuse in order to reduce even more the salary of workers and reduce the cost for the employers.

While new forms of grassroots unions seem to be able to tackle many difficulties of the deregulated labor market, it seems that resistance does not necessarily occur in specific workplaces. Perhaps we should reconceptualize labor struggles, since the sociological and anthropological accounts of immaterial and precarious labor, as they have been developed by post-operaist theorists and others including mostly forms of cognitive and affective work, have reshaped our perceptions of work time and work space. Precarity escapes time and space barriers: it is an intruder in the space of leisure since it erodes any distinction between working and non-working time, and it has led to a total eclipse of the struggle for workers' rights. The system of wage labor and the corresponding welfare system produced a space-fixated work subjectivity (based on normal, full-time, wage employment) measured according to working time. Precarious labor implodes this subjectivity on various levels. It is not space-fixated, the precarious worker works in a multiplicity of locales, and their work cannot be quantified and remunerated according to the system of wage labor measurement.

There has been an effort, particularly by precarious activists, to build a subject that could be considered as the dominant form of the contemporary (post-Fordist) working class:

> The precariat is to postfordism what proletariat was to fordism: flexible, temporary, part-time, and self-employed workers are the new social group which is required and reproduced by the neoliberal and post-industrial economic transformation. It is the critical mass that emerges from globalization, while demolished factories and neighborhoods are being substituted by offices and commercial areas. They are service workers in supermarkets and chains, cognitive workers operating in the information industry.[49]

Conclusion

"The crisis consists precisely in the fact that the old is dying and the new cannot be born in this interregnum [when] a great variety of morbid symptoms appear."

Antonio Gramsci, *Selections from the Prison Notebooks*[50]

We have described the short history of the two labor worlds that comprise the logistical world under construction in "one of Europe's top five container-shipping hubs."[51] It is important to note that labor struggles occurred mostly in the lost "Paradise": most of them were focused on preserving the Paradise, avoiding degradation to the status of the neighboring Hell. Piraeus port, in its simplicity (one of the clearest cases of the foreign direct investment so much sought by Greek governments) and its complexity (there is undoubtedly a latent war among different actors who from their position and in their own interests have raised obstacles to the completion of the Piraeus Port-Thriassion Freight Centre project), can open avenues of research where labor regimes, labor struggles, sovereignty, and above all crisis, can be revisited. And they must be revisited, since up to now, the explanations provided are either deterministic or/and bound hand and foot by facilitating, yet repressive models.

We have tried through broader speculations to highlight that the need described above is intensified by an aporia that occurs whenever someone tries to explain the most blatant contradiction that characterizes austerity-and-crisis Greece: how is it possible that the most unexpected, violent and hopeful "cries for freedom" coincide with the most repressive, disappointing, and hopeless outcomes of the social antagonism?[52] In other words, how can revolutionary developments be so close to and intertwined with reactionary regressions? What we have tried to demonstrate in this short account which stems from our specific case study is that for better or for worse the answers remain open. To put it differently, even in conjunctures where/when time flies—and this is the case of the last few years in Greece—the future seems to last forever![53]

Notes

1 Antonis Liakos, "Griechenland und Europa. Im Knäuel der Krisenreaktionskräfte—Vorurteile und Richtigstellungen" (Greece and Europe. Entanglements of crisis reactions—prejudices and corrections). *Lettre International* 95 (2011), pp. 19–24. See also Athina Athanasiou, "Rethinking Greece: Athena Athanasiou on social struggles and critical resistance," *Greek Left Review* (2016), https://greekleftreview.wordpress.com/2016/02/28/rethinking-greece-athena-athanasiou-on-social-struggles-and-critical-resistance/ (accessed June 14, 2017).

2 Berenberg Bank, "Macro views," May 20, 2011, quoted by Stefan Kaufmann,

"*Schummel-Griechen machen unseren Euro kaputt.*" *Beliebte Irrtümer in der Schuldenkrise* ("*The Cheating Greeks are Destroying our Euro*": *Popular Mistakes in the Debt Crisis*), Berlin: Rosa-Luxemburg-Stiftung, 2012), p. 15.

3 Margarita Argiropoulou, "Τα λάθη των προβλέψεων του ΔΝΤ για την ελληνική οικονομία, επισημαίνει το Μαξίμου" ("The mistakes of the IMF forecasts for the Greek economy, points out Maximus"), *Dikaiologitika*, December 13, 2006, www.dikaiologitika.gr/eidhseis/politikes-eidhseis/134486/idoy-ta-egklimatika-lathi-tou-dnt-gia-tin-ellada. (accessed June 14, 2017).

4 Kathimerini, "IMF admits to misjudging economic performance," April 21, 2017.

5 Carolin Philipp, *Spaces of Resistance. Framing Crisis and Activism in Greece*, PhD thesis, University of Kassel, Germany, 2017.

6 Randolph Duke addressing Wilson in the John Landis film, *Trading Places* (1983).

7 Sol Trumbo Vila and Matthijs Peters, *The Privatising Industry in Europe* (Amsterdam: Transnational Institute, 2016), p. 21.

8 See Hellenic Republic Asset Development Fund: www.hradf.com/en/fund

9 EFSYN, "Χαμηλά ο κυβερνητικός πήχης για το Ελληνικό" ("The government's bar for Elliniko airport is low") March 21, 2014; Hellenic Republic Asset Development Fund, "Lamda Development is nominated Preferred Investor for the acquisition of the share capital of Hellinikon S.A.," press release, March 31, 2014, www.hradf.com/storage/files/uploads/03d983c86a53f1a3baa68be2c8aa9a9b.pdf (accessed December 1, 2017).

10 Costis Hadjimichalis, "Uneven geographical development and socio-spatial justice and solidarity: European regions after the 2009 financial crisis," *European Urban and Regional Studies* 48(3) (2011), pp. 254–74, at p. 173.

11 Aris Chatzistefanou and Katerina Kitidi, *Catastroika: Privatization Goes Public*, documentary film, 127 minutes (2012).

12 Reuters, "Greece completes privatisation of gambling monopoly OPAP," August 12, 2013.

13 Niels Kadritzke, "Privatisierungsschwindel in Griechenland" ("The privatization scam in Greece"), *Le monde diplomatique* (2016).

14 The left parliamentarian Fabio de Masi demanded clarification in the European parliament: parliamentary question on "Role of Lufthansa Consulting in connection with the privatisation of 14 Greek airports," 2015, www.europarl.europa.eu/sides/getDoc.do?pubRef=-//EP//TEXT+WQ+E-2015-013122+0+DOC+XML+V0//DE; www.europarl.europa.eu/sides/getDoc.do?type=WQ&reference=E-2015-013122&language=EN (accessed December 1, 2017).

15 Giannis Kimpouropoulos, "Πώς οι ιδιωτικοποιήσεις «φεσώνουν» το κράτος" ("How the privatizers are kidding with the state"), Dikaiologitika, October 2,2016.

16 *Kathimerini*, "Charges filed over privatization fund property deal", July 20, 2016, http://www.ekathimerini.com/199761/article/ekathimerini/news/

charges-filed-over-privatization-fund-property-deal (accessed December 28, 2017).

17 *Kathimerini*, "Επιστολή δυσφορίας από Ε.Ε. προς Αθήνα" ("Discontent letter from EU to Athens"), May 20, 2016, www.kathimerini.gr/861672/article/epikairothta/politikh/epistolh-dysforias-apo-ee-pros-a8hna (accessed December 28, 2017).

18 *Paron*, "Χαρίζουν τον ολπ στους Κινέζους" ("They are giving the OLP to the Chinese as a gift"), March 16, 2014.

19 Kadritzke (2016).

20 *Kathimerini*, "Πώληση ολπ στην Cosco έναντι 368,5 εκατ" ("Selling of OLP to Cosco for €368.5 million"), January 21, 2016.

21 *Neues Deutschland*, "Thessaloniki unterm Hammer" ("Thessaloniki for sale"), April 26, 2017.

22 *Guardian*, "Chinese carrier Cosco is transforming Piraeus—and has eyes on Thessaloniki," June 19, 2014.

23 International Association of Ports and Harbours, "World port traffic data," 2015, www.iaphworldports.org/iaph/wp-content/uploads/WorldPort-Traffic-Data-for-IAPH-using-LL-data2015.pdf (accessed December 1, 2017); Lloyd's List, "One Hundred Ports 2017", https://lloydslist.maritime intelligence.informa.com/one-hundred-container-ports-2017 (accessed December 28, 2017)

24 Pavlos Hatzopoulos, Nelli Kambouri, and Ursula Huws, "The containment of labour in accelerated global supply chains: the case of Piraeus Port", *Work Organisation, Labour and Globalisation* 8(1) (Summer 2014), pp. 5–21, at p. 6.

25 Susannah Verney, "Greece: a new era," *Mediterranean Politics* 2(1) (1997), pp. 193–200.

26 Karl-Heinz Roth, "Griechenland und die Euro-Krise" ("Greece and the euro crisis"), *Soʒial Geschichte Online* 6 (2011), pp. 156–76, at p. 157.

27 Mithilesh Kumar, "Laboring for logistics: the discontents of dreams of infrastructure," unpublished workshop paper, Kolkata Research Group (2016).

28 See for OLP in 2014, "China's Cosco, five other suitors express interest in Piraeus Port," *Reuters*, April 28, http://in.reuters.com/article/2014/04/28/greece-privatisation-piraeus-idINL6N0NK2KQ20140428; and for 2016, "Cosco-led port of Piraeus in Greece posts higher results for 2016," *Tomos News*, May 20, www.tornosnews.gr/en/tourism-businesses/new-investments/25400-cosco-led-port-of-piraeus-in-greece-posts-higher-results-for-2016.html (both accessed December 1, 2017).

29 "Terminals and Offices for Cosco Pacific," www.coscopac.com.hk/eng/business/terminal_portfolio.php

30 John Kelly and Kestin Hamann, "General strikes in Western Europe 1980–2008," paper for the European Regional Congress of the International Industrial Relations Association, Copenhagen, June 28–July 1, 2010, https://pseudoerasmus.files.wordpress.com/2015/02/europe-strikes.pdf (accessed December 1, 2017).

31 *Neues Deutschland*, " Im Hafen gibt es immer Arbeit" ("In a port, there's always work"), July, 20, 2017.

32 Lefteris Kretsos, "Grassroots unionism in the context of economic crisis in Greece," *Labour History* 52 (2011), p. 274.

33 Dimitris Dalakoglou and Antonis Vradis (eds.), *Revolt and Crisis in Greece: Between a Present Yet to Pass and a Future Still to Come* (Oakland , Calif./ Edinburgh: AK Press and Occupied London, 2011); Kretsos (2011), p. 268.

34 Kretsos (2011), p. 267.

35 For an analytical account of grassroots unions, see Kretsos (2011).

36 B. Neilson and N. Rossiter, "Precarity as a political concept, or, Fordism as exception", *Theory, Culture and Society*, special issue on "Precarity and Cultural Work", 25(7–8) (2008), p. 51.

37 Precarias a la Deriva, "A la Deriva por los Circuitos de la Precariedad Femenina," ("A drift through the circuits of female precarity") (2004), p. 48. www.flacsoandes.edu.ec/generoycultura/Publicaciones/Publicacionesprofesoras/Profesorasasociadas/Perez-Orozco-Amaia/Libros/Precarias_a_la_Deriva_%20Amaia_Perez%20Orozco.pdf (accessed December 1, 2017).

38 N. Trimikliniotis, D. Parsanoglou, and V. S. Tsianos, "Mobile commons and/in precarious spaces: mapping migrant struggles, digitalities and social resistance," *Critical Sociology* 42(7–8), (2016), pp. 1035–49.

39 Carolin Philipp, "Metal scrappers: connectivity and flexibility of the marginalised," *Logistical Worlds*, December 15, 2014, http://logisticalworlds.org/blogs/metal-scrappers (accessed December 1, 2017). See also Precarias a la Deriva (2004), p. 17.

40 For more on the personnel and administrative structure, see the company's website: http://olp.gr/en/the-port-of-piraeus/organization-structure/item/641-organization-structure

41 http://dockers.gr/

42 The Minister of Mercantile Marine, Manolis Kefaloyannis, published in June 2005 a list of OLP dockworkers, some of whom had an annual income over 140,000 euros: see "OLP: Kefaloyannis' lists with high wages", *Euro2Day*, June 9, 2005, www.euro2day.gr/news/enterprises/article/81407/olp-listes-kefalogiannh-gia-misthoys-retire.html. This type of argument reappears every time there is a strike or a major development with regard to the status of the port. See for example regarding the strikes against the enactment of the concession agreement in November 2009, *Kathimerini*, "The privileges that keep the port closed," November 8, 2009, www.kathimerini.gr/375623/article/oikonomia/ellhnikh-oikonomia/ta-pronomia-poy-kratoyn-kleisto-to-limani (both sites accessed December 1, 2017).

43 *Prin*, interview of former employee Dimitris Batsoulis by Leonidas Vatikiotis, "Fear and slave trade—Cosco transformed Piraeus into Dachau—they fire whoever protests", June 2, 2013, http://leonidasvatikiotis.wordpress.com/2013/06/03/%CF%86%CF%8C%CE%B2%CE%BF%CF%82-%CE%BA%CE%B1%CE%B9-%CE%B4%CE%B-

F%CF%85%CE%BB%CE%B5%CE%BC%CF%80%CF%8C%CF%81%CE
%B9%CE%BF-%CE%BD%CF%84%CE%B1%CF%87%CE%AC%CE%B-
F%CF%85-%CE%AD%CE%BA%CE%B1%CE%BD%CE%B5-%CF%84/ (accessed
December 1, 2017).

44 Reuters, "EU promises tough line on U.S., China while pushing for free
trade," June 23, 2017.

45 *Ethnos*, "Οι Βρυξέλλες «μπλοκάρουν» την ιδιωτικοποίηση του ολπ"
("Brussels 'blocks' the privatization of OLP"), December 13, 2013.

46 Lefteris Kretsos, "Grassroots unionism in the context of economic crisis in
Greece," *Labor History* 52(3) (2011), pp. 265–86, at p. 266. Kretsos challenges
the supposed strength of Greek labor protection as ideologically driven in
order to neoliberally destroy labor protection. Christos Ioannou, "Employment regulation and labour relations in Greece," Hellenic Observatory,
London School of Economics, November 3, 2009, www.lse.ac.uk/europea-
nInstitute/research/hellenicObservatory/pdf/Seminars/IOANNOU-ppt.pdf
(accessed December 1, 2017).

47 Chrisos Boukalas and Julian Müller, "Undoing labour in Greece: memoranda, workfare and Eurozone 'competitiveness,'" *Global Labour Journal*
6(3) (2015), pp. 390–405.

48 Boukalas and Müller (2015).

49 Maria-Isabel Casas-Cortes and Sebastian Cobarrubias, "Drifting through
the Knowledge Machine", in Stephen Shukaitis and David Graeber (eds.),
Constituent Imagination: Militant Investigations//Collective Theorization
(Oakland, Calif.: AK Press, 2007), pp. 112–26.

50 Antonio Gramsci, *Selections from the Prison Notebooks*, ed. and trans. Quentin
Hoare and Geoffrey Nowell Smith (London: Lawrence & Wishart, 1971).

51 Jonathan Stearns, "Piraeus port has 'geostrategic' edge as Greece pushes
logistics", *Bloomberg Businessweek*, February 24, 2014, www.ekathimerini.
com/158125/article/ekathimerini/business/piraeus-port-has-geostrate-
gic-edge-as-greece-pushes-logistics (accessed December 28, 2017).

52 Immanuel Wallerstein, *The End of the World as We Know It: Social Science
for the Twentieth-First Century* (Minneapolis, Minn.: University of Minnesota
Press, 1999), p. 154.

53 Louis Althusser, *The Future Lasts Forever: A Memoir* (New York: New Press,
1993).

10

Contested Logistics? Neoliberal Modernization and Resistance in the Port City of Valparaíso

Jorge Budrovich Sáez and Hernán Cuevas Valenzuela

Introduction: Valparaíso and capitalist development

One of the concrete ways in which the global dimension of capitalist market expansion can be perceived is through its infrastructure. Roads, railways, cables, channels, ports, among others, are the vital organs of capitalist development strategies. When carried out on concrete territories, these lead to disputes and conflicts which nurture forms of violence, negotiations, and resistance which constitute the background of the so-called prehistory of humanity. In this regard, ports are an exemplar: as the popular saying states, "A port, a history."[1]

In this chapter we focus on the case of Valparaíso, the historic port city located in central Chile just 118 kilometers from the capital, Santiago. Because of the radical nature of the economic and labor reforms implemented and the depth of the social and political changes experienced there, the port city of Valparaíso is a privileged case study for observing the operations of capital and the resistance that these generate in society.

In our interpretation, the changes and development of Valparaíso can be best understood based on three concepts: neoliberalization, extraction, and logistics, three master logics that govern or structure social processes in Valparaíso. Here we study the logics of neoliberalization, extraction, and logistics in the port sector, and in particular we analyze their coupling in the concrete operations of capital that take place in Valparaíso. This linking of neoliberalization, logistics, and extraction has contributed to the consolidation of a specific version of capitalism and a specific port model that complements it.

When we refer to logistics and extraction, we are not only including specific economic sectors such as transport and supply chain management (logistics), or the extraction of raw materials and primary production (extraction). Instead, we are referring to two systemic underground and fundamental trends, dynamic or logics that underlie and structure phenomenic heterogeneity.[2] Similarly, for us, neoliberalization does not only appoint an economic doctrine or ideology, but covers an economicist form of political rationality that is deployed in heterogeneous practices and devices that constitute subjectivities and social worlds based on mechanisms for commodification, mercantilization, and competition. In other worlds, these are general, cross-cutting structuring mechanisms and processes that have a global presence, and are also characteristic of the installation and unfolding of capitalism in Chile.

Extraction, logistics, neoliberalization

For E. Gudynas, extractivism is characterized by the exploitation of large volumes or high-intensity exploitation of primary materials or natural resources that depend on enclave economies and are exported as commodities.[3] More than extractivism understood as a development model, Gudynas refers to extractivist activities or sectors which are anchored locally and positioned globally as well. The most dynamic sectors of the Chilean economy such as mining, agro-industry, fishing, aquiculture, and the forestry industry are representative of extractive activities. Here we expand the scope of the concept to understand extraction as a social logic that refers to any violent appropriation or procurement of the value of raw materials and forms of life that exist in the biosphere, including the surface and depths of the land and ocean.[4] In this sense, mass tourism to and the gentrification of Valparaíso can also be understood as extractive activities in which the community's ways of life, identity, history, and material and symbolic heritage become values to be appropriated and commercialized on a large scale.[5]

Ports serve a crucial logistical function for extractive sectors.

Extractive activity that is oriented towards large-scale production for export requires logistical facilities that ensure that maritime transport can be provided at a good price. But what is logistics? Logistics has been defined as the part of the supply chain that refers to the planning, implementation, and control of efficiency for effective circulation and storage of goods, services, and information from the point of origin to the point of consumption.[6] In this strict sense, logistics refers fundamentally to the optimization of cargo transport, and the services and information related to that operation. In a broader sense, logistics refers to practices that organize the operations of capital to maximize the transfer, transportation, communication, coordination, and distribution of data, ideas, people, and objects.

Logistics points to the dissolution of the distinction between production and circulation in capital operations. Logistics allows economic activities to be fragmented, externalized, and scheduled in a deterritorialized manner according to the competitive advantages of each economy so that the parts and/or processes can then be articulated for the benefit of capital.[7] The development of containers as an intermodal transportation innovation, which facilitated this post-Fordist scheme of production, has brought about a series of innovations in port logistics infrastructure in order to reduce transportation costs in international trade. Containerization has also promoted the replacement of weight (tonnes) with logistics activity that is more centered on volume (measured as TEU, twenty foot equivalent) and the efficient administration of container mobility in space and time.

Containerization has affected the new designs of cargo ships, and has forced the adaptation of infrastructure and expansion of berthing facilities in Valparaíso. It has also led to the adoption of gantry cranes for high tonnage, the modification of loading and unloading work processes, the automation of work (and resulting decrease in labor), standardization of cargo, modernization of merchandise control forms, and the intensive use of space in logistical support sites outside of the port.[8] The art of logistics can be better understood as the optimizing rationality of resources, which is based on cost–benefit analysis to achieve efficient mobility and transfer of objects, people, and data in time and space. This calculating rationality of logistics is very much aligned with the economicist rationality of neoliberalism.

Following Brenner and colleagues, we define neoliberalization as a complex of processes and practices which intensify the commodification and mercantilization of varied spheres of life (society and nature) and produce unequal regulation of the economy through state interventions.[9] These interventions can range from delay in the public sector to a sectoral strategic planning role. But the characteristic is that they always function in accordance with the interests of the business sector. Over the past few decades, public policy regarding ports in Chile is an example of neoliberalization because public ports saw the majority of their activities privatized through a public concessions policy that attracted the interest of major investors. As such, the construction of logistics infrastructure and increased flexibility and (de)regulation of the labor market have followed the logic of mercantilization and the expansion of an economicist rationality founded on the principle of competition generalized as a criterion of efficiency (economics).[10] As we shall see, the characteristic instruments of the neoliberalization of the port sector in Chile favor linkage between the principles of competition and mercantilization, and the social logics of extraction and logistics.

The successful coupling of these social logics—extraction, logistics, and neoliberalization—is an incidental result. It requires an effort of political coordination and multiple negotiations among agents with different and even opposing interests.

The Chilean port model

Various authors have stated that the "successful" development strategy implemented in Chile over the past 30 years is based on commercial openness and the export capacity of a handful of economic sectors that have been able to use their competitive advantages.[11] It also has been said that over the last few decades, the economy has grown and the export matrix, which was traditionally dominated by copper mining, has diversified.

From this perspective, the design and implementation of port policies in Chile forms part of a national development strategy based on an open and export-based economy that seeks to successfully insert itself in the context of global capitalism. In order to achieve that success, it is fundamental to set competitive port tariffs that benefit the other sectors of the economy. From this perspective, the main organizer of public policy in relation to ports has been the promotion of the country's competitiveness. Investment in ports and the majority of the major investments in infrastructure that have been made in Chile are focused on facilitating development and competition among private projects, with the understanding that these make development and the competitiveness of the national economy more dynamic.[12]

However, in view of the evident environmental and social costs of this strategy and persistent social inequality, over the past few years international institutions, think-tanks, intellectuals, and social and political movements have critically reevaluated the results of this development strategy. In the context of this renewed discussion of development in Chile, it is surprising that we lack detailed studies that discuss the fundamental role that sea ports and their modernization have played in the development of this controversial strategy of economic development, given that its importance has been fundamental to Chile's economic growth.

A recent government report identified 73 ports on Chilean coasts. Of these, 63 are private and operate on the basis of public coastline concessions. The ten most important ports are former Chilean Port Enterprise (EMPORCHI) facilities. These are still state property and are managed by autonomous public port companies that form part of the Public Companies System. Of these, eight operate on the basis of private concessions for the berthing facilities, which were transferred to private operators for 20 or more years based on competitive public bidding processes. In these ports, each public port company functions in practice as a port maritime authority, and manages the contracts with private port terminal concessionaires.[13]

The ports of San Antonio and Valparaíso are multi-purpose ports which process various types of cargo and present a high level of complexity. As a result, they bring together diverse global supply chains, and form part of complex logistics chains that include a series of cargo capacity and consolidation logistics areas, two central logistics corridors (Route 68 between Valparaíso and Santiago and Route 78 between San Antonio and Santiago), a highway transport network, and secondarily, a cargo railway transportation network. As is the case of other Chilean ports, their operations are determined by their territorial specialization. San Antonio and Valparaíso handle an enormous amount of the commercial activity generated mainly (though not solely) by Metropolitan Santiago and its over 6 million consumers, mining and agriculture, and export (of mainly fruit products). The latter is a seasonal activity that takes place between November and April.

These ports generate a logistical triangulation with Greater Santiago and the central zone of Chile. Chilean ports lack an institutional planning, cooperation, and coordination agency that would incorporate them under a broader strategic gaze. Based on our analysis, we have concluded that the operation of the port of Valparaíso can be better understood as a dynamic of coordination in competition with the neighboring port of San Antonio. Coordination in competition is a form of relating and interaction between public and private agencies, and between the state and the market, that is a result of a formulation of neoliberal public policies, along with institutional regulations that favor private enterprise and competition as fundamental mechanisms for introducing economic efficiency. Its application in public policy on investment in logistics infrastructure and port management is what articulates the different waves of neoliberal modernization of Chile's port sector.[14] What were these modernizing waves?

In 1981, Pinochet's military dictatorship restructured the state port system. Law 18.042 promoted the entry of private companies into state-run ports that had been managed by EMPORCHI, in order to engage in a variety of port operations. The following year, Law 18.032 abolished the port licensing system for stowage, which had granted union workers broad control over jobs and hiring in Chilean ports. These reforms also had the effect of liberalizing port activity. Specifically, greater competition was introduced between operating companies, and the labor market became more flexible and liberalized, also introducing competition among workers.

A second modernization wave, this time promoted under democracy, began in 1997 through the implementation of Law 19.542, which produced the decentralization of the administration of the ten state-run ports that belonged to EMPORCHI. This reform consolidated the virtual privatization of port activity in the main state-run ports by establishing that port tasks had to be conducted by private companies under the principle of subsidiarity of the state.[15] This strategy of privatizing port development couples perfectly with the current phase of development of global capitalism.

In practice, Chile's public port policy has involved a form of privatization of the coastline and port-logistics operations. As such, the neoliberalism that really exists in Chile has been built by the state. This economic regime has been constituted as a hybrid that has been installed in a sociocultural and economic context that facilitated active intervention on the part of the state after 1997 in order to promote private investment and logistics enterprise, the regulation of the sector, the creation of a logistics services market or quasi-market, and a public-private alliance.[16] In short, the state policy has favored a process of neoliberalization of the ports, applying measures that are less aligned with neoclassical orthodoxy, but that certainly continue to be coherent with market fundamentalism and with the principle of competition as the best mechanism for introducing economic efficiency and promoting the country's competitiveness.[17]

The Valparaíso Port Development Plan

Various government agencies including the National Council on Innovation for Development (CNID), the Ministry of Transportation and Telecommunications (MTT), and Empresa Puerto Valparaiso (EPV, the Valparaiso Port Company) have noted in their most recent reports the importance and prioritized nature of logistics investment and the development of ports at the national level.[18] The port of Valparaíso has two cargo and passenger terminals. Public and private investments have been made in the renewal and maintenance of port infrastructure (Terminals 1 and 2). Given the lack of port space in Valparaíso, a logistics model was implemented that privileged the formation of an area external to the port (dry port). The new external areas for cargo stockpiling, which are known as ZEAL, have been connected to the port and land transport circuits through a cargo computerization and management system (Port Community System).

Two private concessionaires handle cargo transfer: Terminal Pacífico Sur (TPS), which specializes in containerized cargo, and Terminal Cerros de Valparaíso (TCVAL), a specialist in fractioned cargo (it also plans to specialize in containerized cargo). In addition, both terminals receive cruise ships managed by the concessionaire TPV. These companies have made investments that have revolutionized the operation of the port. Between 1998 and 2000, TPS made a series of modernizations to the infrastructure in the Terminal 1 sites. It also replaced the machinery and acquired five gantry cranes and two mobile Gottwald cranes. In addition to this updating of technology, machinery, and berthing areas, the authorities and EPV argued that the logistics model of Valparaíso, which connects the port to the ZEAL area located outside of the port zone, allow for high levels of cargo transfer efficiency and partly relieve the pressure on the city created by modern port activity, which is intensive in land use. But in order to make that model feasible, significant public investment was required that no private entity would provide. In other words, government officials and EPV leadership view this public investment as a requirement for attracting and facilitating private investment in the port. In its subsidiary role in the private sector, the Chilean government made a very significant investment in the La Pólvora highway and extensive tunnel under Artillería and Playa Ancha through the Ministry of Public Works (MOP).

As a result, this logistics model has involved an important transfer of public funds to facilitate the activity and accumulation of private capital in the port.[19] However, to date it is not entirely clear whether the expected benefits from private investment will be obtained through the EPV's ambitious projects for the development of the port. It is possible that this mode of port governance and form of coordination in competition that the privatization of port operations took in Valparaíso is causing some of the inefficiencies and coordination difficulties between logistics stakeholders with various interests. In other words, it seems that the principle of competition generalized and applied to the different phases of the logistics circuit—including labor relations and infrastructure investment—is not functioning as an economic efficiency mechanism in Valparaíso.

The model has achieved two objectives. First, it has partly freed the state of its responsibility to produce infrastructure investment in order to allocate it to other socially more profitable purposes, and second, it has promoted private enterprise and the accumulation of capital in the port through the privatization of port activity.

The "Valparaíso Port Development Plan" seeks to transform the city's coastline. Its focus is fundamentally logistical: satisfying the demand for cargo transfer in the short, medium, and long term. This demand is related to the development of extractivist export sectors in central Chile, mainly mining and agro-industry. The commercial exchange generated by the country's central area, which includes Metropolitan Santiago, is also very significant. The development plan includes the following projects, which are already operational:

- extension of Site 3 of Terminal 1, concession granted to TPS
- ZEAL L platform for control and coordination of truck entry and exit through port terminals (ZEAL Sociedad Concesionaria S.A.)

- southern access through La Pólvora, the road that connects Route 68 (the highway to Santiago) to ZEAL and the port.[20]
- a new terminal built by Valparaíso Terminal de Pasajeros (VTP) (to open in 2015).

These projects, which are under way or have been executed, are joined by the following scheduled investment projects:

- Terminal 2 expansion to be handled by the concession company TCVAL (private investment, scheduled to open in 2017)
- improved accessibility and construction of a new subterranean viaduct under the Muelle Prat sector through the southern access tunnel exit (public investment, scheduled to open in 2016)
- Puerto Barón Mall and Recreation Area, which includes opening up the coastline to urban use and the development of commercial activities (private investment, scheduled to open in 2015)
- Large-Scale Port (private and public) investment, to become operational in 2024.[21]

Access to the Large-Scale Port through the Cabritería Gorge would require a significant public investment to generate connectivity via Santos Ossa and Route 68, which is known as the northern access project. It is clear that the deadlines have been pushed back. This is where we once again find inefficiencies and "dark" statistics within this modernization process.

Logistics has been the subject of corporate and economic fora, interviews with political figures and academics in the field of engineering, and is positioned to emerge as a major pending issue.[22] The social and political effects of this "logistical crusade," and especially its limitations, inefficiencies, and resistance, are beginning to be felt as the implementations and operation conditions are put into practice. The current debate over what have been called "clean cargoes," which dates back a few years, underscores the conflicts of interest among the various companies that participate in the management of the logistics chain, the state-run port company, and the workers' unions, which see jobs threatened. As such, since late 2014, news around the conflict has appeared almost daily in the local press, mainly in *El Mercurio de Valparaíso*. This may be the first "logistics conflict" that has developed in Valparaíso.

This model of port governance shows the limitations of the state and its company EPV in Valparaíso in regard to promoting what the authority itself has identified as its goal: planning cargo systems as a tool for the country's competitiveness. The socio-labor and urban conflicts that affect Valparaíso, and the social resistance that port logistics development plans generate, are especially illustrative of the limitations of the development strategy implemented in Chile over the past few decades. These are also limitations inherent in their unique articulation of the logics of neoliberalization, extraction, and logistics.

Social conflict in the port sector

A recent Port Chamber (CAMPORT) study states that a positive correlation has been demonstrated between "efficient and expedited logistics and the growth of international trade." In addition, the authors affirm that efficient port logistics produce favorable effects in other "internal economic activities, in the quality of the infrastructure, technological innovation and the development of local economies." From this perspective, which is at once general and economicist, port logistics development only presents net benefits. An interruption in the logistics chain has a significant impact on the competitiveness of a set of productive activities.[23]

The export development and commercial openness strategy that has characterized Chile over the past few decades requires ensuring the security of free trade in order to maintain continuous, efficient connectivity with the global economy that is free of obstacles. Natural disasters, events of *force majeure*, and strikes by port workers can seriously compromise this connectivity. The critical position that port sector workers occupy in the logistics chains of the main extractive export sectors of the Chilean economy—mining, agro-industry, forestry, fishing and aquiculture—give them a significant structural power over logistics operations and extractive operations. This explains their capacity to mobilize and threaten the economic system, as well as the responses of the state and business sector, and attempts to strip power from the port union system.[24]

As a result, the port model implemented in Chile, which supports the strategy of commercial openness, has tried to erase the power of port workers' unions as part of the strategies of control and security of free trade. This response to union power achieved by port workers has a history. Under the strict control of the military dictatorship, a labor legislation reform was implemented in the port sector between 1978 and 1981 that favored flexible and precarious port work, the introduction of an unprecedented night shift, and the weakening of unions and the collective bargaining tools that they had historically used.[25] Up to 3,000 workers were employed in the port of Valparaíso in the 1970s. While it is impossible to determine precisely how many people currently work there, estimates suggest that the two terminals employ approximately 750. It is impossible to determine the contractual status of those individuals. We know that the number of full-time salaried workers with an open-ended contract and benefits is around 280, and the rest are temporary workers with precarious jobs. The stories that we have collected suggest that there was an abysmal salary drop between the 1970s and the 1981 reform. Currently, pay per shift in Chilean ports varies significantly depending on the specialty. Valparaíso's port offers about CLP 40,000, but we also found that some earned less than CLP 30,000 (US$45 per 7.5 hour shift based on the value of the dollar in 2016).

We have evidence that suggests that Valparaíso port workers understand that the structural, technological, and legislative changes experienced since the 1970s have had an enormous impact on the modification of the labor regime that regulates port work. They are also aware that the weakening of port unions is another effect of these changes. According to the testimonies of retired stevedores from the port of Valparaíso, the appearance of containers, cranes, and computer control in the 1980s is associated with the pressure of technological development on the ports and competitiveness on the international stage. In general, the loss of social benefits is related to the neoliberal impact, and not without a dose of unease which oscillates between the memory of dispute over labor conditions under the Popular Unity government and deprecation of the labor identity itself.[26]

This set of significant socio-economic, legislative, political, technological, infrastructure, and logistics administration changes came together to produce a profound social and economic restructuring, and drastically affected various organizations of port workers in Valparaíso. The modernization of the port, which is currently visible in its growing use of technology, has developed alongside a change in the labor regime of port workers, placing them in a situation of job precariousness and growing vulnerability in regard to capital.[27]

Until recently, a significant amount of the public discussion by citizen organizations regarding the investment projects promoted by the state-run EPV focused on opposition to the Puerto Barón Mall project. The logistics investment projects and their impacts on operations hardly appear in the disputes in the public sphere, or on the agenda of the social and citizen organizations that dispute the port-city's development, with the recent exception of stakeholders involved in what has been called the "clean cargo conflict." This should not come as a surprise to anyone who considers the technical nature of the matter, and how it differs from the public issues that tend to be of interest to civil society. This situation seems to be changing because a significant number of citizen organizations and opinion leaders have expressed their discontentment over plans for port modernization in Valparaíso in recent years.

According to some of the dockworker leaders, the citizens' movement that opposes the expansion of Terminal 2 does not understand the relevance of the logistical dimension of economic development. Normal citizens, their representatives and spokespersons, also do not understand the complexities of global logistical chains. In addition, there is a rampant antagonism between, first, a laissez-faire neoliberal position supported by the chief executives of port concessionaries and EPV's development plan, which favors logistical investment against all odds; and second, a more cautious position that favors a centralized, long- term national strategic planning on port development as proposed by the Unión Portuaria. This latter position considers the satisfaction of the real needs of investment in infrastructure, as demanded by the slow growth rate of international trade over the last few years. Yet, in a different line of antagonism, these labor leaders also point to a disagreement with the speculative perspective on the problem of architects, urban analysts, and the intellectual elite, who misunderstand the technical problems of the global logistical chain.

Conclusions

Although Chile has been described as a neoliberal "model," this broad description does not capture the complexities of the coordination between the social logics of extraction, logistics, and neoliberalization, or the relationships between the state, market, and society that these have favored. As we have seen based on the case of Valparaíso and the port sector, the social logics of extraction, logistics, and neoliberalization have produced important changes that have caused an economic and social restructuring in the port city.

On the other hand, it is necessary to clarify the fact that this neoliberal "model" was not even neoclassical in an orthodox sense during the dictatorship. In contrast to the popularized version, new and more precise assessments of the Chilean case suggest that it is more internally varied.[28] The public policies on port logistics cannot be understood under the supposition of a minimal state or ideologically doctrinal anti-state neoliberal model. Instead of developing as an experience of mere reduction and reversal of the state, as was the case with other privatized areas of the Chilean economy, the process of liberalization implemented in public ports since the 1980s and in successive waves of neoliberal modernization has promoted a port logistics model based on a philosophy of public–private cooperation. This model maintains coherence with some of the cardinal principles of neoliberalism, such as the idea of generalized competitiveness, marketization, the superiority of the market as the mechanism to assign resources, and unrestricted support for the business sector and private enterprise.[29] This public policy has been built over a long period of time and through various administrations as a political project from and with government support, and not simply against or at the expense of the state.[30]

One of the consequences of port public policy has been that the ten historical public ports that belonged to EMPORCHI, which included Valparaíso, do not currently share a general coordination and management regime. As a result, they compete with private ports and with each other. As we have seen, this situation of the public ports, which we call "coordination in competition," has its origins in the privatizing reforms of port activity implemented during the 1980s under Pinochet's neoliberal dictatorship. However, their expansion and consolidation took place under democracy, with the 1997 port reform and the development plans and investment in infrastructure promoted by the various state port companies in the successive public bids that granted private concessions for the port terminals.[31] It was this policy that solidified the privatization of logistics–port activity. As a result, while Chilean public ports compete for investment and over tariffs, we find the same holdings and family economic groups that control the main extractivist export sectors among the competing economic agents that invest in and operate the ports.

While this port model seems to have generated short and

medium-term benefits for the large holdings that control the main extractivist sectors of the economy, the logic of generalized competition applied in Chilean ports, which lacks a strategic national vision, has generated numerous flashpoints of social conflict, especially labor, urban, and economic coordination problems among public policy agents and companies. The port city of Valparaíso seems to concentrate those problems, which makes it an excellent example of the limits of this articulation among the social logics of neoliberalization, extraction, and logistics.

The more politicized factions of dockworker unions struggle, aware of the need to reconnect to the forgotten traditions of workers' movements' demands, and in this process they perceive some new chances opened by what they call a generational replacement. Enmeshed in capitalist contradictions and in this complex process of identity formation, these factions learn how to make some progress. Social struggles associated with extractivism, the resistance of indigenous communities, and logistics restructuring, are part of the political imaginary of these factions nowadays. These emerging new struggles need to be taken into account by dockworkers for the building of future alliances.

Notes

1   A. Mah, *Port Cities and Global Legacies: Urban Identity, Waterfront Work, and Radicalism* (Basingstoke: Palgrave Macmillan, 2014).

2   S. Sassen, *Expulsions: Brutality and Complexity in the Global Economy* (Cambridge: Belknap Press, 2014), pp. 6–9, 220.

3   See E. Gudynas, "Estado compensador y nuevos extractivismos. Las ambivalencias del progresismo sudamericano" (Compensatory state and new extractivisms. Ambivalences of the South American progressivism), *Nueva Sociedad* 237 (2012), pp. 128–46.; H. Cuevas and D. Julián, "Extractivismo y teoría social en América Latina. Una entrevista a Eduardo Gudynas" ("*Extractivism and Social Theory in Latin America. An interview with Eduardo Gudynas*"), *Pléyade* 18 (2016), pp. 269–88./

4   S. Mezzadra and B. Neilson, "Extraction, logistics, finance: global crisis and the politics of operations," *Radical Philosophy* 78 (2013), pp. 8–18.

5   R. Sharpley and P. R. Stone, *The Darker Side of Travel: The Theory and Practice of Dark Tourism* (Bristol, UK/Buffalo, N.Y.: Channel View, 2009).

6   G. Grappi, *Logistica* (Rome: Ediesse, 2016).

7   R. LeKashman and J. F. Stolle, "The total cost approach to distribution," *Business Horizons* (Winter 1965), pp. 33–46.

8   See Empresa Puerto Valparaiso (EPV), *Plan de Desarrollo del Puerto de Valparaíso. Contenido, Logros y Desafíos, 1912–2012* (Port of Valparaíso

Development Plan) (Valparaíso: EPV, 2012); S. Bologna, *Crisis de la clase media y posfordismo* (*Crisis of the Middle Class and Post-Fordism*) (Madrid: Akal, 2006); M. Levinson, *The Box* (Princeton, N.J.: Princeton University Press, 2006).

9 N. Brenner et al., "Variegated neoliberalisation: geographies, modalities, pathways," *Global Networks* 10(2) (2010), pp. 182–222.

10 K. Polanyi, *La gran transformación. Los orígenes políticos y económicos de nuestro tiempo* (*The Great Transformation: The Political and Economic Origins of Our Time*) (Mexico: FCE, 2003); W. Brown, *Undoing the Demos* (Cambridge, Mass.: MIT Press, 2015).

11 F. Larrain and R. Vergara (eds.), *La Transformación Económica de Chile* (*The Economic Transformation of Chile*) (Santiago: Centro de Estudios Públicos, 2001).

12 E. Engel, R. Fischer, and A. Galetovic, "El Programa Chileno de Concesiones de Infraestructura: Evaluación, Experiencias y Perspectivas" ("The Chilean program of infrastructure concessions: evaluation, experiences and perspectives") in Larraín and Vergara (2001); MTT, Transport Subsecretariat, Government of Chile, Law no. 19.542, Moderniza el sector portuario estatal, 2011. http://bcn.cl/1uxch

13 MTT (2011); Comisión Estrategia 2030 de Puertos su Logística, Logística y puertos: una plataforma estratégica de desarrollo para Chile (2030 Strategy for Ports and Logistics Comision. Logistics and Ports: A Development Strategic Platform for Chile) (Santiago: CEPL, 2015); Consejo Nacional de Innovación para El Desarrollo (CNID, National Council of Innovation for Development), *Informe de la Comisión de Innovación para Puertos y su Logística* (*Report of the Commission for Innovation of the Ports and their Logistics*) (Santiago: CNID, 2015).

14 Engel et al. (2001).

15 MTT (2011).

16 Brenner et al. (2010); L. Wacquant, "Three steps to a historical anthropology of actually existing neoliberalism," *Social Anthropology/Anthropologie Sociale* 20(1) (2012), pp. 66–79.

17 F. Block and M. Somers, *The Power of Market Fundamentalism: Karl Polanyi's Critique* (Cambridge, Mass.: Harvard University Press, 2014).

18 CNID (2015); MTT, Transport Subsecretariat, Government of Chile, *Plan nacional de desarrollo portuario* (*National Plan of Port Development*) (2013), www.mtt.gob.cl/wp-content/uploads/2014/02/desarrollo_portuario_06_02_14_1.pdf; EPV (2012); EPV, Memoria gestión 2016 Puerto Valparaíso (Corporate memory 2016 of the Valparaíso Port Company), 2017, www.puertovalparaiso.cl/img/media/1493726124_Memoria%20Puerto%20Valparaiso%202016.pdf (both accessed December 1, 2017).

19 See K. Dörre, "Landnahme: un concepto para el análisis de la dinámica capitalista, o: superando a Polanyi con Polanyi" (Landnahme: a concept for the analysis of capitalist development; or overcoming Polanyi with Polanyi),

Política 54(2) (2016), pp. 13–48; D. Harvey, *A Brief History of Neoliberalism* (Oxford: Oxford University Press, 2005).

20 EPV, *Reporte de sostenibilidad 2014 (Report on Sustainability 2014)* (Santiago: EPV, 2015), www.puertovalparaiso.cl/descargas/articulo/134 (accessed December 1, 2017).

21 EPV (2012).

22 O. Merk (ed.), *The Competitiveness of Global Port-Cities: Synthesis Report* (Paris: OECD, 2013), www.oecd.org/gov/regional-policy/Competitive-ness-of-Global-Port-Cities-Synthesis-Report.pdf (accessed December 1, 2017). MTT (2011); Comision Estrategia 2030 de Puertos Y Su Logistica, *Logística y puertos: una plataforma estratégica de desarrollo para Chile* (Santiago: CNID, 2015); CNID (2015); *Informe de la Comisión de Innovación para Puertos y su Logística (Report of the Commission for Innovation of the Ports and their Logistics)* (Santiago, 2016).

23 CAMPORT, *Innovaciones institucionales en el sector marítimo portuario (Institutional Change in the Maritime Port Sector)* (Santiago: CAMPORT, 2017).

24 See H. Cuevas and V. Leal (eds.), "Transformaciones en el Sindicalismo del Puerto de Valparaíso: la Práctica Sindical de la Nombrada" ("Transformations of unionism in the Port of Valparaíso: the labor union practice of 'La Nombrada'") (forthcoming); B. J. Silver, *Forces of Labour* (Cambidge: Cambridge University Press, 2003); S. Schmalz and K. Dorre (eds.). "El planteamiento de los recursos del poder" ("The power resources approach") (forthcoming).

25 V. Leal and C. Aguirre, Estiba y desestiba. Trabajo y relatos del Valparaíso que fue (1938–1981) (Loading and unloading: labor and stories from the Valparaíso that does not exist any longer) (Valparaíso: CNCA, 2012).

26 Leal and Aguirre (2012), pp. 84–8.

27 See Leal and Aguirre (2012); K. Dörre, "La Precariedad: ¿centro de la cuestión cocial en el siglo XXI?" ("Is precarity the core social question of the 21st century?") *Actuel Marx/ Intervenciones* 8 (2nd semester, 2009), pp. 79–108; G. Standing, *The Precariat: The New Dangerous Class* (London: Bloomsbury, 2011).

28 A. Maillet, "Más allá del 'modelo' chileno: una aproximación multi-sectorial a las relaciones Estado-mercado" ("Beyond the chilean 'mode': a multi-sectorial approximation to state–market relations") *Revista de Sociologia e Política* 23(55) (2015), pp. 53–73.

29 Block and Somers (2014); Brenner et al. (2010); Brown (2015).

30 See Harvey (2005).

31 MTT (2011).

Further reading

Cepal Caf Ocde, *Perspectivas económicas de América Latina 2014. Logística y competitividad para el desarrollo (Latin American Economic Outlook 2014:*

Logistics and Competitiveness for Development), 2014, DOI: http://dx.doi.org/10.1787/leo-2014-es; O.

Cowen, D. (2014) *The Deadly Life of Logistics*. Minneapolis, Minn.: Minnesota University Press.

Davies, W. (2014) *The Limits of Neoliberalism: Authority, Sovereignty and the Logic of Competition*. London: Sage.

Standing, G. (2012) "The precariat: from denizens to citizens?" *Polity* 44(4), pp. 588–608.

Universidad Adolfo Ibanez (UAI)–EPV (2015) *Estudio impacto económico y socio-cultural de la actividad portuaria. Informe final. Documento preparado para Puerto Valparaíso.* (*Study of the Economic and sociocultural Impact of the Port Activity. Final report. Document prepared for Puerto Valparaíso*), Santiago: UAI.

11

Logistics Workers' Struggles in Turkey: Neoliberalism and Counterstrategies

Çağatay Edgücan Şahin and Pekin Bengisu Tepe

A general overview of unions and struggles in neoliberal Turkey

The imposition of neoliberalism began in the aftermath of the 1980 military coup when Halit Narin, a representative of the biggest employers' association in Turkey, said, "Now it's our turn to laugh," revealing the class character of the coup.[1] The coup leaders first targeted class unionism. Turkey's most militant federation, *Devrimci İşçi Sendikaları Konfederasyonu* (Disk: the Confederation of Progressive Trade Unions), and other labor organizations which opposed the state's official ideology (some sort of corporatism) were banned.[2] Not until 1992 was Disk permitted to resume its activities. Collective labor laws were also changed in this period, to secure capital accumulation.

This neoliberal era in Turkey was marked by growing unemployment, rising informal employment, increased flexibility, precarity, subcontracted—*taşeron*—work, and lower wages. These policies deepened in the 1990s and 2000s as the Turkish working class encountered a catastrophic decline in wages and job standards. In 2017, national unemployment was at 11.7 percent, 21.4 percent among young people, and informal employment was at 33.1 percent.[3] Following the coup, privatizations expanded, and unions, whose members were threatened with unemployment, lost power. From 2002 to 2016, membership in the three largest public servant confederations shifted: *Kamu Emekçileri Sendikaları Konfederasyonu* (Kesk: the Confederation of Public Employees Trade Unions) decreased by 16 percent, Türkiye Kamu-Sen increased by 29 percent, and *Memur Sendikaları Konfederasyonu* (Memur-Sen Confederation of Public Servants Trade Unions) increased by 2,129 percent, from 41,871 members in 2002 to 956,032 members in 2016, which is quite extraordinary under neoliberalism.[4]

The main reason that Kesk lost members while the other two confederations gained can be understood in the context of Kesk's class unionism strategy and other confederations' wage unionism strategy, as well as their steady positions in corporatist relations. The number of unionized public servants was 1,756,934, 69.2 percent of all public servants, in July 2017.[5] While Turkey's population nearly doubled from 43 million just before the coup to 79 million in 2016, the number of unionized workers in the private sector declined from 5.7 million in 1980 to 1,623,638 in 2017, 11.97 percent of all private-sector workers, according to official data.[6]

The Turkish government has banned strikes in key sectors. In 2012, a government regulation banned strikes in the transportation sector, and finally in 2016, the right to strike was abolished by decree. Thus, all strikes in "urban public transportation" were banned indefinitely. This was in violation of national and international labor laws.[7]

The pressure on strikes is not limited to banning them in some sectors. Strikes are quite often ordered to be postponed via statutory decrees in Turkey's industrial relations system. The Council of Ministers may also extend collective labor agreements to other businesses by statutory decree, but this is quite rare. So unions cannot declare a strike when they are having problems with employers over acquired rights. In these cases, the union and workers have to pursue a court case against the employer, but the legal process usually takes months. In summary, over the past two decades the Turkish government has helped establish flexible labor markets, securing the interests of capital through decreasing the power of unions.

General overview of the logistics and transportation unions

Turkey's strategic location in Eurasia connects 1.6 billion people with a gross domestic product (GDP) of $27 trillion within a four-hour flight radius of the country's borders. This area handles more than US$8 trillion of foreign trade, corresponding to around half of the total world trade. Over $100 billion, or 12 percent of Turkey's 2016 GDP of $857 billion, relates to logistics industries.[8] Indeed, Turkey is a "logistics hub" for international companies due to its unique position on the main trade routes and its proximity to European, Eurasian, and Middle Eastern markets. It is expected that Turkey's position will be maintained by a cheap labor force and environmental laws that are "favorable" to foreign capital. The investments of multinational cargo companies reveal the significance of Turkey to world trade. Deutsche Post plans to invest €100 million in DHL Turkey by 2020.[9] DHL provides comprehensive technical facilities for the storage and transportation of medicines for pharmaceutical companies. The unionization efforts at DHL have the potential to buttress unionization campaigns more broadly in pharmaceutical companies.[10]

But most European-based companies in Turkey oppose unionization since the primary motivation for investing in Turkey is cheap and unorganized labor.[11] Given the country's strategic location in the supply chain, the government anti-union strategies in aviation, ports, and railways are vital to foreign investment. From 1975 to 2015, the deunionization of railroad workers was a visible example of this strategy, as employment in the sector decreased 65 percent from 67,642 to 24,000. Moreover, logistics firms shifted to subcontracting as the main form of employment in aviation, railways, and ports. In the spring of 1996, the International Transport Workers' Federation (ITF) issued a final declaration that Turkish privatizations, subcontracting, flexible and atypical forms of work, illicit labor, fake firm closures, forced retirement, deunionization, redundancies, and difficulties in union organizing in the private sector have contributed to declining wages and higher levels of accidents.[12] The lower staffing levels in particular have increased accidents, especially on the railways.[13]

According to Law of Trade Unions and Collective Labor Agreements (TUCLA) No. 6356, dated 2012, some branches were combined and the number of branches of activities decreased from 28 to 20, and there is a double threshold regulation: unless a union has at least 1 percent of the workers in the sector/branch (which is known as the sectoral threshold), and also has at least 50 percent of the workers in a specific workplace, or if the union is organized in an enterprise which includes several workplaces, more than 40 percent of all workers in the enterprise, it does not have the authority to engage in collective bargaining.[14] The sectoral unionization threshold was also reduced under TUCLA from 10 percent to 3 percent, and finally in June 2015 a constitutional court decision further reduced the level of unionized workers to 1 percent by combining land transportation, air transportation, and maritime transportation into one "transport branch." This regulation might seem in favor of unions at first glance, but it must be appreciated that the figure is evaluated across combined branches. The regulation combined workers in different branches like railroad transportation, airways, and road transportation into one big branch: transportation. Thus the total number of workers in the transportation branch increased, and some of the unions like *Nakliyat-Is,* which represents 10 percent of road transportation workers, could not achieve 1 percent of membership across the entire transportation branch.

In Turkey the logistics industry is classified into two branches of activity: transportation, employing 732,639, and shipbuilding and maritime transportation, warehousing, and storage, employing 167,779, for a total of 900,418 workers in July 2017, which is approximately 6.6 percent of Turkey's total private-sector workers of 13,581,554.[15] There are 15 logistics unions (including four for public servants). Six of the 11 private-sector workers' unions (four in transport and two in shipbuilding and maritime transportation, warehousing, and storage) are subject to the sectoral threshold. Even though all unions are permitted to organize, in these two branches they are concentrated in the following specific areas: 1) *Oz Taşıma-İş* (transportation and logistics, 21,349 members); 2) *Hava-İş* (aviation, 21,329 members); 3) *Demiryol-İş* (railroads, 15,927 members); 4) *Tümtis* (all transport and warehouse workers, 8,538 members); 5) *Türk Deniz-İş* (maritime, 6,541 members); and 6) *Liman-İş* (docks and warehouse workers, 4,263 members). The other five private-sector unions have 6,995 members in total, and *Nakliyat-İş* (all transport and warehouse workers) and *Karsan-İş* (cargo workers) have 4,423 and 2,408 members respectively. All of the unions except *Karsan-İş* (which appears to be an employer-backed union[16]), are members of ITF, and only *Nakliyat-İş* is also a member of the World Federation of Trade Unions (WFTU).

Under TUCLA, transportation sector workers include taxi drivers, who are typically difficult to organize. If taxi drivers are excluded from transportation sector, there are only 307,719 workers employed in transportation instead of 732,639, and there are 162,424 workers in the shipbuilding and maritime transportation, warehousing, and storage branches, increasing the percentage of unionized workers in transportation to 18.8 percent, which is over 50 percent higher than Turkey's overall unionization rate of 12.2 percent.

There are 28,069 laborers and three major unions in the transportation public sector. *Ulaştırma Memur-Sen* (UMS) has 9,955 members, *Türk Ulaşım-Sen* (TUS) has 7,775 members, and *Birleşik Taşımacılık Sendikası* (BTS) has 1,768 members. Almost 70 percent of all laborers are unionized in the public sector, while 8,571 laborers are unorganized.

Unionization at the enterprise level is important for the logistics sector in general, because of legal regulations which appear to be aimed at liquidating small businesses, which also encourages monopolization as multinational companies increase their market shares. Unionizing in companies like UPS is extremely important for *Tümtis*, which wants to be a center of working-class struggle and the labor movement. As of 2011, UPS has six subcontractors and uses 256 agencies. In addition to its permanent workers, the company is also recruiting workers under fixed-term employment contracts, corresponding to a highly flexible labor regime, a strategy which compounds the difficulty for unions in gaining a majority of signed-up workers. *Tümtis*'s main motivation is not limited to signing collective labor agreements with employers, it also hopes to accelerate class consciousness and union awareness in order to save the future of the working class.[17] The issue of accelerating class consciousness is quite important because if it cannot be achieved, the struggle between workers and companies will look like a struggle between "the nineteeth-century working class and the twenty-first century's or Age of Industry 4.0's capital":

> Logistics is an industry of interest for international monopolies, and competition among these monopolies is a fact. Generally unskilled workers work in logistics and warehouses. Thus, usually the wages are low and the work places a lot of physical stress on the workers, with one major exception: port workers. Because most of them are skilled workers. (Interview no. 4, February 17, 2017, Istanbul)

Workers, unions, and resistance against capital in neoliberal Turkey

In the mid-1980s unionizing practices in warehouses started to gain momentum. In response, from the 1990s, firms started to change their networks of organization in transportation and logistics. In 1985 and 1986 firms started to pressure unions to prevent their obtaining authorization to represent workers, while unions pursued some exceptional tactics against firms:

In 1987, Topkapı-Istanbul transport warehouses were in operation and 1100 workers were working in 110 workplaces, and Tümtis has organized 37 of 110. The biggest employer was employing 55 workers. In the majority of the workplaces, employers were only hiring six or seven workers. When unionization started in one of these workplaces, employers were increasing the total number of workers by hiring their children as workers on paper while half of the workers were already working informally. After an uphill struggle, [the] union signed collective labor agreements in authorized workplaces, and union representatives also signed a number of contracts of service with employers which guarantee the same conditions (in terms of the Turkish Code of Obligations) in unauthorized workplaces. Once the union was able to stop work at the logistics center in Istanbul, the other firms in other cities which the union tried to organize were forced to compromise with the union because the employers in Istanbul were forcing these firms to do so to avoid facing unfair competition. In the 1980s, all workflow in logistics went through warehouses. Then the cargo companies emerged, as a response from capital. (Interview no. 2, February 16, 2017, Istanbul)

The wave of industrial action by workers in cargo-handling firms against employers' union-busting strategies began in Istanbul and Ankara in the 1990s and spread throughout the country. The "Yurtiçi Kargo Resistance" which lasted for seven months in 1992,[18] and "Aras Kargo Resistance," were among the actions. In both cases, as soon as unionization began, employers pursued union busting as a response. The term "resistance" here means "resistance against union busting," and covers the activities of the laid-off unionized workers. These two companies are still among the largest cargo companies in the country. In the resistance in Ankara, workers camped out in tents in front of the firm's headquarters into the night. In response, the employers hired armed security guards to break the resistance. Then the resistance peaked with occupation of the transhipment center. Police forces intervened to hustle away the workers who were occupying the transhipment center. At the end of this struggle, union branch management changed and militant workers gained positions in the trade union bureaucracy.[19]

In the 2000s the main emerging problems in the logistics industry were deregulation and illicit employment. The facts underlined by the leader of the *Tümtis* union which organized a transport branch are:

The most frustrating problems in transportation and warehouse sectors are the deregulated working conditions and informal employment. Illicit employment is quite common in transportation. On the other hand, even if the workers legally work in the firms, the articles of the Turkish Labor Law No.4857 are feasible in terms of flexibility, and the employers are pushing it to the limits at every chance they have. For example, the work day starts at a certain time, but the time of leaving is not specified, which means it can be specified "by parties," I mean only employers of course. … The vast majority of workers are employed for 12–13 hours a day on the minimum wage, and there are no social benefits in the transportation and warehouse industry …. When a union starts to organize in a cargo company and tries to get a majority and authorization, the employer also starts union-busting activities, and fires unionized workers immediately. Workers fired in this way are not involved in calculating whether there is a majority! Subcontracted work makes things worse, and is already widespread in the industry. (Interview no. 3, February 16, 2017, Istanbul)

It has been emphasized that the success of the *Tümtis* union in organizing subcontracted workers in the Mersin International Port in Southern Turkey led to the port transportation branch being separated from land and air transportation and combined with storage and warehousing in drawing up TUCLA No. 6356:[20]

There were almost 2,000 workers employed in the privatized Mersin International Port, and there were two unions in two branches: one was road transportation, the other was maritime transportation. The *Tümtis* union organized the subcontracted workers in the road transportation branch, and signed a collective labor agreement with the employer. *Tümtis* also invited the *Liman-İş* union to Mersin Port to organize the permanent workers of the main employer in maritime transportation. So the employer transferred subcontracted workers to the main firm in order to prevent *Tümtis* from gaining recognition at Mersin International Port. Then *Tümtis* signed a protocol with the employer on behalf of its ex-members to guarantee their acquired rights. Even though *Tümtis* lost its members because of the change in the branch of activity, the winners became the workers who had permanent employment in the end. On the other hand, the unionization in Mersin Port which was ended in 2007 when the port was privatized was established again, with 2,000 workers in total. However, employers were afraid of the possibility of unionizing all the workers in the road transportation branch in *Tümtis*. Then the employers warned the legislators during the discussion of the proposed new collective labor law that they believed the presence of a union like

Tümtis in ports would harm the country's trade, and the maritime branch was excluded from transport in the new collective labor law. (Combined comments from Interview no. 3, February 16, 2017, and Interview no. 5, February 17, 2017, both Istanbul)

The public-sector union BTS experienced a similar pattern in reorganizing under TUCLA No. 6356. The BTS head at the time underlined that railroads, aviation, and road transportation, which were treated as separate before TUCLA, were combined to form a "transport sector," but maritime, warehousing, and storage were separated, although they too are obviously a critical part of global logistics.[21] The head also pointed out that the shipbuilding sector, which might more logically have been treated as part of the "metal-working" sector, was also put into the maritime, warehousing, and storage sector. In addition to that, the enterprises of railway maintenance and rail systems, locomotive and wagon maintenance and repair enterprises, were combined in the transport sector, but somehow enterprises concerned with the maintenance and repair of aircraft and on-road vehicles were not included there. After this segmentation and reorganization of sectors, the *Liman-İş* union, which had been a member of *Türk-İş* (the Confederation of Turkish Trade Unions) for years, transferred to the *Hak-İş* Trade Union Confederation, which has close ties with government.[22] To sum up, the underlying purpose of the new legislation introduced in 2012 appears to have been to prevent unions from organizing in the logistics industry.

Employer anti-union strategies

In Turkey, employers seek to prevent unionization in three primary ways. First, they establish separate companies and transfer unionized workers; second, they use anti-democratic laws against trade unions: objecting to the threshold and re-enumerating the number of workers by appealing to the labor court or objecting to unions' branch of activity; and third, they try to force workers to quit their union, and if they refuse, fire them without compensation.[23] Although employers could face imprisonment of six months for breaking the labor laws, in practice this penal imposition is rare in Turkey. On the contrary, there are cases according to Turkish Penal Code article 117 in which "violation of the freedom to work and labor" is used against the unions.[24]

Companies with foreign capital avoid unionization through extending the authorization process, while pressuring workers to quit their unions; laying off unionized workers or threatening dismissals; helping to organize company (compliant) unions; shifting production out of union jurisdictions; and withdrawing from the market and re-entering the market again under a new registration:

> After *Liman-İş* applied for authorization in Teknosa Storage, the employer laid off some of the militant workers. If the employer objects to the branch of activity, then the collective labor agreement process stops until the appeal is finalized, according to TUCLA. In short, unionization problems can be solved only if the workers start an actual resistance in warehouses. Otherwise, it is difficult to deal with employers within the limits of this legal system. (Interview no. 5, February 17, 2017, Istanbul)

> Some of the logistics companies are registered in the "shipbuilding and maritime transportation, warehousing, and storage" branches, while others are registered in "transport," and some others even registered in "commerce, offices, education, and fine arts." Even if the company is involved in transportation, it might not be registered in the transport branch, or the company might divide its main business into several different branches of activities, thus making it difficult to unionize. When a union wants to determine the branch of activity of the firm first, it may take several months.... It is obvious that this is a very useful way of union busting. (Interview no. 3, February 16, 2017, Istanbul)

While union challenges are supposed to be heard within two months, this often extends to two years in practice. For this reason, the workers grow weary as employers pressurize them, and resign from their union or quit their jobs.[25]

> *Demiryol-İş* union signed six collective labor contracts in a row in Konya Metropolitan Municipality, and while the last contract was still in operation workers were transferred to Öz Taşıma-İş union, thus there was a contract but there were no workers to benefit from it. ... In another case the employer registered its enterprise in the food industry branch, but actually it is in logistics. (Interview no. 7, March 16, 2017, Ankara)

> Warehouses are the least unionized workplaces in the industry. Branch of activity changes by employers is the main strategy. For instance, 3,500 workers were in the warehouses of LcWaikiki. When *Liman-İş* union

almost had authorization to start collective bargaining, the employer changed its branch of activity to retail sales (in the commerce, offices, education, and fine arts branch) and combined warehouse workers with store workers. The employer simply justified the request by claiming that the firm also has many stores, not only warehouses. Even though Tümtis union had requested determination of the branch of activity before, and it was determined as warehouses, that's the reality unions face most of the time. So *Liman-İş* started to unionize the workers, but the employer switched its branch of activity from warehouses to retail sales in a night! Not only did *Liman-İş* lose its members in this case, but also store workers were included in the new branch and the number of total workers has risen to 25,000 in the company. (Interview no. 5, February 17, 2017, Istanbul)

A striking example of the interpretation of laws by the judiciary in ways that favor the employer is the case of *Tümtis*'s jailed union branch manager. *Tümtis*'s branch managers were taken into custody on the grounds that "they are guilty of increasing pressure on employers by increasing the number of union members!" and "establishing a criminal organization" (an expression that directly refers unionizing activities):

We, as *Tümtis*, were unionizing at Horoz Kargo Ankara. In November 2007, 14 branch managers of our union were detained for seven months on the basis of an employers' complaint that we were preventing freedom of labor because of an action that took place on a Sunday, which is a holiday. Union managers were tried, found guilty and sentenced to six years in prison. On the other hand, those who made these decisions were dismissed from the profession and also arrested a while after. ... We are now demanding a retrial. (Interview no. 3, February 16, 2017, Istanbul)

Five years after this trial and after the judges were dismissed, the Supreme Court upheld the sentences, demonstrating that union struggles are the main target.[26] Some members of the Turkish Parliament opposed the final court order, and there are still some efforts at solidarity with the union both in Turkey and internationally. But the union organizers remain in jail.

Unionizing cargo companies may have positive effects in other industries. Although cargo and transportation workers are isolated from the production-based workforce, as a result of flexible production, they are critical and decisive for unionization, especially unionized cargo workers in international companies. Therefore, organizing cargo and logistics workers will be a victory for the entire working class.[27] The fact is that as the worker mobilizations succeed, there is more powerful action against employers' union-busting activities in other unionizing campaigns. Borusan Logistics is a common carrier of Huawei, Pirelli, Limango, L'Oreal and many other international and local companies. During a dispute, all Borusan Holdings workplaces were accepted as resistance areas by the *Nakliyat-İş* union. Workers occupied the Borusan Culture and Arts Center, and customers of the company were visited and informed of the organizing drive by employees and customers, and even demonstrated at a Borusan Philharmonic Orchestra concert. After continuous action for one month the employer relented and settled with the union.[28]

What are the lessons of the struggles in logistics? First, unions continue to pursue the legal process as well as pursuing national and international-level strategies for unionizing. Unions can still take advantage of legal loopholes such as "primary employers share the responsibility with subcontractors for payments" and "workers may use their right to leave the job if they are not paid for a period of 20 days (which is not a strike)" in favor of workers. Second, unions must unionize secretly until the last moment, to protect key worker organizers from employers. Third, union activists need to organize in workplaces and in their neighborhoods, as the *Tümtis* union does. Fourth, workers and their union should camp out in front of the workplaces, to pressurize employers until problems are resolved. During a strike at UPS, the wives of the majority of workers, and even the children of some of them, began to work to support their families.[29] If this strategy can be carried out (that is, workers and their families can manage to ensure they make a living during strikes), success can be achieved in the struggle against multinational corporations, such as UPS, which is concerned about its global reputation.

Sometimes global action decisions can be more useful than the local announced action itself, and create more pressure on the employer. Ken Hall, a senior manager of the American Teamsters Union, suggested a postponement of an announced global day of action on December 16, 2010, because of the ongoing mediation between UPS senior managers and *Tümtis*. This initiative was successful, and 151 workers came back to work on February 1, 2011, after the second round of talks which had started in December.[30] As a next step, a collective labor agreement was signed. Another form of support from the international community could be pressure on clients of the company. On the other hand, in the case of UPS, two big German customers (Volkswagen and Toshiba) only sent letters in support to UPS, and not to its workers.[31]

Some aspects have an effect on the tendency of law enforcement officers to interfere with the action. They include the scale of an enterprise and the nature of the action, including whether it is spreading. Yet the most common problem for workers and union representatives is still the changes in the stated branch of activity which employers can make online. Unions first apply to the Ministry of Labor and Social Security for determination of the branch of activity in which the firm is located (if it has not been determined before), and after the determination, the authorization period for the collective labor agreement starts. Even if a firm has signed a collective labor agreement which is still in operation, the firm may change its branch of activity for a new period, simply by making a statement and request.

There are countless cases of unions experiencing a loss of members because of branch of activity changes for next term. In the process that starts with the determination of the branch of activity, it is frequently observed that the militant workers are immediately laid off by the company. In some cases such as the unionization at Mersin International Port, where subcontracted workers were organized in a union, the main employer cancelled the subcontracting agreement and transferred all the workers to become permanent staff of the main firm in order to remove the union. Of course, even if the union loses representation in cases like this, the workers have achieved employment security as the result of the union's struggle, which is an obvious achievement in neoliberal Turkey. Skilled workers are also subject to employer union busting. In transportation and logistics a strict "blacklist" policy is in force for skilled workers who perform critical tasks.

Conclusion

Since 2000 the logistics labor process has been influenced by government, employer, and union developments. Government powers are used against workers through legislative, executive, and judicial actions. The government combines and separates industrial sectors to hinder unionization. Regulations are enacted to ban strikes and severely limit labor and organizing rights. The government uses executive powers to postpone and ban strikes through calling a state of emergency. Judicial powers severely delay lawsuits over authorization processes, impinging on labor freedoms and the success of organizing campaigns.

Companies also pursue strategies against labor and unions, within the neoliberal legal framework, through subcontracting, union busting, the creation of company-dominated "yellow" unions, and dismissing militant unionized workers despite the law and international conventions. Turkey's dominant union model in logistics will experience serious challenges in near future owing to the authoritarian legal framework, and widespread subcontracting in both public and private enterprises.

One rapidly growing public servants "union" is the exception to this situation, and the state of emergency making things worse for class unionism, and even for bureaucratic unionism since the state of emergency was declared. Given the bureaucratic tradition in unions, some public servants are not eager to join them. But Turkey's neoliberal economic model is challenging the business unionism model. For example, Türkiye Denizciler Sendikası (TDS, the Turkish sailors union), a union organized in maritime transportation which did not strike for 66 years, has initiated a strike in Izmir ports, interrupting intercity ferry services.[32]

There is some evidence that the militant workers in the field may push their unions to cooperate rather than compete with one another. If these workers can push their unions towards this agenda, unions might stop "stealing the members of the other unions," and may have a chance to focus on unionizing unorganized workers. This rank and file movement will be challenged by the tradition of business unionism, and union bureaucracy, both of which are supported by employers.

The ideological differences between union administrations and rank and file members are reflected in the struggle. However, militant workers from different unions may make these differences insignificant if they show class solidarity.

In such an environment, unions will not be successful in protecting workers' rights exclusively through legislative, executive, and judicial struggles. Thus unions have to consider legitimate means to create a wide range of strategies both nationally and worldwide, and focus on doing as well as possible in their current circumstances.

Future privatizations might have a huge effect on the labor process in logistics. New waves of privatization in logistics will increase the number of subcontracted workers. This will also impact on regional minimum wage and migrant workers (one of the main reasons for the support for "yellow" unionism in both the private and public sectors), strike bans, and the state of emergency. On the other hand, the tensions between militant workers and the union bureaucracy can be felt directly. Despite the insufficiency of the national minimum wage, discussions on regulating the minimum wage on a regional basis still continuing, and transforming the system of severance pay in favor of employers is another issue on the table. If these regulations are achieved, and because of the strike ban in some industries, we can expect colorful and also illegal mass actions from workers and public servants at the same time. In a process like this, the tendency to militancy might be strengthened in both unionized and unorganized workers.

The workers who are forced to come together because of the material working and living conditions are united by the threat of unemployment, the possibility of determining the minimum wage at the regional level, the possibility that severance pay will be lost and creating a severance fund, and finally the postponement of strikes and strike bans. This is the current agenda of capital in Turkey, but some parts of the working classes (for example, despite the decreasing number, we can count most public servants in this category) have yet to experience it in the way that subcontracted workers do. The question here is, is there a possibility that would make the struggles in the near future sustainable? There is no definitive answer to this question, and we can argue that the answer lies in unionizing subcontracted workers. It is extremely important for the public authority to keep this tension sustainable and within certain limits, because Turkey's fragile economy is likely to be highly adversely affected by massive workers' movements in logistics.

The privatization of Turkish State Railways and the introduction of market conditions, and the search for quicker profits, the construction and privatization of connections between railways and ports, and also strike bans in logistics, can be evaluated as direct government interventions in the sector to accelerate capital accumulation. Subcontracting, the new personnel regime in public enterprises, also supports this thesis. When public servants lose their job security, they tend to go on strike—but privatization and de-unionization have decreased the number of strikes. That is a central reason for the decline in worker militancy and union struggles from the 1990s to the 2000s. Through growing subcontracting workers in public enterprises are seeing a decline in their wages and conditions, which are gradually equalizing at the bottom for all workers in logistics. Therefore, given the centrality of logistics to Turkey's economy, unions and workers have the potential to join with workers who share similar conditions in other industries to resist and act together on the least common denominators: wages, work conditions, and especially job security.

Interviews cited

No. 2, an ex-leader of *Tümtis* union, February 16, 2017, Istanbul.

No. 3, a leader of Tümtis union, February 16, 2017, Istanbul.

No. 4, a leader of *Nakliyat-İş* union, February 17, 2017, Istanbul.

No. 5, specialist working for *Liman-İş* union, February 17, 2017, Istanbul.

No. 7, press and public relations specialist of *Demiryol-İş* union, March 16, 2017, Ankara.

Notes

1 *Türkiye Sanayici ve İşadamları Derneği* (Tüsiad-Turkish Industry and Business Association).

2 M. Ş. Güzel, *Workers' Movement in Turkey: 1908–1984* (Istanbul: Kaynak, 1996), pp. 255–7 (in Turkish).

3 TUIK, "Workforce statistics, March 2017," June 15, 2017, www.tuik.gov.tr/PreHaberBultenleri.do?id=24628 (accessed June 20, 2017) (in Turkish).

4 A. Çelik, "What's happening in public servants unions?" *Selüloz-İş* union, 2016, http://selulozis.org.tr/yazilar/memur-sendikaciliginda-neler-oluyor-aziz-celik/ (accessed February 3, 2017) (in Turkish).

5 *RG. Official Gazette*, "A document on the member statistics of public servants unions and confederations by July 2017, according to the Law on Public Servants' Trade Unions No. 4688," www.resmigazete.gov.tr/eskiler/2017/07/20170705-4.pdf (accessed July 14, 2017) (in Turkish).

6 MLSS, "A description of the number of workers' and union members by branch of activities by July 2017, according to the Law on Trade Unions and Collective Bargaining Agreements No. 6356," www.csgb.gov.tr/media/5605/2017-temmuz-ay?-?statistigi.pdf (accessed August 5, 2017) (in Turkish).

7 On May 29, 2012, *Hava-İş* Union members exercised their constitutional rights and began direct action at Turkish Airlines (THY) to secure their right to safe flight (BTS, Working Report on the BTS Kesk United Transport Employees' Union 6th Ordinary General Assembly: April 20–24, 2013, Ankara, in Turkish, p. 130). This direct action was declared illegal by the THY administration, and smartphone messages were sent to 305 employees terminating

their contracts without notice. After a long struggle and solidarity efforts, all of the workers regained their jobs. So, if we combine the position of executive power and the latest changes in the legal framework, we can argue that there is unionism without strikes in these sectors now.

8   See INVEST, "Transportation and logistics," Republic of Turkey Prime Ministry Investment Support and Promotion Agency, 2017, www.invest.gov.tr/en-us/Sectors/Pages/TransportationAndLogistics.aspx (accessed July 12, 2017); Hürriyet, "Logistics sector shrank in 2016," January 3, 2017, www.hurriyet.com.tr/lojistik-sektoru-2016da-daraldi-40325658, (accessed April 5, 2017) (in Turkish).

9   Tümtis, "General condition of the transport industry," 29th Ordinary General Assembly Working Report, 18–19 April 2015: 2011–2015 period (Istanbul: Tümtis, 2015), pp. 92–4 (in Turkish).

10 Tümtis, "Presentation," 28th Ordinary General Assembly Working Report, 16–17: 2008–2011 period (Istanbul: Tümtis, 2011), p. 49 (in Turkish).

11 Tümtis (2015), p. 95.

12 Demiryol-İş, The History of Demiryol-İş Union 1952–2012 60th Year (Ankara: Demiryol-İş, 2012), p. 257 (in Turkish).

13 BTS Kesk United Transport Employees' Union, 7th Ordinary General Assembly Working Report, May 30–31, 2015 (Ankara, 2015), pp. 28–9 (in Turkish).

14 Law on Trade Unions and Collective Labor Agreements (TUCLA), No. 6356, 2012.

15 MLSS (2017).

16 According to media resources. See Evrensel, "The boss has established Karsan-Is union, and pushed the workers to be enroll in it: MNG Kargo-İş!", January 2, 2016, www.evrensel.net/haber/268930/patron-karsan-isi-kurdu-iscilere-uye-ol-baskisi-yapti-mng-kargo-is, (accessed March 3, 2017) (in Turkish).

17 Tümtis (2011), pp. 26–7.

18 Nakliyat-İş, "Nakliyat-İş moves forward to DISK's name, its history and its struggle tradition," Education Series No. 1 (Istanbul: Nakliyat-İş, n.d.), pp. 7–40 (in Turkish), at p. 13.

19 Nakliyat-İş (n.d.).

20 Tümtis (2011), pp, 26, 50, 62; Tümtis (2015), p. 121.

21 N. Karakurt, "A new game on the branch of activity bylaws" (in Turkish), United Transport Employees' Union (BTS), July 23, 2013, www.bts.org.tr/index.php/açiklamalarimiz/genel-merkez-açiklamalari/item/807-i%C5%9Fkollar%C4%B1-y%C3%B6netmeli%C4%9Finde-yeni-oyun.html (accessed March 15, 2017)

22 N. Karakurt, "A new game on the branch of activity bylaws," United Transport Employees' Union (BTS), July 23,2013, www.bts.org.tr/index.php/a%C3%A7iklamalarimiz/genel-merkez-a%C3%A7iklamalari/item/807-i%C5%9Fkollar%C4%B1y%C3%B6netmeli%C4%9Finde-yeni-oyun.html (accessed March 15, 2017) (in Turkish).

23 *Tümtis* (2011), p. 54.
24 A. Çelik, "Judicial stroke on unionism", *Birgün Daily Newspaper*, 2017, www.birgun.net/haber-detay/sendikaciliga-yargi-darbesi-151671.html (accessed April 25, 2017) (in Turkish).
25 K. Oztürk, "A real guarantee for acquired rights is real democracy," *Tümtis Workers' Power Journal* 38 (June 2017), p. 5 (in Turkish).
26 *Tümtis*, "Union activities cannot be punished, imprisonment against our branch managers is inadmissible!" *Tümtis Worker's Power Journal* 38 (June 2017), p. 7 (in Turkish).
27 Tümtis (2015), p. 95.
28 *Nakliyat-İş*, Disk *Nakliyat-İş* Union 11th Ordinary General Assembly Working Report: 2012–2015 Period, January 27, 2016, pp. 30–1 (Istanbul: *Nakliyat-İş*) (in Turkish).
29 *Tümtis* (2011), p. 65.
30 *Tümtis* (2011), pp. 71–2.
31 *Tümtis* (2011), pp. 54–5.
32 *Hürriyet*, "Strike handicap in maritime transportation", July 11,2017, www.hurriyet.com.tr/deniz-ulasimina-grev-engeli-40516971 (accessed July 12, 2017) (in Turkish).

Part IV

New Organizing Strategies for the Global Supply Chain

12

"The Drivers Who Move This Country Can Also Stop It": The Struggle of Tanker Drivers in Indonesia

Abu Mufakhir,
Alfian Al'ayubby Pelu, and Fahmi Panimbang

The labor movement in Indonesia has been recovering from dictatorship since 1998, and ever since, a wave of strikes have been taking place in many towns and cities that have involved several million workers. In the face of internal fragmentation and external challenges, the labor movement has been vibrant in shaping the country's political dynamic. A young generation of union leaders have also challenged the existing organizational culture of the conservative union, and transformed it to generate meaningful changes for the workers and even for local communities.[1] Direct action has been practised increasingly in recent years, where workers have had relatively new experiences with factory raids that took place for seven months in over a hundred factories in 2012, and two successful general strikes in 2012 and 2013 that engaged 2 million and 3 million workers respectively. Moreover, toll road blockades and industrial zone blockades are also among the popular forms of workers' protests in Indonesia to articulate their political aspirations.[2] Despite of this development, transport and logistics workers' struggles in the country are newly emerging, especially those in state-owned enterprises.

In early November 2016 a strike by 800 fuel tanker drivers at the world's largest fuel terminal situated in Jakarta was threatening to leave petrol stations across the capital and its neighboring cities short of fuel, and would have sparked fears that it could lead to a fuel crisis. The tanker strike, which lasted for 18 days, focused on Greater Jakarta (the cities of Jakarta, Bogor, Depok, and Tangerang), with some support from other oil depots in other cities. The strike action, which was held after a series of negotiations with the management, demanded improvement in working conditions, a pay rise, employment of the drivers with permanent status, and implementation of a pension scheme. The drivers were responsible for delivering dangerous fuel to hundreds of petrol stations, yet living precariously on dismal wages, with poor working conditions.

This chapter discusses the struggle of fuel tanker drivers in several cities in Indonesia, with a focus on the Plumpang depot in Jakarta, the world's largest fuel terminal. The chapter explains the origins of organizing tanker drivers, which led to the formation of the fuel tanker drivers' union. It highlights their organizing strategies and the building of solidarity between tanker drivers across Indonesia in order to exert their collective influence to achieve their rights. Although a series of industrial actions by the drivers was not quite successful in bringing about significant change, their collective action was a remarkable experience and the start of a journey, which led them to where they are today; gaining strength and confidence with increased capacity for protest mobilization.

PT Pertamina and Indonesia's oil industry

The oil and gas industry continues to be a fundamental part of the Indonesian economy. Indonesia has been active in the oil and gas sector for more than 132 years, following the first commercial oil discovery in North Sumatra in 1885. Indonesia continues to be an important player in the global oil and gas industry, and holds verified oil reserves of 3.7 billion barrels. Recently, Indonesia was ranked in the top 20 of the world's oil producers. Investment in the oil and gas industry reached US$22.2 billion in 2015 and around US$23.9 billion in 2016. However, state revenue from the oil industry has been declining, from 24.84 percent in 2006 to only 3.44 percent in 2016.[3]

During the dictatorship era (1967–98), PT Pertamina (an acronym of Perusahaan Tambang Minyak Negara or State Oil Mining Company), was a state-owned entity with the task of managing Indonesia's oil and gas development. Established in 1968, it was Indonesia's sole state oil company, responsible for managing businesses and production-sharing agreements, but with little involvement in production itself. Oil was already an important and "unlimited" source of funds for the Suharto government early in the New Order (dictatorship) period, but the sudden increase in oil prices in 1973 gave Pertamina enormous wealth. An investigation in 1970 sharply criticized Pertamina for loose auditing, failure to pass on profits to the government, and for the luxurious lifestyle of its senior executives.[4] Recently, Pertamina's executives were found guilty of being embroiled in various embezzlement and corruption cases.[5] It was estimated that in two years alone, in the mid-1990s, Pertamina lost nearly US$5 billion through inefficiency and corruption.[6] The Suharto regime consolidated its politics and economic interests with strong connections to the military, which controlled many strategic state-owned companies such as Pertamina.

Following the ousting of Suharto in 1998, the new government made an effort to end Pertamina's oil monopoly. Despite the democratization push from the population, the new administration embraced a

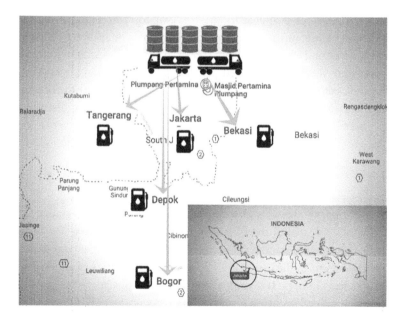

Map 12.1 Plumpang depot and its fuel distribution in Greater Jakarta

market-oriented economy. Thus, Indonesia's double transition towards a free market economy and a (neo) liberal democracy occurred under pressure from the International Monetary Fund (IMF) and the World Bank during the Asian financial crisis in 1997, which forced Indonesia to adopt austerity measures and a structural adjustment program. In October 2001, the legislature passed the Oil and Gas Act, giving Pertamina two years to transform itself into a state-owned commercial enterprise, surrendering control over foreign and local oil companies, and relinquishing its downstream role to a separate regulatory agency. The legislation was also intended to privatize and break Pertamina's monopoly by handing the control of production-sharing contracts to an agency created under the Office of the President.

Law No. 22/2001 formally liberalized the downstream sector (processing, transportation, storage, and trading) by opening it up to foreign capital and ending the state ownership of Pertamina. The first licenses for the retail sale of petroleum products were granted to Shell and Petronas of Malaysia in 2004. In the interests of the private sector, the fuel subsidy for citizens was reformed and significantly reduced by the Joko Widodo government's subsidy reform.[7] Following its privatization, Pertamina continues to dominate the oil and gas sector. In the retail and distribution sector for petroleum products, Pertamina maintains its two huge fuel terminals in Jakarta, Tanjung Priok depot and Plumpang depot (see Map 12.1). While the first depot stores and distributes liquefied petroleum gas (LPG) for the non-industrial sector, the second depot at Plumpang stores and distributes fuel, also for the non-industrial sector. This chapter only discusses the second (Plumpang depot), where the action of tanker drivers took place.

Plumpang depot, the world's largest fuel terminal

The Plumpang depot is the largest non-industrial fuel terminal in Indonesia. Located in the Plumpang area in North Jakarta, it is only 1 km from the international seaport of Tanjung Priok, the largest and busiest seaport in the country. This depot was built in 1972 and began its operation in 1974. It distributes fuel to all petrol stations in the capital, Jakarta, and its neighboring cities of Bogor, Depok, Tangerang, and Bekasi. The Plumpang depot has 27 storage tanks with a capacity of 18,000 kiloliters (18 million liters) of fuel. It is the world's largest fuel storage depot, with a capacity to serve the fuel requirements of at least 17.5 million motor vehicles a day in Greater Jakarta. The motor vehicles running in Greater Jakarta need at least 9 million liters of fuel every day.[8]

The fuel stored at the Plumpang depot comes partly from two oil refineries in Balongan and Cilacap, both located in Central Java. The oil is transported through underground pipelines over a distance of 200 km. The remainder comes from several other oil refineries, and is transported by sea tankers. The vast storage and distribution capacity of the Plumpang depot has made the status of the depot that of a vital and highly protected facility. Conservative data shows the number of petrol stations in Greater Jakarta that are in partnership with Pertamina to be about 314.[9] However, according to several tanker drivers, there are at least 850 petrol stations in Greater Jakarta area that are controlled by, or in partnership with, PT Pertamina.[10] All of these petrol stations are supplied from the Plumpang depot. The average fuel pump has sufficient capacity for two days, so it requires punctual supply in order to maintain adequate storage and distribution. Once the pump faces a complete or partial shortage, it takes one week for the pump to recover its normal function. This shows the crucial role of the Plumpang depot, which depends heavily on tanker drivers, whose role is to distribute the fuel on a daily basis. Each tanker has a fuel capacity of at least 24,000 liters.

At the Plumpang depot there are three different companies which have interconnected relations. The first is the management of Pertamina, which deals with the technical and operational functions of the depot, its infrastructure, and the supply from the oil refineries. The second is PT Pertamina Patra Niaga (PPN), a subsidiary of Pertamina which is responsible for tanker management, depot management, and the distribution of the fuel to petrol stations. The third is an outsourcing company that receives subcontracting work from PPN, which is mainly the provision of payroll services for the workers and tanker drivers at the depot. This company has changed regularly, depending on how efficient it is in dealing with the drivers' demands. In fact, PPN has the power to appoint the vendor, which handles the payroll. In the last five years, the outsourcing company or the vendor at the Plumpang depot has changed three times. Since March 2017, the outsourcing company has been PT Garda Utama Nasional (GUN). Previously, it was outsourced to PT Sapta Sarana Sejahtera (SSS).[11]

Precarious work of Pertamina's tanker drivers

Indonesia's fuel distribution is the most complex in the world. There are about 1,200 drivers working at the fuel terminal at Plumpang, operating approximately 800 road tankers.[12] Each tanker is operated by one driver and an assistant who is required to have good stamina and a high degree of discipline, to be punctual in Jakarta's poor traffic conditions, and to master the roads to petrol station destinations that are spread across the cities, in order to transport the fuel punctually. As Cowen identified, the job characteristics in the distribution and logistics sector, such as fuel distribution, are on a "just-in-time" basis, where commodities are coordinated and distributed as required. As "just-in-time" becomes more widely implemented, processes and commodities have to be efficiently coordinated, and transported quickly and reliably.[13]

On average, the drivers have been working for the company for more than seven years. Despite this long period of service, they are still illegally employed, with an insecure and irregular status. Their employment contract is for only one year, with a renewal process each year. The drivers' employment relationship is with an outsourcing company, which is designated by PPN, although the tanker fleet is owned by PPN. This is the reality of a flexible labor market regime. Referring to Labour Law 13/2003 (article 66), the work of these drivers is the company's core business, thus it is illegal for it to be outsourced.

Prior to the privatization of Pertamina, the drivers were employed by a transport company which leased the fuel tankers to Pertamina depots. Since 2007, when Pertamina's subsidiary PPN took over the management,[14] drivers who previously worked for PPN gradually transferred their employment to the outsourcing company. The drivers claim to be earning much less than previously, as their salary has declined to below even the minimum wage. Some allowances were also reduced to a meager IDR25,000 (less than US$2).[15] On the other hand, the net profits of Pertamina and its subsidiary PPN have increased every year. PPN even declared that its net profit in 2015 was the largest in the company's history.[16] The drivers and workers' union believes the huge profit accrued by Pertamina and PPN is the result of sweated labor.

Tanker drivers make three round-trips a day on average, working a total of over 12 hours a day on the road, excluding loading time in the depot and unloading at petrol stations. Given this situation, the company always opts out of its responsibility. If a serious road accident occurs where a driver's leg is amputated, the company does not cover the insurance for the worker, or even if the worker is severely injured or killed. In 2016, an accident caused a tanker explosion which burned the driver and his assistant. The workers were on sick leave during their recovery from the accident, but their wages were not paid. The company argued that the workers were taking days off.[17] In addition, the drivers are responsible for the tanker maintenance. They have to bear the cost of repairs if an accident occurs.

Some of the features of industrial relations in Indonesia's post-dictatorship phase are that they are liberal, flexible, and decentralized.[18] A flexible labor market policy was implemented to create a "friendlier" pro-business environment. Since the enactment of Law No. 13/2003 which legalized contract work and enabled labor outsourcing practices to take effect, employers turned more workers into casual and contract labor, hence there is a more precarious workforce. Since 2003, it has been the norm for companies to have three groups of workers: permanent, contract, and outsourced (agency) workers. Each has a different employment status and consequently different wages and benefits, despite their doing the same work. An outsourced worker is hired not directly by a company, but through an employment agency. The worker remains the employee of the employment agency and is temporarily contracted to work for a company. Thus, the company is not responsible for the worker's social security payments or for providing medical insurance, paid holidays, paid sick leave, or any other benefit provided to regular workers, as required by law. And importantly, in practice the employment agency that contracted out the worker does not provide them with any of those benefits either.

A contract worker, which is one level "better" than an outsourced one, is hired by the company, but unlike a permanent/regular worker does not receive any benefits—they just receive wages that are a little higher than the wages of outsourced workers, and are hired directly. Therefore, outsourced workers are paid less than contract workers, who in turn are paid less than the permanent workers, who receive minimum wages and several benefits such as transport allowances and annual bonuses. The practice of using a large number of outsourced workers, contract workers, and recent graduates (such as apprentices and trainees) as full-time workers who are usually paid less than the minimum wage puts tremendous downward pressure on the wages of all workers. Numerous sources indicate that the typical composition of labor in an Indonesian company is 20 percent permanent, 30 percent contract, and 50 percent cent outsourced (agency) workers. A study has shown a drastic increase of contract and agency workers in many companies. Even those with permanent employment status were transformed into contract workers by the management in order to cut labor costs. Such practices occurred even before the enactment of Law No. 13/2003; however, the law legalized the practice.[19]

The origin of drivers organizing

Back in 2008, the tanker drivers at the Plumpang depot established a union named Indonesian Tank Transport Workers' Union (SBTTI) in response to the change in the company management that was seen to affect the workers. For two years the SBTTI union functioned at the Plumpang depot. It organized a number of protests against poor working conditions, but with very little influence. In 2010, some SBTTI organizers were dismissed and transferred by PPN management to other depots, leaving other union organizers and members feeling insecure. The union then ceased to function. However, it is interesting to observe that the organizers who were transferred to other depots, such as Surabaya in East Java, Yogyakarta in the center of Java, and other big cities, apparently continued to organize. At the new depots, they secretly organized and consolidated the workers, built connections, and expanded communication between tanker drivers in various depots.

These organizing and consolidation efforts gradually paid off.[20] In mid-2011, the drivers formed an informal association (*paguyuban*), the Association for the Solidarity of Indonesia Fuel Tanker Drivers. In contrast to SBTTI, whose coverage was limited to workers at the Plumpang depot, the *paguyuban* covers workers nationally, although its members are mainly in key depots across Java Island. Java is the most densely populated part of Indonesia, and is the world's 13th largest island. Official data in 2007 recorded that the islands' 132 million inhabitants constituted 58.3 percent of the entire population of Indonesia.[21] Later, tanker drivers in other depots decided to join the *paguyuban* because they faced the same problems, and they began to realize that it was not sufficient to organize only in their own area.

In 2012, the drivers' association, or *paguyuban*, held a simultaneous strike action at almost all Pertamina depots in Java, which called for minimum wages and employment status demands which had not been met, for drivers responsible for delivering dangerous fuel in harsh working conditions. This was the first major strike in the fuel retail sector in the post-authoritarian period which engaged almost all depots in Java. However, the strike action failed and was curtailed. Many organizers were dismissed, leaving another threat for the drivers. Following the massive dismissal, direct actions were reduced and the organizers began to launch several legal battles against the company, but to no avail.[22] Efforts through legal and formal mechanisms were not successful.

In May 2015, the drivers' informal association at the Plumpang depot formed a branch of the Transport and Seaport Workers Union (SBTPI), which is affiliated with the Federation of Transport and Seaport Workers Union (FBTPI). Under the SBTPI union, they continued to reorganize and consolidate the drivers. At first, out of 1,200 drivers at the depot, only 92 joined the union.[23] In February 2016 the union courageously fought with the management by launching a legal action claiming loose audits and lack of transparency in the PPN workers' cooperative. The cooperative issue was intentionally chosen as it was not directly related to labor relations, and thus it would not trigger the usual backlash. The union encouraged re-election of the co-operative committee.[24] During the re-election process, several union organizers were elected to several positions, gaining more confidence for the union to prepare further steps strategically. Not long after this, the number of union members was increased to 300 workers.

In March 2016, the union began to confidently demand its members' rights. First, a case was filed to claim a compensation payment for an occupational accident that occurred in 2015, which killed a driver; management had never paid any compensation to the victim's family. Second, the union claimed workers' rights to social security (BPJS Health). Many of the drivers have received BPJS cards, but they are not eligible to access the health services in hospitals, as they are actually not registered in the BPJS social security database. At that time the outsourcing company was PT SSS, which was replaced by PT GUN. Third, the union demanded that management pay wages according to the minimum wage regulations, as throughout 2015 and early 2016, drivers were paid less than the minimum wage. Soon after these demands were made by the union, four union leaders and organizers were dismissed from their jobs. In response to this, the union prepared to hold a strike on March 24, 2016, to demand that the four union leaders be reinstated. Surprisingly they were reinstated before the strike took place. This was the first time in the history of the Plumpang depot that a reinstatement had occurred. More workers joined in the union.

In June 2016, the union submitted a list of basic rights violations at the Plumpang depot to the North Jakarta Manpower Office. As the officer ignored the union letter, hundreds of workers held a continuous protest in front of the office. A memorandum of understanding was issued by the Manpower Office in September 2016. There were 12 issues based on the inspection. The Manpower Office mandated that management fulfil workers' rights, including 8-hour working days, pension and health insurance, rights to collective bargaining, and improved working conditions. However, PPN management refused to meet the demands. They argued that the vendor or the outsourcing company (GUN) was responsible for meeting the workers' demands. Workers did not receive an answer to their demands until they decided to hold further industrial action.

A series of industrial strikes

Several meetings of union leaders, organizers, and members were held to discuss union strategies. Strike action was then agreed to be held from November 1–18, 2016. The strike involved more than 800 drivers out of 1,200. They set up a massive tent for the workers' station and camp, located alongside the wall of the depot. Every day, workers gathered at the workers' station for discussions. Solidarity emerged, coming from various labor organizations and unions within the federation as well as outside the federation.

The management (PPN and GUN) responded to the union move with the usual threats of massive dismissals. They did whatever was necessary to secure stocks of fuel. First, to avoid the disruption of fuel distribution, the management deployed substitute drivers, a "reserve army of drivers from various oil depots across Java, Sumatra, and Sulawesi islands."[25] Second, some of the fuel supply for Jakarta's neighboring cities of Bogor, Depok, Tangerang, and Bekasi was supplied from the nearby depots of Cikampek and Merak, thus the substitute drivers focused only on the fuel supply to the petrol stations throughout the capital. Third, the management started to recruit new tanker drivers to be stationed at the Plumpang depot with several promises of incentives such as regular status and decent wages. Later it was found that the incentives were bogus, as the "labor recruitment mafia" in management still carried out the long-time practice of charging the new drivers amounts between IDR15–20 million (US$1,100–1,500).[26]

With all these efforts, the management managed to handle the impact of the strike. Some of the strikers from depots in Merak (Banten), Cikampek (West Java), and Bandung (West Java) returned home, but most of the strikers continued on the picket line. Sometimes they went in motorbike convoys to blockade the road, causing traffic congestion for hours. They also went to the headquarters of Pertamina and PPN to pressure the authorities and employers. This also served to keep the spirit of struggle and their solidarity alive. There were, of course, some minor disruptions and delays in fuel deliveries, as the substitute drivers were not familiar with the roads and pump destinations. Several road tanker accidents were seen during this period. A number of government officials visited the strikers to negotiate, including officials from the Coordinating Ministry for Political, Legal, and Security Affairs, the Ministry of Manpower, and the National Police. This proves that the Plumpang depot is vital, as it is the sole source of fuel supply for the capital, the country's economic and political centre.[27]

On the 11th day, the strikers staged a rally in front of the State Palace. Representatives were received by one of the deputies in the Office of the Presidential Staff, saying they would facilitate a negotiation with Pertamina. The negotiation with Pertamina and PPN materialized on the 15th day of the strike. The union demanded that the company (1) ensure there will be no intimidation against the strikers; (2) provide additional payment for overtime work; (3) appoint the drivers as permanent employees; (4) provide decent wages and allowances; and (5) provide a pension scheme. The company refused to meet the demands, and no agreement was achieved.

On the 18th day, another negotiation was facilitated by the Ministry of Manpower. The management of PPN looked friendly, saying that some of the demands would be fulfilled, except changing the drivers' status to regular, which would be negotiated later. As the strike ended and the drivers returned to their workplace, the union observed that most of the demands had not been implemented. Union leaders are preparing their response thoughtfully.

The backlash from the employers

The PPN and GUN managements were greatly disturbed, and there was an intense backlash from them. They had taken the threat of the drivers' strike seriously and tried to consolidate their power. They are aware that the growing capacity of drivers and other workers in mobilizing protests at the Plumpang depot is a serious risk to their business. The fact that many depots operate as part of Pertamina's supply chain, especially such a strategic and vital business operation as the Plumpang depot, means that a disruption in fuel distribution in one depot affects the entire production, transportation, storage, and trading of fuel products nationally. The national government and Pertamina recognize how disruptive the situation could be, given the status of the Plumpang depot as vital and highly protected. They are also worried that if the demands of workers are met, it would be followed by similar demands from workers in other depots.

In early February 2017, the management fired 32 drivers and suspended another 64 workers who were all over 55 years of age. This was anticipated, and the union responded quickly. A series of negotiations and continual protest have managed to reinstate all the workers. Counterattacks also took place in other depots, such as in Bandung. Eleven union organizers at the Padalarang depot in Bandung were suspended from their jobs because of their involvement in the Labour Day celebration at the Plumpang depot in Jakarta. Labour Day is a public holiday, and the workers had submitted a letter requesting permission to take a day off on May 1. The union negotiated with the management in Bandung, but with no result. The union leaders at the Plumpang depot helped by going to the PPN headquarters in Jakarta and successfully reinstated the 11 organizers to their jobs. During the negotiation, the union also raised concerns by workers at different depots.

Not long after that, in early June 2017, another backlash by management occurred at the Plumpang and Merak depots, where 350 drivers were dismissed. It was claimed they were no longer qualified for the jobs. The union believes this was just a management strategy to threaten the drivers. This moved the union and drivers in various depots in different cities to hold an even bigger strike on June19–26, 2017. The time to strike was chosen to test whether the union could spark fears of fuel shortages during the fourth week of the Muslim fasting month, which is close to the Idul Fitri holiday and festivities, where fuel is in high demand by millions of Greater Jakarta residents who drive home at this time. However, management did whatever was necessary to secure the fuel stock, at great expense in terms of funds and resources. The eight-day strike, although it occurred with much better preparation and resource mobilization, had only a minor impact.

Despite these challenges, the union and workers realized that their collective actions provided a remarkable level of experience for them.

Consolidating power

One of the key union strategies following the series of strikes was to focus on internal consolidation. On December 10 and 11, 2016, in accordance with the celebration of Human Rights Day, the union held a mass assembly in Jakarta which involved union leaders and organizers from six key depots in three major islands of Sumatra (Lampung), Sulawesi (Makassar), and Java (port of Merak in Banten, Padalarang in West Java, and Plumpang in Jakarta). They are aware that Java is vital for consolidation, as the island holds more than half the total population of Indonesia. During the assembly and the aftermath, consolidation was built when organizers shared their on-the-ground experiences with each other, followed by a plan for union education. In March 2017, they had another mass assembly with more workers involved. New representatives from other depots also participated, including those from Jambi (Sumatra), Ujung Berung (West Java), and Tegal (Central Java).

The series of industrial actions by drivers has forced Pertamina, PPN, and their outsourcing company to negotiate with and listen to the drivers—for the first time in Pertamina workers' history. The Plumpang depot and its organizing capacity have been the backbone of the drivers' power, but it has also gradually transferred to other depots in other cities. The collective experience of strikes and resistance has taught them that grassroots labor organizing is necessary for success in the union's political struggle. The political task for the drivers' union is to document their experiences for continuous learning, and to develop them into more effective strategies for the future. But the most urgent task now is to decide how to respond to the usual counterattacks from the state and capital.

Notes

1   Fahmi Panimbang, Labour struggles in Asia," in F. Panimbang ed.), *Resistance on the Continent of Labour: Strategies and Initiatives of Labour Organizing in Asia* (Hong Kong: Asia Monitor Resource Centre, 2017).

2   Fahmi Panimbang and Abu Mufakhir, "Labour strikes in post-authoritarian Indonesia, 1998–2013." In Jörg Nowak et al. (eds.), *Strikes and Workers Movements in the 21st Century* (London: Rowman & Littlefield, 2018).

3 Ministry of Finance, quoted in PWC, "Oil and gas in Indonesia" (Jakarta: PWC Indonesia, 2016), www.pwc.com/id/en/energy-utilities-mining/assets/May%202016/PwC%20Indonesia-oil-and-gas-guide-2016.pdf (accessed June 25, 2017).

4 Robert Cribb and Audrey Kahin, *Historical Dictionary of Indonesia*, 2nd edn (Maryland: Scarecrow Press, 2004).

5 Maya Ayu Puspitasari, "Polisi Periksa Mantan Dirut Pertamina, Alasannya…" ("Police to interrogate former CEO of Pertamina, the reason is…"], *Tempo*, July 25, 2017.

6 Cribb and Kahin (2004).

7 PWC (2016).

8 Jakarta Central Bureau of Statistics, "Transportation statistics of Jakarta" (Jakarta: BPS Provinsi Jakarta, 2015), http://jakarta.bps.go.id/backend/pdf_publikasi/Statistik-Transportasi-DKI-Jakarta-2015.pdf (accessed May 5, 2017); Fiki Ariyanti, "Depo Plumpang Tak Operasi, Jakarta Bisa Lumpuh Tanpa BBM Seminggu" ("Plumpang depot ceased to function, Jakarta without fuel for a week might paralyze the city"), *Liputan6*, May 8, 2017, http://bisnis.liputan6.com/read/2944712/depo-plumpang-tak-operasi-jakarta-bisa-lumpuh-tanpa-bbm-seminggu (accessed May 9, 2017).

9 Portal Data Terpadu Pemerintah Provinsi DKI Jakarta, "Data SPBU Pertamina Provinsi DKI Jakarta Tahun 2014" ("Data of Jakarta gas stations, 2014") (2017), http://data.jakarta.go.id/dataset/data-spbu-pertamina-provinsi-dki-jakarta/resource/oc1df4bc-3cc8-4d43-8809-ae039c768067 (accessed May 6, 2017).

10 Interview, SP and DW (labor organizers), April 29, 2017.

11 Interview, TS (labor organizer), May 5, 2017.

12 Interview, SP (labor organizer), April 29, 2016; interview, TS (labor organizer), May 5, 2017.

13 Deborah Cowen, *The Deadly Life of Logistics: Mapping Violence in Global Trade* (Minneapolis, Minn.: University of Minnesota Press, 2014).

14 Pertamina Patra Niaga, "Tentang Perusahaan Kami" ("About our company") (2017a), www.pertaminapatraniaga.com/about-us-id-ID/company-history-id-ID/ (accessed June 9, 2017).

15 Interview, GT (labor organizer), May 12, 2017; interview, DI (labor organizer), April 29, 2017; interview, SP (labor organizer), June 9, 217.

16 Pertamina Patra Niaga, "Laba Bersih Terbesar dalam Sejarah Perusahaan" ("The largest net profit in company's history") (2017b), www.pertaminapatraniaga.com/news-and-events-id-ID/latest-news-id-ID-2/laba-bersih-terbesar-dalam-sejarah-perusahaan-id-ID/ (accessed May 20, 2017).

17 Afik Irwanto, "Kisah Sunyi Awak Mobil Tangk" ("The tank truck drivers' soliloquy") (2017), https://fbtpi.org/kisah-sunyi-awak-mobil-tangki/ (accessed June 6, 2017).

18 Indrasari Tjandraningsih, "Industrial relations in the democratizing era," pp. 244–66 in Aris Ananta, Muljana Soekarni, and Sjamsul Arifin (eds.),

The Indonesian Economy: Entering a New Era (Singapore: Bank Indonesia, Jakarta, and Institute of Southeast Asian Studies, 2011).

19 Panimbang and Mufakhir (2018); Tjandraningsih (2011).

20 Interview, TS (labor organizer), May 5, 2017

21 Iem Brown (ed.), *The Territories of Indonesia* (London: Routledge, 2009).

22 Interview, OB (labor organizer), May 3, 2017.

23 Interview, TS (labor organizer), May 22, 2017.

24 Interview, TS (labor organizer), May 22, 2017.

25 Interview, TS (labor organizer), May 5, 2017.

26 Interview, GT (labor organizer), May 12, 2017.

27 Dunia Energi, "Beban Plumpang Terlalu Besar, Pertamina Kaji Bangun Depo Tambahan" {"Plumpang depot's workload is too heavy, Pertamina studies to build an additional depot"), 2017, www.dunia-energi.com/be-ban-plumpang-terlalu-besar-pertamina-kaji-bangun-depo-tambahan/ (accessed May 20, 2017).

13

Lessons Learned from Eight Years of Experimental Organizing in Southern California's Logistics Sector

Sheheryar Kaoosji

Introduction

On January 20, 2009 the US labor movement, a critical part of the coalition that helped Barack Obama win the presidency, felt ascendant. Though the American Federation of Labor and Congress of Industrial Organizations (AFL-CIO), after a series of faltering reform movements, had split, with seven unions establishing Change to Win (CTW), an initiative focused on identifying new large-scale organizing opportunities, labor had an ally in the White House, and a list of reforms for Congress to take up. In the depths of a recession rooted in inequality and a failing economic system, a new-era progressive policy felt possible.

Around that same time, Teamsters, community leaders, and environmental advocates were celebrating the rollout of an example of such progressive policy: the Clean Trucks Program (CTP) at the ports of Los Angeles and Long Beach. Approximately 16,000 port drivers had, for decades, faced misclassification as independent contractors, moving goods for the largest companies in the world. The CTP required trucking companies serving the port to replace old, dirty diesel trucks with new, lower-emission vehicles, removing tons of pollutants from the air in poor communities near the twin ports of Los Angeles and Long Beach, and at the same time provided drivers with a path to employment, and a sustainable future. And just as that moment of creation of a model policy for just sustainable goods movement, its undoing began. On March 30, 2009, two months after Obama's inauguration and six months after the CTP was initiated, the Ninth Circuit Court of Appeals, upon hearing a challenge by the American Trucking Association (ATA), enjoined the CTP's employee mandate, keeping drivers deprived of their rights and gutting the economic logic of the program.

At that same moment in late January 2009, I sat in a basement in Fontana, California, 50 miles east of Los Angeles, handing out packets of turf to canvassers from the local Teamsters, community activists, and students. We were canvassing among the 100,000 warehouse workers in the Inland Empire, the largest population of warehouse workers in the United States, most of them unorganized and many of them temps. The goal was to organize a pool of workers who could push the Congress and president to pass the Employee Free Choice Act (EFCA)—a policy called "Card Check" to allow workers to unionize more easily. The timing for this mobilization placed us in the midst of an economic crash with no end in sight. Organizers visited unemployed, homeless, and temporary workers. We brought them together to take action—to run into a warehouse where their fellow workers were being mistreated or helping shut down a major industrial intersection, to risk arrest for the mere potential of a good job. It was also a moment of great opportunity and experiment—but one that ultimately failed to spark a movement, or affect the policy debate in Washington DC.

Over the past eight years, the unions at CTW established organizing efforts among goods movement workers throughout Southern California, the hub through which $500 billion in goods pass through each year—43 percent of the goods that enter the country. These efforts were resourced with strategic researchers and experienced organizers, and supported by motivated community partners. While we made significant impacts on the way the goods movement sector operates, we clearly fell short of the ambitious original vision of sparking organizing of production and retail workers using the power of the supply chain. This chapter analyses the experiences of these two distinct yet related efforts, with the perspective of eight years of lessons learned from somebody who worked on both projects and remains committed to organizing in the goods movement sector of Southern California.[1] These two projects were intended to make significant, strategic changes in a sector that is critical to our global economy. While the optimism of these projects at their outset was not realistic, the central strategy was correct. These efforts have fallen short but if we look closely, we can see a path forward.

Regulation and organizing in the goods movement sector

Goods movement has always been provided with special treatment by US regulators, from the commerce clause of the Constitution, to the railroads gaining special protections based on their value as the driver of commerce and empire. In 1935, Franklin Roosevelt signed the Motor Carrier Act, setting rates for regional trips and regulating trucking as a public utility.[2] Under this regime, the national organizing of trucking became possible, with a floor for costs protecting the sector participants and driver wages. The Teamsters found great success organizing in this context, starting with Local 574 in Minneapolis, Minnesota in 1934.[3]

The power the Teamsters built was based in constant organizing and growth in trucking and in the sites of pickup and delivery for the drivers. This depended on the opportunity gained from the threat of secondary pickets—when drivers come across pickets at a gate and refuse to deliver or pick up at a factory, warehouse, or store, created pressure on the employer to allow the goods to move—at any cost. The cost, of course, was a Teamster contract—a model replicated throughout the nation, most famously by Jimmy Hoffa's organizing efforts throughout the Midwest. But trucking was not the only sector of the economy impacted by the innovations of the Teamsters. The actions of these drivers at strategic sites moved Teamster organizing into manufacturing, food processing and dairies, coalmines and sawmills. Pickets at delivery sites made warehouse workers and retail workers into union members.

By the end of the 1930s, large sectors of production had wage parity and the rush of organizing had slowed. Through the Second World War, the labor movement was frozen by a no-strike agreement. Four years of pent-up wage stagnation amidst a war-fueled economic expansion exploded in 1946 in thousands of strikes, more than during any year in the 1930s. Republicans took Congress and came up with a response, the Taft-Hartley Labor Management Relations Act, signed by President Truman in 1947. Crucially, Taft-Hartley banned the secondary picket, devastating this organizing model.

Taft-Hartley ended the unions' ability to easily leverage organizing wins out of existing members. But the price controls remained, and trucking and warehousing were, through the 1970s, an occupation of the middle class. In 1980, Jimmy Carter deregulated the trucking industry with his own Motor Carrier Act, removing price controls, causing the bottom to fall out, with unionized trucking firms rapidly dissolving. This was further reinforced by Bill Clinton's signing of the Federal Aviation Administration Authorization Act in 1995, which, among other things, barred state or local authorities from regulating prices, routes, and services related to goods movement.

It is in this context—an ascendant policy regime designed to facilitate goods movement at all costs, based in laws signed by Democrats to reduce labor power in goods movement—that the Port Trucking and WWU campaigns currently operate.

Port trucking

In 1937, the Teamsters targeted the drivers at the Ports of Los Angeles and Long Beach, whose stevedores had been organized into the International Longshore and Warehouse Union (ILWU) three years earlier. Because the 1935 Motor Carrier Act prevented goods from being diverted to other markets, work stoppages were effective in bringing the trucking industry to the table. Longshoremen stopped work in solidarity with these activities, putting pressure on the shippers.[4]

While Taft-Hartley undercut the ability of unions to keep growing at the pace they held in the 1930s, the Motor Carrier Act created a framework within which organized truck drivers were a powerful force in commerce. This culminated with the Teamsters' establishment in 1964 of a national Master Freight Agreement with common carriers across the country, which at one point covered over 400,000 drivers.[5] The Carter administration's Interstate Commerce Commission began to remove barriers to entry in the sector, culminating in the Motor Carrier Act of 1980, which removed the price floors and routes that underpinned the sector. Deregulation was accomplished to cut costs for the companies who were moving their goods, and turned the trucking sector upside down. This affected port trucking deeply, with new entrants undercutting existing union carriers. Within five years, the last holdout had declared bankruptcy, and a new system of independent contractor drivers had taken hold, with drivers quickly becoming among the lowest paid workers in the area.

Through the next quarter-century, the culture and economy of the port changed drastically. Drivers were paid by the load, driving old trucks they financed themselves. As Southern California changed with the influx of Latinos in the 1980s, the workforce also changed. Central American men, in particular, flooded into the sector and created a culture able to simultaneously contain, on one pole, individualism and entrepreneurism, and at the same time fierce and radical solidarity exhibited through regular wildcat strikes. These occurred despite the fact that as independent contractors, any form of collective action by drivers was legally actionable collusion. This scared unions away from organizing these workers, and their efforts instead focused on bringing back the employee model. Various efforts were tried and failed, most prominently the efforts by the Communication Workers of America in 1996 to partner with a financier interested in establishing a trucking company that would employ drivers.[6]

In 2007, CTW, the Teamsters, and community and environmental partners approached the twin ports of Los Angeles and Long Beach with a plan to implement a CTP. In order to address the massive environmental impact created by 16,000 diesel trucks on the low-income communities around the port, the policy mandated new, environmentally cleaner trucks. In order to address the cost of the new trucks, it required that the trucks be part of a large company's fleet, not financed directly by drivers, who were to be classified as employees. This policy addressed labor, environmental, and community needs in one neat package.

This policy was embraced by Antonio Villaraigosa, the former union organizer and first Latino mayor in modern Los Angeles history. Long Beach Mayor Bob Foster resisted the employee mandate but moved forward with the CTP. The ATA sued Los Angeles and claimed the City had no authority to mandate the employment status of drivers. The litigation invoked the issue of federal pre-emption by the 1979 Motor Carrier Act and its renewal, the Federal Aviation Administration Authorization Act of 1994 (FAAAA). Despite the refusal of the litigators of the environmental movement to take their victory and walk away, in 2009 and 2010, the Ninth Circuit determined that the FAAAA pre-empted the employee mandate, and ruled it illegal.

The core of the policy gone, many expected the Teamsters to move on from the port. The Teamsters, led by General President Jim Hoffa, instead looked for a new path. They first looked at federal legislation, the Clean Ports Act, which would have affirmatively excluded drivers from this pre-emption.[7] These efforts were precluded with the election of a Republican House of Representatives in 2010.[8] In 2011–12, the union pivoted to organizing one of the largest employee-based companies at the port, Toll Global, establishing the first union contract at the port in a generation. Then, addressing the vast majority of drivers who remained misclassified, the union and its local partner, the Los Angeles Alliance for A New Economy (LAANE), landed on a legal strategy rooted in challenging the employment model as illegal, and gaining determinations of drivers as employees by the California Labor Commissioner in 2012–13.

By 2017, thousands of port drivers have been involved with claims of misclassification through the California Labor Commissioner (an administrative process), or private litigation as individuals or classes. Almost every one of these claims has resulted in determinations of employee status and thousands per year in back wages and illegal deductions owed. These findings have consistently been affirmed on appeal by the courts.[9] Findings of employee status do not magically change a driver's situation, but they create legal grounding for organizing. And as companies the Teamsters have organized have hired on their drivers, they create living examples, paid by the hour with benefits and 40-hour work weeks, Social Security, workers' compensation, and unemployment benefits, right there at the port terminal.

After determining that drivers were indeed treated as employees based on established legal tests, the drivers at several companies began to take collective actions—filing wage claims, making delegations to management, and by late 2013 going on strike, bolstered by a then-pending charge to the National Labor Relations Board (NLRB) that confirmed they were misclassified as independent contractors. The board made a determination in early 2014 affirming the drivers as employees, and as such allowed them to strike, though the drivers by that time had already successfully returned to work without incident.

These actions spread, and over a dozen companies have experienced strikes since then, with no NLRB pushback. Teamsters have utilized the ambulatory picket, using a rule that allows them to follow trucks and picket at their terminus. Port strikes have become famous in the LA labor movement as massive operations, with up to 20 primary and ambulatory picket teams operating at any given time manned with strikers, rank and file Teamsters, union allies, and community supporters, across container terminals, truckyards, railyards, and warehouses.

These efforts have changed the region in several ways. With almost every company at the port facing litigation, dozens are moving to an employment model, and ending misclassification. Wages have also risen steadily, and hundreds of unionized port drivers stand as an example of the possibilities at one of the hardest places to organize in the country. Hundreds of rank and file Teamsters join the pickets every strike, and the campaign has built an expertise in the industry and presence in the community. Port drivers are part of positive change where it was said to be impossible.

Warehouse Workers United

The Inland Empire's goods movement sector grew up as the overflow from the port distribution expanded beyond the Harbor region. The Inland Empire, consisting of San Bernardino and Riverside counties, has a long history of relatively low wages and poor working conditions. While there are thousands of union members in the region, its labor movement lacks the cohesion and power that exists in Los Angeles. Warehousing exploded in the early 2000s, thriving in a region hungry for jobs, loose with development subsidies, and low on regulation. Many of the 100,000 workers in the 300-plus warehouses in the Inland Empire have consistent, regular, decent-paying jobs. But others, perhaps 30 percent, move from job to job, with little or no permanent employment relationship.[10] These workers are employed through staffing agencies, paid the minimum wage or slightly above. They are provided with no benefits, and consistently have to fight to keep their employment. The use of these staffing agencies was originally justified by the industry to account for the ups and downs of goods movement, but their presence now functions to create a permanent underclass in the sector—a pool of hungry temps willing to do any job offered, and a credible threat to undercut the conditions of the directly employed.

Warehouse Workers United's (WWU's) first efforts in 2009 were framed in the context of public action in support of broad labor law reform, specifically the EFCA. While we were able to organize workers to speak up in remarkably difficult conditions, there was little effort to address the issues they dealt with on a daily basis. A strategy born before the recession was not modified to address the crisis at hand, and made little impact.

While it was clear that the original campaign theory was flawed, ctw continued to support small-scale organizing through 2010 as we built worker relationships and roots in the community. At that point, things were clearly not moving as quickly as hoped. Organizing at the ports was delayed by litigation, and it became clear that EFCA had no chance of moving in Congress. With the project threatened, the United Food and Commercial Workers (UFCW) approached ctw about integrating the warehouse project into their plans for a Walmart campaign—for the first time, seriously organizing Walmart store workers. The UFCW "adopted" the project, while the Teamsters focused on the Ports.

This relationship produced the most significant of WWU's efforts. Not coincidentally, these activities took place as part of a comprehensive campaign against an apex retailer, Walmart, integrating retail organizing, warehouse worker organizing in Chicago, community and capital strategies.[11] This campaign and the rest of the UFCW's efforts from 2011 to 2013 represent a legitimate, if limited, effort to take on a global firm at many levels. A focus on Walmart brought us to a cluster of about a dozen warehouses operated by third party logistics (3PL) companies. Warehouse Workers For Justice, a similar group outside Chicago, joined the effort and took on Walmart 3PLs in their region. The UFCW established OUR Walmart, a project to bring together retail workers in a new association. The UFCW also established national and global relationships to align anti-Walmart efforts. WWU established partnerships with production workers in the Walmart supply chain, especially in Bangladesh and Cambodia.

Our strategy was based in highlighting Walmart's responsibility for problems in the warehouses through legal action and public messaging, and drawing the contrast between the largest company in the world and the poverty of the workers in their supply chain. On one hand, Walmart is one of the most technologically advanced goods movement companies in the world. Walmart's warehouses utilized the benefits of the computerized and centrally coordinated systems of freight movement.

At the same time, the efficiency that makes Walmart a model in the sector exhibits itself in cutthroat vendor and labor relations focused on cutting costs. We found several Walmart facilities in the region that only employed workers through staffing agencies. Consistently, workers identified the Walmart-serving 3PL warehouses in the region as offering among the lowest-paying, most dangerous, and least reliable jobs.

The rampant and strategic use of temp agencies became exacerbated under the labor law under which the warehouse industry operated. The NLRB excluded temp workers from its scope with its 2004 Oakwood decision, ruling that in the context of a union campaign, the eligibility for organizing of temp workers was up to the manager of the workplace.[12] This effectively kept union organizers out of the warehouse sector, because any employer could quickly bring in more temps to displace direct employees in the case of a campaign or strike.[13]

Our strategy started with bringing workers together to file complaints on health and safety, or wages and hours, which helped surface issues workers wanted to organize around. These were also areas workers could gain support with workers across the warehouse, and create government investigations that brought public scrutiny on the company and support for workers. We jointly filed these complaints against both the staffing agency and warehouse operator because they supervised the workers most of the time. These actions were publicized through the UFCW and CTW's growing social media and global networks, making warehouse workers the "hidden face of Walmart."

The most spectacular example of this was at Schneider National, a major logistics company that operates a cluster of warehouses dedicated to Walmart in the Mira Loma area of Riverside County. These warehouses operate together as the largest Walmart distribution facility west of the Mississippi. At Schneider, the fact and necessity of Walmart's deep control of its logistics contractors led to its being found legally responsible for the conditions in the warehouse. Schneider employed workers from two staffing agencies, Rogers Premier and Impact Logistics. Because they worked on piece rates, workers reported working long hours—sometimes 24 hours straight—with stretches of unpaid time broken when containers arrived at the warehouse from the port. The piece rate system, coupled with the lack of breaks and overtime, resulted in so many violations stacked upon each other that potential damages were nearly incalculable.

Workers filed a class action suit in October 2011 in Federal Court against the staffing agencies.[14] The judge granted a temporary injunction at the filing of the suit, requiring the companies move to hourly pay while the case was being tried. Workers identified Schneider managers as the shot-callers, and the court named Schneider a codefendant about a year later. In 2014, the court determined that Walmart itself would be included as a co-defendant, despite being two layers removed. Soon after this finding but before class certification and trial, the parties settled, with workers receiving $21 million.[15]

The other aspect of our strategy was to bring back a long-ignored tactic available to workers: the Unfair Labor Practice (ULP) strike. ULP strikes are legal, and workers' jobs are protected if a genuine unfair labor practice has occurred. A militant minority of workers at these warehouses, who had faced retaliation over their claims on health and safety, or wages and hours, were able to take action through ULP strikes, first from NFI Crossdock workers in September 2012, and centered on a 50-mile march to Los Angeles. In 2013, workers at Olivet International, a Walmart supplier a few miles away, joined the campaign. These actions were centered on the Walmart cluster, and created real risk of disruption for Walmart. Strikes that summer in warehouses in California and Illinois unearthed the ULP strike and created the opportunity for these workers to reclaim power through radical action, resulting in increased wages, and improved health and safety conditions. They also intrigued the broader left, leading to a major action by Occupy Riverside and community allies in early 2012, when hundreds of activists shut down the entire Walmart cluster for a day.[16]

In 2012–13, our efforts were significant enough to elicit a response from the company. A Walmart executive vice president met with warehouse workers in 2012—a first for workers organizing anywhere in the company's structure. The company established an office to address working conditions in its 3PL system, something that signaled interest in engaging with the issues we raised and sensitivity to these problems, especially when these problems were made public. However, these efforts were difficult to sustain, as temporary workers moved on from these workplaces and campaign energy flagged. In 2013, the UFCW left CTW to rejoin the AFL-CIO. Support for WWU went with it. The following year, the union abandoned OUR Walmart and any effort to organize Walmart workers.

Lessons learned

Supply chain campaigning without secondary pickets

The current organizing of the supply chain clearly suffers from the lack of the secondary picket as a tool. However, WWU's efforts show that a campaign can still target the retailer or manufacturer at the top of the supply chain. Our efforts were able to identify critical strategies to campaign against such an ubiquitous firm.

By bringing low-wage warehouse workers into the national spotlight, we were able to affect the company's image just as they were embarking on an effort to expand into major urban centers including Los Angeles and Chicago, areas with large numbers of Latinos and other people of color, and high union density. The efficiency through which workers can be affected by a campaign aimed at the top of the chain is a critical lesson that is often ignored. Only the retailer has the power and capital to make a decision that changes conditions for thousands of workers. While we were not resourced to sustain a battle against Walmart, we were able to make significant gains, and changed warehouse and retail jobs at Walmart in significant ways.

A different effort to move up the supply chain was exhibited by the Teamsters' organizing of Shippers Transport Express, a major port trucking company owned by us-based terminal operator SSA Marine, which in 2014 became the first company at the port to change its business model from misclassifying port drivers to employing them. Critically, SSA and its chief executive were named in a class action suit as co-defendants, with a claim that they had taken millions of dollars in illegal deductions. This effort, coordinated with driver actions, led the company into conversation with the union, and led to a settlement of the claims and a union contract.[17] These drivers are members of Teamsters Local 848, and make over $25 per hour with full benefits and pension, driving safe and clean trucks as a model to the rest of the port industry.

Use government policy when possible but don't depend on it

When the Obama administration started, the labor movement focused on EFCA but also other issues. In goods movement, we saw the New Deal institutions of the National Labor Relations Act (NLRA) and US Department of Labor (DOL) take on misclassification in a serious way in response to action on the ground, not lobbying. DOL issued advice memos on misclassification and joint employment, and participated in strategic litigation (including Schneider and Shippers Transport).[18] This points to a path forward in which such methods of exploitation are reduced and examined by the federal government. The Port

Trucking campaign used the NLRA to gain findings of employment among drivers, creating the justification for collective action. Similarly, WWU used NLRA rulings of joint employment to connect the actions of contract warehouses with their temp agencies. Without depending on National Labor Relations Board (NLRB) elections, the campaigns used the federal act to bolster cases for reform.

Both the Warehouse and Ports project have repeatedly utilized the ULP strike to take strong, meaningful action among unorganized workers—something that rarely happened until 2012. The Teamsters have similarly expanded the ambulatory picket (following the trucks) to become a tool of disruption at port terminals. Utilizing the remaining tools available under the law has returned some of the power workers lost with the banning of secondary picketing.

Don't count on politics to save you

CTW was established in part in opposition to the AFL-CIO's limitless funding for Democrat politicians with no payoff. This mindset dissipated with the election of President Obama and the great opportunity that the filibuster-proof majority Democrats held in the Senate in 2009. But there was still no payoff. EFCA never moved, and the Ports Campaign's efforts to exempt port drivers from the FAAAA were stymied.

The hundreds of warehouse workers we mobilized in 2009 were one of the few pools of workers who stood up for EFCA. Who did not mobilize for EFCA? About 15 million union members, easily identified and mobilized through the well-staffed, institutional union locals across the country affiliated with the AFL-CIO and CTW. EFCA never came up for a vote in the Senate. Local and state policy, while effective, is limited, again and again, by NLRA and FAAAA preemption. The restraints of the federal government—obvious now—were always there and powerful. If the labor movement had the power to remove them, we would be in ascendant power and setting a progressive agenda.

Solidarity ain't easy

The cohesion of the labor movement, which has never been a strength in the United States, is a critical factor for successful supply chain organizing. The fact that CTW's effort came out of a split in the labor movement created inherent weaknesses that we are only beginning to overcome. A decade after the decisive 2003 PMA lockout, the ILWU has been unwilling to take a risk of a stoppage in support of the 15 port driver strikes that have raised ambulatory pickets at ILWU terminals since 2013. Solidarity, already strained, is further imperiled by the Teamsters' leaving the AFL-CIO and then the ILWU's own 2013 exit from the federation, which also crucially excluded them from the local LA County Federation of Labor.

With few unionized or organizing drivers to engage with, WWU was unable to project supply chain power in meaningful ways. Even when we could track products from the port to the warehouses, there were not enough interactions in the sea of containers flowing through the region every day to affect disruptions. Without pools of workers coming into contact on a regular basis, such action is unrealistic and short-lived.

Conclusion: turning inward

The most important fact of goods movement organizing is that it is not an industry in itself, but is important only as the relationship between production and sale. If workers in contiguous parts of the supply chain can see each other taking action, the possibility for disruption exists. This sounds simple but almost never happens in the United States. Picket lines are rare and the sector is massive, moving over 50,000 containers through hundreds of facilities each day.

While the organizing efforts in these sectors did not produce anything like what CTW projected in 2006, we have nevertheless built movements. In a moment of profound weakness for the labor movement, diversification and innovation are needed for the next round of action. The Ports and Warehouse projects represent nodes of action in critical points of the nation's economy.

We now see that our early efforts were over-optimistic, and built on a weak foundation. Only after a few years of experimentation are we building our toolkits. Yet the Trump era is looking to be one of retrenchment for unions.[19] Right-to-work laws, laws, and court rulings weakening public union membership rules, and other administrative efforts, will result in unions facing a choice: organize your own members, or die.

The lesson of the last eight years (and the last 80), is that it really doesn't matter who is in the White House or Congress. Only focused, sustained organizing with local investment blended with a national or global strategy can affect capital at the level necessary to make real change. Perhaps that is beyond the capacity of the labor movement as currently situated. Only such organizing efforts—and many of them, not just one or two—will result in a movement ready to organize "on scale."

The warehouse and port trucking campaigns, at their best, spurred these kinds of efforts and built lasting solidarity across race, industry, and class. In the past two years, Teamsters and the Warehouse Worker Resource Center (WWU's nonprofit descendant) have partnered, organizing misclassified port drivers and temporary warehouse workers side by side on a critical property at the Port of Los Angeles operated by California Cartage. They have delegated their common managers and company owner, struck together, filed lawsuits against their employer, and stood together to call on the city to address issues of wage theft and retaliation. Focusing on replicating these efforts is our best hope to gain lasting and beneficial results, and create partnerships and institutions able to overcome the power of the companies that rule the supply chain, and the governments that facilitate them.

The courageous and creative worker leaders in these campaigns have stood up to the largest companies in the world and won. Some of the greatest moments of these organizing campaigns have been when they have joined with workers from other parts of the country and the world, as well as community members and environmental allies to strategize, organize, and demonstrate power. Such efforts for solidarity across long distances and in the midst of intense campaigns are difficult to organize but crucial in a moment like this, when resources are tightening and progressive movements must support each other if we are to survive.

Notes

1   I was a research analyst and campaign coordinator with the Warehouse Workers United campaign from 2008–13, and founded and currently co-direct the Warehouse Worker Resource Center, dedicated to supporting low-wage workers through education, advocacy, and action. I worked on the Ports project in a later iteration from 2014–17, as project director with Los Angeles Alliance for a New Economy (LAANE).
2   John Richard Felton and Dale Anderson (eds.), *Regulation and Deregulation of the Motor Carrier Industry* (Iowa City: Iowa State University Press, 1989).

3   See Farrell Dobbs, *Teamster Power* (New York: Monad Press, 1977).

4   Scott Cummings, "Preemptive strike: law in the campaign for clean trucks," *4 UC Irvine Law Review* (2015), p. 958.

5   Barry T. Hirsch, "Trucking regulation, unionization, and labor earnings: 1973–85," *Journal of Human Resources* 23(3) (Summer 1988), pp. 296–319, www2.gsu.edu/~ecobth/PaperReprints/TruckingRegulation.pdf (accessed December 2, 2017).

6   Cummings (2015), p. 1003.

7   Cummings (2015), p. 1128.

8   Cummings (2015), p. 1125.

9   Rebecca Smith, Paul Marvy, and Jon Zerolnick, "The big rig overhaul," National Employment Law Project, February 2014, www.nelp.org/content/uploads/2015/03/Big-Rig-Overhaul-Misclassification-Port-Truck-Drivers-Labor-Law-Enforcement.pdf (accessed December 2, 2017).

10 Juan De Lara. "Warehouse work: path to the middle class or road to economic insecurity?" USC Program for Environmental and Regional Equity (PERE), September 2013. https://dornsife.usc.edu/assets/sites/242/docs/WarehouseWorkerPay_web.pdf

11 Yana Kunichoff and Jesse Menendez, "Walmart warehouse workers fight for the future of work," Truth-Out, October 3, 2012,www.truth-out.org/news/item/11920-walmart-warehouse-workers-fight-for-the-future-of-work (accessed December 2, 2017).

12 US National Labor Relations Board. H.S. CARE L.L.C., d/b/a Oakwood Care Center and N&W Agency, Inc. and New York's Health and Human Service Union, 1199, Service Employees International Union, AFL–CIO, Petitioner. Case 29–RC–10101, Decision on Review and Order, November 19, 2004, https://apps.nlrb.gov/link/document.aspx/09031d4580022ea1 (accessed December 2, 2017).

13 This decision was reversed in Miller and Anderson, Inc. in 2016, creating a short window in which temp workers are organizable, though a union election involving temps now runs the risk of being the case that is brought to the new board to reverse the ruling.

14 Carrillo v. Schneider Logistics, Inc. (C.D.Cal. 10-31-2011). Filed October 17, 2011. https://casetext.com/case/carrillo-v-schneider-logistics

15 Ricardo Lopez, "Workers reach $21 million settlement against Walmart, warehouses," *Los Angeles Times*, May 14, 2014, www.latimes.com/business/la-fi-wal-mart-warehouse-workers-20140515-story.html (accessed December 2, 2017).

16 Arun Gupta and Michelle Fawcett, "Occupy invades 'America's Storage Shed,'" Salon.com, March 1, 2012, www.salon.com/2012/03/02/occupy_invades_americas_storage_shed/ (accessed December 2, 2017).

17 Karen Robles Meeks, "Los Angeles, Long Beach port truck drivers agree to unionization process with firm," *Long Beach Press Telegram*, January 6, 2015, www.presstelegram.com/business/20150106/los-angeles-long-beach-port-

truck-drivers-agree-to-unionization-process-with-firm (accessed December 2, 2017).

18 David Weil, Chief Investigator. "Improving workplace conditions through strategic litigation, Boston University, a report to the Wage and Hour Division," May 2010. https://www.dol.gov/whd/resources/strategic Enforcement.pdf

19 Perhaps an unintentional turn to "Fortress unionism," proposed by former Port Trucking campaigner Rich Yeselson in *Democracy Journal*, Summer 2013: http://democracyjournal.org/magazine/29/fortress-unionism/ (accessed December 2, 2017).

14

Struggles and Grassroots Organizing in an Extended European Choke Point

Carlotta Benvegnù and Niccolò Cuppini

In recent years, the Italian labor market has been particularly affected by a series of processes that have profoundly weakened labor power: the casualization of the workforce and the erosion of the welfare state, the long-term effects of the global economic crisis which began in 2007–08, the delocalization of production activities, and the weakening of collective bargaining. In this context, the Italian logistics industry seemed to be the most advanced point of this tendency, given the wide recourse to subcontracting, the spreading of illegal practices, and the employment of recently arrived migrant workers lacking legal protections. However, even if this scenario seems to confirm that the "logistics revolution" is one of the key tools in the long global offensive against labor, it is precisely along logistics organizational structures that the system of coordination, communication, and transport has opened capital up to the danger of disruption. Northern Italy's logistics space is nowadays a "frontier zone" suspended in an uncertain equilibrium, owing to the confluence of two apparently contradictory processes: logistics is one of the sectors with the most precarious and difficult labor conditions, but at the same time it shows one of the most powerful contemporary examples of labor conflictual organization.

This chapter is organized in four parts. First, we discuss the territorial context of these logistics struggles. Second, we present a concise chronology of the most relevant moments of conflict and the trajectory of the workers' organizing. Third, we offer a description of the labor force in the logistics sector and the processes of unionization, and explain the strategies that logistics employers are adopting to respond to workers' organizing; we also trace some hypotheses around the tendencies of this conflict. Finally, we conclude with some more general political reflections about the potential and limits of these logistics struggles.

To grasp the conditions of possibility for the emergence of these logistics struggles in Northern Italy it is necessary to contextualize them in the specificities of this territory. Usually, talking about logistics necessitates a focus on specific places, generally ports, single logistics warehouses, or at least the so-called "logistics cities," indicating a sort of bounded space, generally conceived as an *ex novo* urban park, an area where logistics activities are concentrated. Alongside this conception there is a tendency to conceptualize the nexus between territory and logistics as something quite new, and logistical spaces are framed as the fresh production of a series of "exceptions" in the urban tissue.

However, Italian logistics struggles allow us to reverse this perspective. The map of the strikes and their interconnections show a "logistical fabric" that leads us to reconceptualize logistics as an organizing principle of contemporary urban territories, making them locations or terminals of logistics activities. Boris Vormann states that:

> Just-in-time production has recreated the city in its image [and as commodities] are shipped from their point of production to the point of sale, they pass through and depend on the urban hubs and bottlenecks of international trade, in turn reshaping the physical layout and the multiscalar governance logics of global cities.[1]

In this way the whole contemporary city is becoming a hub, and there is at play a "logisticalization" of the urban fabric which has completely subverted the established Italian landscape.[2] It is not a coincidence, then, that one of the main Italian newspapers has referred to Northern Italy as the "logistics valley." Here, logistics assembles different businesses, labor forces, software systems, and cultural contexts to produce a governance regime, understood as a set of practices of knowledge and power that constitute a space "above, beyond, between and across states."[3]

Italian logistics struggles have been concentrated in the north of the country, within a huge valley traversed by the River Po. The Po valley region[4] is enclosed by mountain ranges to the north (the Alps) and south (the Apennines), and bounded by two different seas: to the west, the Tyrrhenian Sea, and to the east, the Adriatic. The Po valley region is of geostrategic importance for Europe in the global economy. It is the principal junction that connects the Mediterranean Sea with the Continent and vice versa because of a series of tunnels located in the Alps, and many ports on the two shores (for example Genoa, Ravenna, Venice, and Trieste). However, what makes this area a crucial node for the articulation and grounding of global flows, and a platform for "global connections," is above all its "internal" urban configuration.

Following Jean Gottman, we maintain that Northern Italy can be configured as a megalopolis, with a complex logistical matrix of centers and peripheries, intermodal transport terminals, warehouses, IT infrastructure, container parks, and shipping ports, interspersed with suburbs, green belts, roads, railways, water systems, and barren land.[5] Milan is the epicenter of this megalopolis, but "more distant cities from Milan can also act as centers of value for leading LSPs [logistics service providers], such as the national crossroad of Bologna."[6] Italy is located within the global logistics network primarily through the presence of large foreign global operators, but at the same time it remains an economy that acts mainly on a national scale, and even in some cases a local one.[7]

Given this context, in recent years we have witnessed a multiplication of operational sites (warehouses), even if the management functions are concentrated in few places. "Value, information and power are on one side concentrated but, on the other side, are also very selectively distributed to certain places in the national space, depending on their sectorial and geographical specificities."[8] It is precisely this continuum of concentrated and extended logistical textures and nodes that constitutes this Italian megalopolis as a logistics land bridge where commodities are mostly moved via road transportation.

The construction and evolution of this enlarged European choke point was made possible by an interlacing of private investments and public interventions. The iconic emblem of the region is the model of the Interporto, a major intermodal transportation and logistics hub constructed since the 1970s close to almost every major city in Northern Italy, thanks to public–private partnerships. The Interporto is one of the first cases of political logistics planning in Europe, and it is linked to the crisis of the Fordist model and to the cities' necessity to escape increasing gridlocks. However, the realization of this logistical territory in Northern Italy has been also accomplished through a neoliberal logic of urbanization, making possible the proliferation of warehouse construction without any public oversight. This dynamic has enlarged a widespread metropolis.

It is possible to feel this territorial particularity also from the words of the logistics workers. A Senegalese migrant warehouse worker, who has lived in Italy almost 20 years and worked in six different cities, ironically described the Italian landscape as flat and monotonous: "Everything is a warehouse, [or] a small town near a warehouse." In the words of Karim, a Moroccan migrant who belongs to the union si Cobas, "I arrived in Italy in 2009, and I didn't know anything. For years I didn't realize where the city centre was."[9]

Eleonora, an Italian labor activist, puts it this way:

> The chronicles of these struggles refer to very different cities like Piacenza, Bologna, Milan ... but still their scenography never changes. We are talking about industrial peripheries far from the city centre, where a sequence of identical gigantic warehouses are connected by huge streets, where a non-stop queue of trucks passes through, slowed down by the waiting of loading and unloading of commodities. When you reach a picket line, you can perceive the difference between a city and another only from the trip you do and its duration. ... Bologna's Interporto is many kilometers from the city centre, and it is surrounded by many warehouses and small towns, where thousands of logistics workers live. They come from really far away: Morocco, Tunisia, Somalia, Eritrea, Senegal, Pakistan, Bangladesh, Sri Lanka, Romania, Albania .... Once settled down in this region, they rarely go to the city .... Hence, the logistics workers are a sort of army of the underground ready to be enlisted by capital, every day and every night, being completely disconnected from the rest of the social context. Through the struggle they have somehow emerged from the darkness.[10]

According to Saskia Sassen, "the localization of the global creates a set of objective conditions of engagement," empowering the "disadvantaged" to gain presence.[11] In light of this, today's warehouses and logistical hubs throughout Northern Italy are not only places of commodity storage and transportation, but also sites of conflictual organization, showing that under certain conditions, logistics routes (typically pathways of capitalist accumulation) can become paths of training for new worker subjectivities.

The prelude to this phenomena can be traced back to 2008–09 in

Northern Lombardy (the Milan region), when the first contact between rank-and-file unionists and some workers occurred in the food retail sector. These first strikes attained some significant results, planting the seeds for successive organizing steps. However, it is only from 2011–12 that the Italian logistics struggles experienced a decisive crescendo. In 2011 there were two main labor disputes in the Milan hinterland. Again, the warehouses of two Italian supermarket chains (Il Gigante and Esselunga) were the target of the struggles, but in these cases there was a strong intervention by the police to break the picket lines and subvert the strike. Nevertheless, the clashes between workers and police were very visible in the media, which helped spread this relatively new form of unionism. Rather then simply declaring the strike and abstaining from the workplace, the workers instead directly blockaded their warehouses, inflicting important economic losses on their employers.

From July 2011 to 2012 the new epicenter of these struggles became the logistics pole of Piacenza, 70 km south of Milan. This time the strikes erupted against two multinational parcel delivery firms (TNT and GLS), and in the logistics warehouse of Ikea, one of the world's largest furniture retailers. Within a few months, hundreds of workers joined the rank-and-file union SI Cobas, thanks to the informal networks within migrant communities, the support of local social activists, and a feeling of optimism and militancy linked to the ongoing Arab Spring insurrections. In fact, many TNT workers were Egyptian migrants, and during the pickets they were heard to sing, "Here is our Tahrir Square!"

These struggles lasted for months, and the strikers were frequently attacked by the police with tear gas and framed in a negative way by the media. However, the workers again obtained significant improvements in working conditions, and the workers felt a new sensation of being "present" in a context where they have always been seen as strangers, which many of the workers described as "dignity." In the last months of 2012, the echo of these struggles travelled very far due to the mainstream media coverage, the use of social networks by the workers, and the spreading of information between migrant communities and social activists. During the winter of 2012 many other logistics companies (including Artoni, Bartolini, and DHL) registered a process of unionization with Cobas all around the Po valley, especially in the east. One of the most important tools of the union was the solidarity between different warehouses. When there was an important strike in one company, many workers from other companies directly supported it.

On March 22, 2013, the unions announced the first 24-hour general strike in the logistics sector. Across Italy, the warehouses of multinational express delivery companies and other logistics operators were shut down, as trucks were blocked from accessing the warehouse. One banner read, in Italian, English, and Arabic: "Strike and fight for dignity, until victory." The slogans were reminiscent of the Industrial Workers of the World's rallying cry, "An injury to one is an injury to all." A few months later one of the well-known logistics struggles began against Granarolo, a multinational dairy corporation. Given the many delays in morning deliveries of milk to coffee bars, the media named it the "Cappuccino strike." Lasting for over a year, it was a deeply entrenched political battle, which included several police interventions to force out the pickets, leading to many arrests. In addition, there were demonstrations by thousands of workers, solidarity actions, and an organized boycott of the firm. Even if almost every institution explicitly acted against the workers, the outcome of the struggle was quite successful, providing a great visibility and forward momentum to the logistics workers' movement. During 2014 the process of unionization arrived in the western region of Italy, especially in the food retail industry in Turin, and many other companies were afflicted by strikes during the subsequent years.

Mapping the strikes gives an idea of how logistics is a really heterogeneous world. However, between big multinational companies and small local enterprises, the one main common point is the very hard working conditions, primarily linked to the widespread process of subcontracting employment to cooperatives and their intense use of migrant labor. Italian cooperatives, which were founded in the middle of the nineteenth century as an instrument of workers' self-defense, employ migrants as "working members." The expansion of the cooperative movement during recent decades (linked to increasing outsourcing practices, tax breaks, and to the growing pressure on prices in the market) has brought a new business-style approach. Today, in most of the new cooperatives internal democracy and working conditions have deteriorated.[12] Officially, "working members" have permanent contracts, but their concrete employment situation remains highly insecure. As the rehiring of workers is not assured, principal contractors can use the threat of ending the relationship with the cooperative as a way of discouraging industrial action.

For nearly 10 years, workers' struggles have achieved many concrete objectives in terms of improving working conditions, wages, and dignity and power in the workplaces. A crucial turning point in this sense was the agreement stipulated in November 2016 between the Cobas and some of the major express delivery companies. The agreement replaces the previous ones, and improves in many ways on the agreement with the main national trade union confederations. In particular, it introduces a so-called "social clause," which constrains principal contractors to rehire all the workers when it changes subcontractor. However, the application of this agreement is not homogeneous, as it depends on the strength of the union and the specific situation in each workplace.

For example, in March 2017 a protest by workers employed by a haulage cooperative stopped the production of Coca-Cola in Nogara (Verona). The cooperative that won the new contract refused to rehire the employees, who were all members of a rank-and file union (ADL-Cobas). The situation was so critical that the US Embassy in Italy asked the Italian government to solve the conflict. In this case, the protest ended with the hiring of fewer than 10 workers, while the other 35 workers were fired and received about €30,000 (based on seniority) as compensation.

Alongside the intensification of the economic crisis and labor market transformations (namely, the casualization of labor and the weakening of collective bargaining), in Italy the composition of the workforce has also changed immensely, and migrants have become a crucial part of economic processes. In 2014, they made up 10.3 percent of all employees.[13] The logistics sector in Northern Italy has been one of the most affected by this process, with approximately 80 percent of the workforce in many warehouses now migrant workers (mostly from Northern and sub-Saharan Africa, and from Eastern and South-Eastern Asia).

While traditional unions generally tend to consider migrants as "birds of passage"[14] available to work for lower wages and worse working conditions, the long cycle of struggles that has disrupted the Italian logistics sector for almost 10 years would not have been possible without the strong commitment and determination of migrant logistics workers. Indeed, despite the economic crisis, migrant workers do not easily interrupt their migration project, for which they have already endured a difficult process of uprooting, and conversely put in place different strategies of resistance not only for their immediate survival, but also for their long-term ambitions.[15]

In this context, Italian grassroots unions—less bureaucratic and hierarchical than traditional ones—give considerable flexibility to the agency of migrant workers. They have been free to choose their own types of action and their representatives among members of their communities, hence decreasing the distance that can exist between migrant workers and Italian semi-professional shop stewards (especially in terms of language and culture). In this way, community networks that help newcomers to settle in the host society (including for employment), and that are integrated into many workplaces,[16] have been converted into a resource for the union. At the same time ethnic recruitment, built by the management to ensure control over labor through the enforcement of divisions and internal hierarchies, has been turned into a resource for collective organizing.

However, in recent years employers have also been putting in place a range of strategies in order to regain control over labor, and to compensate for productivity that has been lost in terms of costs of labor. Anti-union policies and repression are still used in many cases to discourage unions from organizing across the logistics sector. Two particularly grave events marked the recent period. On September 14, 2016, during a strike at GLS in Piacenza, a worker named Abd el Saleem was killed by a truck that struck him. On January 27, 2017, the national coordinator of SI Cobas was arrested and held in custody for a few days, generating a strong reaction by the union militants, with days of demonstrations, blockades, and strikes.

From 2015 to 2017 , as a response to labor conflicts, companies have also been enacting a general reorganization and innovation in the sector. First, they are trying to attract a labor force with a different composition—hiring workers they consider potentially more docile—using a "narrative" that presents logistics as an opportunity, as a new "cool" and international workplace rather than a stigmatized "migrant job" symbolically placed at the lowest rung of the economic ladder. Those who are targeted with this new rhetoric are mostly young Italians deeply impoverished by the economic crisis.

This search for new labor pools and new combinations in the labor force emerged for the first time in August 2016, when a series of strikes at the logistics warehouses of H&M (a multinational retail clothing company) brought to light a new social composition of the labor force. While most of the workers in the logistics struggles were previously migrants, here many young Italian workers were at the front of the picket line. Moreover, big companies like Amazon are starting to build up their own logistics structures, attracting a similar workforce, and related to this, a new kind of logistics is starting to emerge in this area: a new metropolitan logistics based on the "just-in-time and to the point" logic, especially in online food delivery operated by corporations like Foodora and JustEat.

Second, mechanization, automation, and the use of new technologies are implemented in order to increase control over labor and intensify the labor process. With regard to this question, it is important to underline that logistics faces a kind of "paradox": while it tends toward standardization, and thus to the increasing use of technologies and machines, only living labor can provide the resilience and adaptability required by its processes.[17] However, in recent years many employers—mostly the big multinational delivery companies able to make large investments—started to increase their use of technology and, alongside this, changed their attitude toward grassroots unionism. Then, rather than putting in place anti-union policies and taking on the risk of a labor conflict (and thus of serious economic losses), they are changing their strategy in order to increase productivity and regain control over labor through co-optation or cooperation with the union.

In this sense, the agreement signed in 2016 between Cobas and the major delivery companies can be understood as a first important step in this direction. Finally, a new emerging trend can be observed which again concerns the use of subcontracting to the cooperative system. As the complex inter-firm networks and subcontracting chains that were used in the past to reduce costs become less profitable because labor costs have increased, many big companies are reconsidering the possibility of internalizing labor in order to retake control over the whole labor process.

As stated earlier, the logistical world in this contemporary Italian megalopolis is a field of tensions, and its development is at stake within the conflict between the forces and tendencies we attempted to describe. Rather than a smooth space for commodities' free movement, the potential threat of interruption to logistics circulation has been ongoing for many years. In light of this, some crucial turning points have to be taken into consideration.

First, while the eruption of the global crisis in 2007–08 led to a reduction of labor power and to a deterioration of working conditions in many sectors, the crisis in Italy has been in turn strategically used by the workers. The refusal to accept the threat of the crisis as a way to lower wages and to erode labor rights has rather been a spring of subjectivation for the logistics workers.

Second, as discussed before, struggles have been possible due to a counter-use of ethnic recruitment. The solidarity within migrant communities that connect labor within the region has been a crucial tool to sustain the strikes.

Third, a series of "innovative" practices (or, in some cases, of old practices of the workers' movement almost forgotten today) has been crucial to achieving results: the radicalism of the strikes, with blockades and pickets; the solidarity between different warehouses (workers of different companies going to support a strike in another workplace); and the involvement of many different actors (usually unrelated to capital/labor conflicts) in the struggles (like social centers, activist collectives, and students).

Several different labor disputes are currently ongoing, and the process of unionization is stabilizing or even increasing. The current situation opens up a path for an institutionalization of the logistics unions, which could have very complex consequences. In fact, this poses a risk of co-optation into the emerging Italian logistics system, as well as the risk of a decrease in the long-term power obtained by the workers. Accordingly, we believe that at the moment there is at stake in these disputes a political element that goes beyond the field of labor disputes. For this reason we have focused this chapter on the territorial dimension of these struggles in order to suggest that their force and relevance cannot be understood simply by looking at the workplace level.

In other words, the strength of the Italian logistics struggles, and their ability to play a different melody in the logistics orchestra, has to be found in the connection between workplaces and their social and territorial context. They have expressed, at least partly and in some specific cases, a form of "social power."[18] This means that the logistics workers' "associational power"[19] within workplaces, and their "positional power" (thanks to their strategic position in the cycle of production and distribution)[20] have been important, but they are not sufficient to explain such a prolonged and radical process of struggles and organization. Without the crucial connection to other subjectivities and struggles outside the workplaces, and without the counter-use of migration networks, it would be hard to imagine such a process. This means that workers' power has been built within and outside workplaces at the same time.

To conclude, a more general problem still remains to be discussed.

The other paradox of logistics is that on one hand logistics companies tend to segment their labor force and their territorial locations as much as they can to improve their control over labor. On the other hand, logistical chains are constantly increasing the interdependence between every single link. Within this gap, between the tendency to produce heterogeneization of labor and territories, and the necessity to improve the connection among workers and urban areas, probably lies a new global possibility for labor power. However, given the important diffusion within the Northern Italian megalopolis of logistics struggles, they have not realized a concrete connection with other national contexts. This is a political problem that still remains to be solved.

Nevertheless, it should be stressed that this process of conflictual mobilization gained a fundamental objective: the re-opening of the theme of the strike as a moment and a locus of organization, after decades in which the strike was progressively domesticated and became a disciplined practice. It is precisely within the new forms of the strike that logistics struggles indicate there lies the possibility for connecting with other working sectors. In our mind, it is only within struggle processes that it becomes possible to imagine the structuring of new relationships between workers, social movements, and political organizations, and the reinvention of what striking means and implies could be the framework of processes of recomposition of different subjectivities.

Putting strike back on the scene in our times means taking into consideration two of the elements we highlighted in this chapter: labor and urban territory. It is only starting from their conjunction that it becomes possible to generate a broader struggle. And this us leads to tackle the political problem mentioned before, that of the very possibility of a strategic transnational struggle. Effectively, if we look at social movements of this new millennium, we see a constitutive connection between the urban and the global. From the opposition to the G8 in Genoa 2001 and the millions and millions of people who simultaneously took the streets in 2003 to protest against the war in Iraq, to the sequence of uprisings from 2011 to 2013 (Maghreb and Mashreq, Occupy, the Acampadas, the Greek movement and the Hong Kong one, Gezi Park and the Brazilian movement ...): one of their distinctive characters has been their urban entanglement and the fast "contagion effect" they generated worldwide. However, their resonances did not find the capacity to "root" themselves and give a consistent timing to their interruption of capitalist everyday life. Given these facts, we suggest that for the years to come experimentation with the interconnections between logistics chain disruptions, the extension of new strike forms at the metropolitan level, and the potentialities of global contagion of urban mobilization are issues that could lead to a new wave of emancipative politics.

Notes

1 Boris Vormann, "Infrastructural statecraft and the rise of just-in-time urbanism," *Global Urban History.com*, January 9, 2017, https://globalurbanhistory.com/2017/01/09/infrastructural-statecraft-and-the-rise-of-just-in-time-urbanism/ (accessed December 2, 2017).

2 See Niccolò Cuppini, "Dissolving Bologna: tensions between citizenship and the logistics city," *Citizenship Studies* 21(4) (2017), pp. 495–507.

3 Wendy Larner and William Walters, *Global Governmentality: Governing International Spaces* (London: Routledge, 2004).

4 This geographical conceptualization is elaborated in Niccolò Cuppini, Mattia Frapporti, and Maurilio Pirone, "Logistics struggles in the Po valley region: territorial transformations and processes of antagonistic subjectivation," *South Atlantic Quarterly* 114(1) (2015), pp. 119–34.

5 Recalling Ned Rossiter, *Software, Infrastructure, Labor: A Media Theory of Logistical Nightmares* (New York: Routledge, 2016), p. 35.

6 Sébastien Antoine, Cécile Sillig, and Hilda Ghiara, "Advanced logistics in Italy: a city network analysis," *Tijdschrift voor economische en sociale geografie* (2016).

7 See Rossana Cillo and Lucia Pradella, "New immigrant struggles in Italy's logistics industry," *Comparative European Politics* (2016), pp. 1–17.

8 Antoine et al. (2016).

9 Interview undertaken in Bologna at the Si Cobas headquarters, April 28, 2017.

10 Interview reported in Fulvio Massarelli, *Scarichiamo i padroni* (Unloading the bosses) (Milan: Agenzia X, 2014), p. 111.

11 Saskia Sassen, "Repositioning of citizenship: emergent subjects and spaces for politics," *Berkeley Journal of Sociology* 46 (2002), p. 21.

12 Devi Sacchetto and Marco Semenzin, "Workers' cooperatives in Italy: between solidarity and autocratic centralism," pp.135–55 in P. Ngai, K. Hok Bun, Y. Hairong, and A. Koo (eds.), *Social Economy in China and the World* (Abingdon and New York: Routledge, 2015).

13 Ruth Milkman, "Immigrant workers, precarious work, and the US labor movement," *Globalizations* 8(3) (2011), pp. 361–72.

14 Michael J. Piore, *Birds of Passage: Migrant Labor and Industrial Societies* (Cambridge: Cambridge University Press,1979).

15 Devi Sacchetto and Francesca Alice Vianello, *Navigando a Vista. Migranti nella crisi economica tra lavoro e disoccupazione* (*Sailing in Uncharted Waters: Migrants within the Economic Crisis, between Labor and Unemployment*) (Milan, Italy: FrancoAngeli, 2014).

16 Milkman (2011).

17 Giorgio Grappi, *Logistica* (Roma: Ediesse, 2016).

18 Maurizio Ricciardi, "Appunti per una teoria politica delle migrazioni: potere sociale e politicizzazione della differenza," (Notes towards a political theory of migrations: social power and the politicization of differences) pp. 108–24 in Sandro Chignola and Devi Sacchetto (eds.), *Le reti del valore, Migrazioni, produzione e governo della crisi* (*Value Chains: Migrations, Production, and the Government of the Crisis*) (Rome: Derive Approdi, 2017).

19 Erik Olin Wright, "Working-class power, capitalist-class interests, and class compromise," *American Journal of Sociology* 105(4) (2000), pp. 957–1002.

20 Edna Bonacich and Jake B. Wilson, *Getting the Goods: Ports, Labor, and the Logistics Revolution* (Ithaca, N.Y.: Cornell University Press, 2008).

15

Beyond the Waterfront: Maintaining and Expanding Worker Power in the Maritime Supply Chain

Peter Olney

The fascination with "choke points" or strategic points of intervention is as old as the workers' movement. Strategists have long argued about which workers or occupations are most likely to organize and take action, just as they have recognized that certain economic sectors constitute "weak links" in the economy, with the potential for workers to exercise disproportionate power.

Insight about strategic sectors, commerce, and communication links goes far beyond the confines of revolutionaries and would-be revolutionaries, and is standard fare for a wide range of current professionals, including logistic experts, urban planners, systems analysts, and military planners. Whether conscious or not, it is also standard fare in less reputable occupations like organized crime, where strategic interventions in production and process links are often extremely lucrative.[1]

While this chapter focuses on the maritime logistics chain, and particularly longshore worker power on the docks, its lessons are universal to the discourse on the exercise of working-class power. There are strategic workers and strategic loci in the supply chain and the production process. Such workers and loci are not fixed for all time, but are conditioned by technology, worker political organization, and alliances. Therefore no working-class strategy can be static or frozen in time irrespective of the shifting terrain.

John Womack, one of the world's leading experts on the Mexican revolution of 1910, has written extensively on the topic of strategic position and strategic industries.[2] According to him:

> modern divisions of labor, however they change in modern economies, have some technically "strategic positions" in them. Wherever these positions may be, shifting as they may, what makes them strategically important is that work there (skilled or not) matters much more than work in other positions (skilled or not), because it holds a division of labor technically together, in production. If work there stops, this forces extensive disruption of work elsewhere. And if the disruption happens in an industry "strategic" in production at large, this forces disruption across the entire economy, even internationally.[3]

Chokepoints in flux

This chapter examines the power that longshore unions, particularly the International Longshore and Warehouse Union (ILWU), hold over major maritime ports. But this chapter also argues that strategic choke points are not static and forever. Class conflicts and new technology preclude any strategic position from becoming permanent. Consider the fate of industrial tool and die makers who were once among the most strategic workers in the auto manufacturing process. Today, computer-aided design/computer-aided manufacturing (CAD/CAM) has deskilled that craft and made their work much less strategic. But every new position or node that emerges from new technology brings with it a new group of skilled workers and vulnerable power points.

A similar story exists in the field of maritime logistics, where new technology and years of worker struggles have given rise to new power in new places. Consider the importance of workers who now program the automated machines and robots that are now working on all the terminals in the Port of Rotterdam and have been recently introduced in the Ports of Los Angeles and Long Beach, and increasingly in warehouses across America. Marine clerks who previously controlled the flow of cargo on the waterfront with a clipboard have been supplanted by optical character reader (OCR) bar codes, radio frequency identification, and off-dock control systems operated from thousands of miles away.

The potential agency of these new workers in new settings remains intact. It is the strategist's job to find those chokepoints and organize the incumbent workers there. New technology and new workers create new organizing opportunities for serious strategists. Containerization has had dramatic and far-reaching effects which extend far beyond the docks to workers and communities across the globe. The partial dein dustrialization of America and shift of manufacturing jobs to low-wage countries was made possible in part by the new technology of contain-erization. Offshoring, downsizing, and automation have considerably reduced the power of industrial workers in the United States and other former industrial giants. But domestic markets for manufactured goods remain, and a certain amount of manufacturing continues to take place at home.[4]

Whether produced at home or abroad, goods still need to reach customers and plants. The worldwide movement of goods, supplies, and raw materials, known as logistics, has become a place where the working class can still exercise significant power and leverage. The widespread adoption of powerful computers has given rise to new ef-ficiency techniques, including "just in time" production, "inventory turns" and "supply management." These changes have made the stra-tegic nodes at gateway ports to the United States, like Long Beach and Los Angeles in California, into points of immense potential power for workers.

When the Pacific Maritime Association locked out the ILWU on the West Coast in 2002, the economic impact was swift and immediate.[5] The Bush administration invoked a law known as the Taft Hartley Act, empowering federal courts to suspend lockouts and strikes.[6] Ironically, it was the Bush administration that used this power against employers to quickly open the ports because the damage to the economy was so dramatic. At the auto plants in Fremont, California jointly operated at the time by General Motors and Toyota known as NUMMI, the as-sembly lines shut down in a week because they ran out of parts.[7] In the 15 years since, the amount of Pacific Rim trade coming through West Coast ports has continued to grow, and now amounts to 40 percent of all Pacific Rim imports. No wonder that the impact of a relatively short stoppage was telling. On October 3, 2002, employer labor relations lawyer Steve Cabot squawked about the greed of the working ILWU members, and in a famous quote on NPR's *News Hour* stated, "We're talking about the need to deal with the global competition. It's some-thing that unions for a long time have resisted. And unfortunately in the steel industry, they resisted too long."[8]

Asked whether Mr. Cabot had a point by show host Ray Suarez, the union's spokesperson responded: "Mr. Cabot, in comparing long shoring to the steel industry, perhaps does not understand that you can't move the port of Los Angeles or the port of Long Beach to Singapore. You need a port on the West Coast. These ports are going nowhere. These workers are going nowhere and the employers need to sit down and strike a fair deal."[9]

Who does the choking?

The power of dockworkers and maritime workers is not new, although it has been recently discovered by young activists who have marveled at the capacity of a relatively small workforce to influence global commerce. The power of waterfront workers goes back decades. West Coast dockers struck for a union in 1934, and had a dramatic impact on the flow of cargo. But only when the City and County of San Francisco were paralyzed by a general strike over the death of two waterfront workers was the strike won. West coast longshoremen have a long tradition of exercising power at the point of production for political purposes. In 1937 ILWU members refused to load metal scrap bound for Japan because of the Japanese invasion of China. ILWU members refused to load cargo for apartheid South Africa, and boycotted ships carrying the freight of Central American dictatorships in the 1980s.

"Occupy Oakland" thrilled to the fact that their mass demonstration in the Port of Oakland in November 2011 brought the port to a halt as longshore members refused to cross mass picket lines. Enthralled by this action and disruption, many of the demonstrators thought it was their brilliance and daring that had triumphed, rather than understanding that the unique history and features of longshore unionism enabled the moment. In other words a husband and wife team with their three children and the proper picket signage could also bring a temporary halt to port commerce on a marine terminal while waiting for a contractually mandated arbitration to determine whether the action was *bona fide* and therefore a picket line to respect under the coastwise maritime agreement.

The Occupy protesters in Oakland and many in the realm of academic activism confuse the agency of workers with their own. "Revolutionaries" who have awoken to the power of the international transport system and its strategic nodes are often prone to dismiss the very workers who are necessary to realize that strategic potential.[10] No amount of artistic power mapping can replace the agency, intelligence, and action of those who do the work![11] Many ports are potential choke points in the international supply chain, but not all ports can be choked with the same effect. It is important to recognize that while organization and action at the point of production is crucial, for such action to be successful it must often be coupled with a broader political and societal connection.

The railroads in the United States carry 40 percent of gross national product (GNP), and remain a vital transportation system. Choke points exist in many huge railroad yards around the United States where trains are "humped" or consolidated. The largest such yard is in North Platte, Nebraska. A blockade there would probably be ineffective, as railroad labor has been handcuffed by a rigid Railway Labor Act (RLA) passed in 1926 to prevent strikes in the industry. But it is not only the legal handcuffs that shackle rail labor. The fact that there are 13 craft unions for 132,000 rail workers, all bargaining under separate agreements with the railroads, hampers any solidarity. Militant railroaders go to bed every night praying for the second coming of Eugene Debs, the Socialist candidate for president and railroad organizer who fought for a railroad industrial union. Recent history might be different if Debs had succeeded in organizing the multi-craft American Railway Union (ARU).

Here again we have an example of strategic workers at strategic nodes who have vast potential power to impact capitalism, but remain shackled by legal regimes and fractured internal organization. Eric Olin Wright has written a brilliant essay[12] that establishes a framework in which to think about this dynamic. He distinguishes between "structural" power and "associational" power. Structural power is the power of strategic workers in strategic places in the capitalist system. They have power *per se*, but the question of whether they can successfully leverage and exercise it depends on their associational power: that is, their organization, consciousness, allies, and so on. This interplay is a dynamic way for workers and their allies to think about their work in organizing at strategic choke points.

Challenges to the future of the *ILWU*

There is no question that the ILWU and for that matter the International Longshore Association (ILA) on the East Coast and many other dockworkers' unions around the world still have the capacity to engage in battles with incredible effects on global capitalism. The deeper long-term question is, how best does that power get exercised and to what end? After all, the international capitalist class recognizes the "strategic choke points" and is working overtime to figure out ways to neuter and spay the potency of dock workers. Dockworker unions face the challenge of preserving their power in the face of the introduction of job-eating new technology and the passage of power-restricting legislation. Legislation is pending now in the US Congress that would give governors in maritime states, who determine that commerce is being negatively impacted by port workers' actions, the ability to go to court and seek remedies and injunctive relief under federal Taft Hartley statutes. What is to be done on the waterfront and beyond to preserve and enhance these working people's organizations, which are a precious resource for the whole working class?

The challenges for powerful dockworkers' unions are immense. The ILWU is not alone in facing these powerful trends and enemies. But the ILWU as a proud flagship of solidarity and militancy is a case study in how to respond or not to the forces that are plaguing workers at these strategic nodes. The union presently faces thorny questions about its future:

- Technology is replacing much of traditional longshore labor, so how can the incumbent members and the generations coming after them survive?
- How can the ILWU justify, under intense public scrutiny, the fabulous wages and benefits its members get and deserve, when workers inland are doing many of the same job functions in the marine supply chain at minimum wages and with no benefits?
- How can the ILWU maintain its power in the supply chain if dock jobs are disappearing? Is there a future for ILWU members working off the docks?
- There is significant organized community and environmental opposition to container and bulk traffic that harms the environment and community health. Can the union both preserve jobs and the environment?

History of ILWU organizing along the whole supply chain

A positive answer to these questions can be found by breaking out of treating the workers as isolated individuals clinging to elite status on the waterfront, and instead making common cause with workers all along the logistics supply chain. Often the workers doing key functions along the supply chain away from the docks are first-generation immigrant workers toiling at minimum wage with no benefits and no job rights. This employment apartheid cannot be allowed to stand, and these workers must become part of the community of the organized. Recent years have seen attempts to organize these workers in key geographic logistics centers in Southern California, Metro Chicago, and New Jersey near the ports of New York and New Jersey. All these initiatives were funded by the Change to Win Federation,[13] and were sometimes linked to the national organizing effort among Walmart workers called Our Walmart.

While heroic and creative, these initiatives have all failed to organize any workers because they lack the strategic hammer of port workers backing their exciting community and worker outreach. The Warehouse Workers United (WWU) effort founded in 2009 in Southern California has recently pulled back from its locus in the heavily warehoused Inland Empire to a Warehouse Worker Resource Center based at the Port of Los Angeles. Interestingly the board of directors of the center has union representation from the Service Employees International Union (SEIU) and the Hotel Employees and Restaurant Employees Union (HERE), but no presence of the port power unions, the ILWU or the International Brotherhood of Teamsters (IBT).

Ironically the future for powerful dockworkers lies in conceptualizing themselves as logistics workers and not dockworkers. This is not a new concept for the ILWU. The union led two historic "Marches Inland" on the West Coast mainland and in Hawaii.[14] In San Francisco, the home of the union's glorious and founding 1934 maritime strike and subsequent general strike, the Embarcadero is still a visual and spatial landscape of the challenges that led to the March Inland and the organization of thousands of warehouse and manufacturing workers.

In the wake of the organization of dockworkers the Union crossed the Embarcadero and organized workers in warehouses and manufacturing who were handling and processing the same cargo that was being unloaded on the docks. As Harvey Schwartz points out in his important book *The March Inland*, "The low-paid, unorganized waterfront warehousemen, a potential source of non-union labor for ship-owners, posed a direct threat to the longshoremen. ILA 38-79 militants, therefore felt compelled to help unionize the waterfront warehousemen to insure the substantial gains the longshoremen eventually made from the 1934 tie-up."[15] The Union saw that if those workers were not part of an allied labor organization, its own ability to maintain a grip on dock work would be undermined by the dramatic imbalance in wage costs and the proximity of a potential scab workforce that could be counted on to do the work of dockworkers.

The March Inland on the West Coast resulted in the growth of the ILWU into an industrial power, and the workers in the warehouse division far outnumbered the members on the docks. This large group of members played a crucial role in expanding the mindset of the union, both providing numbers for active political involvement in cities like San Francisco and Seattle, and grounding the union in the reality of the life of the rest of the working class off the docks.

In Hawaii the history is an even starker endorsement of not allowing dockworker power to be isolated spatially and politically. The organization of dockworkers in Hawaii followed on the organization of the West Coast, but again the union recognized that, to use a catch phrase, "no worker is an island." Lou Goldblatt, the brilliant strategist and one of the leaders of the stateside March Inland, saw very clearly that consolidating power on the docks in Hawaii meant successfully organizing workers on the vast sugar and pineapple plantations and production facilities. Goldblatt reflected on his strategy for consolidating power in Hawaii: "One of the conclusions I reached was that longshoring played a different role in Hawaii than it did on the mainland. Instead of being a general industry of longshoring, in Hawaii longshoring was just a branch of the Big Five."[16]

The organizing which took place in 1943–45 made the ILWU the largest union in Hawaii and the most powerful political force on the island. In fact, when the entry of Hawaii as the 50th state in 1959 was debated in the US Congress, many senators and representatives questioned the loyalty of Hawaiians because of the influence of the aforementioned ILWU leader Jack Hall, an open Communist and a gifted organizer who collaborated with Goldblatt in the organization of the pineapple and sugar workers. According to Katy Fox-Hodess, a London-based researcher and writer:

> First of all, Goldblatt's observations illustrate the point that what we mean by "strategic" is highly variable across time and place and depends on historical and spatial particularities that must be understood in any

given context in order to be successful. Secondly it is important to recognize that in many cases it's the "flank" that's responsible for protecting the "fortress."[17]

On the mainland in the 1970s and 1980s the warehouses and factories shut down or moved out of the reach of the ILWU, so the power of the warehouse division was radically reduced. These shutdowns of manufacturing facilities were part of the wave of closures and relocations that hit the whole US manufacturing sector in the late 1970s and early 1980s. In the case of warehousing often the facilities ceased to exist and/or were replaced with third-party logistics providers (3PLS), or the warehouses moved inland to escape the ILWU and other unions. Local 6, the warehouse power local of the Bay Area with 20,000 members in the 1950s, has been reduced to a shell of its former self with fewer than 1,000 members. In Hawaii, the pineapple and sugar plantations have all been plowed under, but the union wielded its state and municipal power to make sure that the hotel and resort workers on the land that once produced those crops became ILWU members. ILWU remains the largest private sector union in Hawaii, and the largest hotel workers' union on the islands.

Modern maritime supply chain employment trends

While power in the strategic choke points remains, the trends in employment show a shrinking on-dock workforce relative to productivity, coupled with a huge growth in other occupations in the supply chain, with workers who are often employed far from the docks. Peter V. Hall has done extensive studies documenting these trends. Hall details the massive growth in container traffic through the West Coast ports. In 1980, 2.1 million TEU[18] were handled in the ports of the West Coast. In 2010, 14.9 million units were handled. This is a 620 percent increase.[19] In this same period of dramatic cargo growth the growth in long shore or on dock employment has grown but at nowhere near the rate of cargo trends. It is important to remember that in 1960 prior to the advent of containerization there were 26,000 longshore workers on the West Coast docks. In 1980 after the establishment of containerization as the dominant mode of cargo movement, there were only 10,245 workers left on the docks. In the period that Hall details from 1980 to 2010, employment grew to only 13,829, a rise of only 35 percent, and puny when compared with the 620 percent increase in production. There is no mystery to this disparity. Containers and massive capital equipment have replaced longshore gangs in the United States and around the world. Before containerization a ship would call for two weeks to be loaded and unloaded. Today the process can take less than 24 hours. While these increases in employment keep pace with regular employment trends, the real job growth action is off dock on the West Coast in three areas:

- Logistics information services: from 1980: 12,816 to 2010: 47,890. This is 274 percent growth. These are information service workers who track the flow of cargo and equipment worldwide. Often they work at inland office centers far from the docks. For example Evergreen, the giant Taiwanese carrier, has a massive information center in Dallas, Texas, far from any port, and purposefully so.
- Warehousing: from1980: 12,738 to 2010: 86,737. This is 581 percent growth. These are inland warehouses and 3PL centers that provide warehouse and order fulfillment services to giant retailers that are clients of the giant carriers that employ dockworkers in the ports.
- Trucking:1980: 156,808 to 2010: 257,673. This is 64 percent growth. The increases in these off-dock sectors are much more in keeping with the triple-digit increases in cargo volumes. These drivers are often called "owner operators" or "independent contractors," and therefore their wages and conditions are eroded because they are treated as pieceworkers and paid by the load, especially in short-haul trucking. Many of them, particularly doing short-haul trucking, were once members of the IBT. After deregulation on 1981 the Teamsters lost control of this short-haul cargo "drayage" sector.[20]

A programmatic response: organize all along the supply chain

The trends over the 30-year period make it clear that there is decreasing employment on the docks relative to the dramatic increase in cargo traffic. The ILWU faces a clear choice. The union along with other powerful dockworkers' unions can hole up on the docks and try to fend off the tide of technology and political attacks, or it can break out of its isolation and organize the industry while it still has strength and power on the waterfront. Such isolation is not just industrial but political as well. The union needs to ally broadly with other unions and new political formations that are challenging neoliberal corporatist politicians.

The ILWU is uniquely positioned because of its power on the docks with Pacific Maritime Association (PMA)[21] employers to again march inland and capture work all along the supply chain. There are thousands of workers in logistics facilities and back offices working for PMA employers handling cargo and information flows. They can become ILWU warehouse and office clerical members. There are hundreds of marine workers on the West Coast and in Alaska and Hawaii working in tug and tow and environmental services who should become part of the Inland Boatmen's Union of the Pacific (IBU), the union's maritime division. They are equally crucial to maintaining the union's power. The union can no longer see itself as a dockworkers union isolated on the waterfront while the cargo chain grows away from it.

In an excellent feature in *The Dispatcher*, the newspaper of the ILWU written in 2004, editor Marcy Rein points out the integrated nature of the industry:

> A new type of company called the "third party logistics" provider (3PL) has sprung up over the last 15 years. These 3PLs may be branches of other firms. American President Lines (APL) Logistics and the container shipping company American President Lines both belong to the Singapore based Neptune Orient Lines (NOL) Group, for example. Many 3PLs grew out of freight forwarders and NVOCCs. (NVOCCs, non-vessel operating common carriers, make arrangements and take responsibility for cargo that travels on vessels owned by other companies.) But 3PLs may not own any ships or trucks or warehouses. These "non-asset based firms" use information and contacts to help other companies use the cargo-handling chain as efficiently and cheaply as possible.[22]

The founders of the ILWU saw the importance of organizing workers all along the supply chain to protect their dockworkers' flanks and to grow their political power and influence. It is important to note that such organizing cannot and will not always be into the ranks of the ILWU. For over 20 years IBT has been waging a nationwide port truckers campaign to unionize the over 40,000 short-haul "drayage" drivers in ports all over the United States. Recently *USA Today* carried a front-page exposé entitled "Rigged" which detailed the horrible conditions and servitude of these drivers.[23] These are strategic flanks, and the ILWU cannot stand idly by and allow this campaign to flounder. The power of the dockworkers must be brought fully to bear to organize these workers.

Training for technology

Even on dock the possibilities exist to build power if the union can capture the new-technology work that is part of the use of robotics and other automated processes.[24] Union members can be retrained to repair the robots and develop the software that programs and runs the robots. Right now the ILWU is not prepared to capture the new jobs in maintenance, programming, electronics, and data management that have arisen because of the implementation of new technologies on dock and near dock. The union needs to invest in its own massive training program partnering with vocational high schools, two-year junior colleges, and degree-granting universities, to prepare its members to be the workforce of the future. The ILWU needs a registered apprenticeship program to train the next generation of workers.

There is no future in fighting the machines. Legendary union leader and one of ILWU's founders Harry Bridges correctly foresaw the advent of containerization, and negotiated a landmark agreement, the Mechanization and Modernization (M&M) agreement, which allowed the introduction of technology but preserved longshore work. Some in the union today have advocated a "John Henry" solution to technology. The thinking is that ILWU crane drivers, the union's most elite segment, can work fast enough to manually outpace the robots.

John Henry was successful in beating the steam engine, but then he dropped dead. The same fate awaits the ILWU if it does not get hip to the realities of technology and develop a positive program to embrace technology and find new employment and training.[25]

Fight for environmentally sound employment

In some ways the biggest threat to the union and the industry lies in the environmental challenges produced by the emissions of trucks and equipment in the harbor areas.[26] Community groups will not stop in their efforts through lawsuits and legislation to abate the pollution that poisons their neighborhoods. The unions can side with these lawsuits and actions, and fight for communities free from pollution, often their own neighborhoods, or defend their employers and perpetuate the problem. The unions cannot be climate change deniers and support every new job created, despite the noxious environmental damage it may cause. The ILWU has led in demanding that ships slow down as they cruise into major container ports in order to reduce toxic exhaust fumes. The ILWU also promoted the "cap and bonnet" program developed by Advanced Cleanup Technologies Inc. in Long Beach to contain effluents from bulk ships tied up at marine terminals. It needs to explore "short sea shipping" as an alternative to environmentally damaging truck trips moving cargo from Southern Californian ports to Northern Californian warehouses.[27] No marginal increase in jobs is worth total isolation from the communities and progressive social forces that surround the ports. After all it is the longshore residential communities that are often hit the hardest by toxic fumes and substances. Making common cause with environmentalists is crucial to realizing a power program and establishing the union as a solid force for working families. Enviro-clean-up is a growth industry, and the union should grow with it!

Core and periphery: a global challenge

These are not challenges unique to the ILWU; rather they are universal, and not only in the maritime logistics industry, but in all industries where unions have power in core employment but have lost or never had power in the periphery. The Communications Workers of America (CWA) have held power among landline workers in the phone industry. They are attempting through bargaining to organize and secure collective agreements for the growing wireless segment. They have struck for the rights to organize these workers.

The ILWU and other dockworker unions have been trailblazers in the past in standing with worldwide revolutionary people's struggles and in strengthening the domestic power of their sisters and brothers in the working class. While dockworkers still wield power at the point of production it is incumbent on them to recognize new structural and employment realities, and adjust their strategies accordingly. Such unions like the ILWU must reconceive themselves as supply chain unions and act and organize accordingly. "An injury to one is an injury to all!"

Acknowledgments

Many thanks to Katy Fox-Hodess, Christina L. Perez, Glenn Perusek, and John Womack, who greatly assisted with content and editing of this chapter.

Notes

1 The final report of the New York State Organized Crime Taskforce, entitled *Corruption and Racketeering in the NYC Construction Industry* (New York: NYU Press, 1990) reveals the manner in which the Mob intervened strategically to block the arrival of cement trucks at large job sites in order to extort money from real estate developers.

2 Womack's work, *Strategic Position and Worker Power (Posicion estrategica y fuerza obrera. Hacia una nueva historia de los movimentos obreros)* (Mexico City, Fonde de Cultura Economica, 2008), is only published in Mexico and has yet to be translated into English for American readers. A translation is sorely needed, and the book would be of great benefit to a whole new generation of organizers and activists. His contribution is to highlight this strategic power but also to recognize its temporal nature, or as he says, "and often not the same places for very long."

3 John Womack, Jr. "Working Power over Production: Labor History, Industrial Work, Economics, Sociology, and Strategic Position," June 2, 2006. XIV International Economic History Congress, Helsinki 2006, Panel 56: The Economics of Latin American Labor. See www.helsinki.fi/iehc2006/papers2/Womack.pdf (accessed December 29, 2017).

4 Manufacturing employment accounted for 32.4 percent of the work force in 1910, but this had been reduced to 8.7 percent of the workforce by 2015 (Bureau of Labor Statistics). See "Employment by industry, 1910 and 2015, www.bls.gov/opub/ted/2016/employment-by-industry-1910-and-2015.htm (accessed December 30, 2017).

5 Peter V. Hall, "'We'd have to sink the ships': impact studies and the 2002 West Coast port lockout," *Economic Development Quarterly*, November 1, 2004.

6 Peter Olney, "On the waterfront analysis of ILWU lockout," *New Labor Forum* (Summer 2003).

7 It is interesting to note that when the ILWU struck in 1971 for 130 days during the height of the Vietnam War, there was an impact on trade, but nowhere near the immediate crisis levels of 2002. This attests to the increased velocities of the supply chain in the intervening years. Anon. *New York Times* "West Coast longshoremen obey writ, return to job," October 10, 1971, www.nytimes.com/1971/10/10/archives/west-coast-longshoremen-obey-writ-return-to-job.html (accessed December 30, 2017).

8 "Update: On the waterfront," *NPR News Hour*, October 3, 2002.

9 *NPR News Hour* with Ray Suarez, October 2002.

10 Jasper Bernes, "Logistics, counter logistics and the communist prospect," *Endnotes* 3.

11 Empire Logistics, "Supply chain infrastructure," www.empirelogistics.org/sci-map (accessed December 4, 2017).

12 Erik Olin Wright, "Working class power, capitalist class interests, and class

compromise," *American Journal of Sociology* 105(4) (January 2000), pp. 957–1002.

13 Change To Win (CTW) was a new labor federation formed by the Service Employees, Teamsters, United Food and Commercial Workers, Farmworkers and Laborers Union when it left the AFL-CIO in 2005.

14 Harvey Schwartz, *The March Inland: Origins of the ILWU Warehouse Division 1934–38* (Berkeley, Calif.: Ink Works Press, 1978).

15 Schwartz (1978), p. 14.

16 The Big Five were the companies that owned sugar and pineapple plantations and processing plants on the islands.

17 Katy Fox-Hodess in email to author, June 11, 2017.

18 TEU are twenty foot equivalent units, the original size of ocean-going containers and the basic measurement unit of container traffic.

19 Hall (2014).

20 "Drayage" is an English term for short-haul truckers, derived from the term donkey dray (or cart).

21 The PMA is the employer association created to collectively bargain with the ILWU and administer the labor agreement. All the major world-class carriers including Maersk, Hyundai, and Evergreen, are members.

22 Marcy Rein, "Desert docks and octopi," *The Dispatcher* 63(1) (January 2005).

23 Brett Murphy, "Rigged," *USA Today*, June 16, 2017.

24 Ryan Petersen's blog post on Flexport asks the question "Why is the port of Rotterdam more automated that the Port of Oakland?" And Erica Phillips writes in the *Wall Street Journal* (March 27, 2016) about automation in the Ports of Los Angeles and Long Beach. Both articles describe the inevitability of the new technology and the difficulties that the employers have experienced in implementing it as has been done in other ports worldwide such as Rotterdam.

25 Raquel Varela, a Portuguese researcher, and Manuel S. Oliveira assert that the introduction of new technology at least in the short run is not cost-effective particularly in low-wage ports, but that the employers make such moves in order to limit the power of labor. Of course in the long run such limits on the power of labor are "cost-effective." Varela and Oliveira suggest that the introduction of technology is damaging to local communities, which often offer public subsidies to support its introduction. See Manuel S. Oliveira and Raquel Varela, "Automation in ports and labor relations in XXI century," https://raquelcardeiravarela.files.wordpress.com/2017/07/studyautomation-2.pdf (accessed December 4, 2017).

26 Morgan Wyenn, "Port of LA approves $10 million in settlement funds to reduce port-related air pollution," blog, NRDC, November 10, 2014, www.nrdc.org/experts/morgan-wyenn/port-la-approves-10-million-settlement-funds-reduce-port-related-air-pollution (accessed December 4, 2017).

27 Short sea shipping refers to a very common maritime practice in many parts of the world where smaller container ships move cargo from large ports to

smaller ports or inland ports. This takes containers off the road and means that ocean-going container ships can call at one port rather than multiple destination points.

Contributor Biographies

Jake Alimahomed-Wilson is an associate professor of sociology at California State University, Long Beach, USA. His research interests are in the areas of logistics, racism and labor, and global workers' struggles. He is the author of *Solidarity Forever? Race, Gender, and Unionism in the Ports of Southern California* (Lexington Books, 2016) and co-author (with Edna Bonacich) of *Getting the Goods: Ports, Labor, and the Logistics Revolution* (Cornell University Press, 2008).

Amazon workers and supporters collectively wrote their chapter based on their experiences as workers in Amazon warehouses in Poland, as activists of a grassroots union, and as co-organizers of Amazon workers' meetings with participants from several European countries.

Carlotta Benvegnù is a PhD candidate in social sciences at the Universities of Padua (Italy) and Paris VIII (France). Her research project compares, through ethnographic fieldwork, the evolutions of the logistics sector in France and in Italy. Her main research interests include sociology of work, labor market segmentation, industrial relations, and migrations.

Andrea Bottalico is a PhD student in economic sociology and labor studies at the University of Milan (Italy). He is the editor of the *Social Enquiry Napoli Monitor* and wrote a book on labor conditions in the oldest shipyard in Europe, *Il fuoco a mare, Ascesa e declino di una città-cantiere del sud-Italia* (Monitor, 2015). His research is on dock labor issues in European ports.

Jorge Budrovich Sáez received his PhD in interdisciplinary studies on thought, culture, and society, from the University of Valparaiso. He is the editor of the *Journal of Humanities* of Valparaiso. His research interests deals with the city-port relation in the context of the logistical, infrastructural and technological restructuration of global supply chains, and the social contestation to it by dockworkers in Valparaiso.

Paul S. Ciccantell is professor of sociology in the Department of Sociology at Western Michigan University, USA. His research examines socioeconomic change over the long term, the evolution of global industries, and the socioeconomic and environmental impacts of global industries, focusing particularly on raw materials extraction and processing, and transport industries.

Peter Cole is professor of history at Western Illinois University, USA, and research associate in the Society, Work and Development Institute, University of the Witwatersrand, South Africa. He authored *Wobblies on the Waterfront: Interracial Unionism in Progressive-Era Philadelphia* (Illinois, 2007) and co-edited *Wobblies of the World: A Global History of the IWW* (Pluto, 2017). He is currently revising *Dockworker Power: Race, Technology, and Unions in Durban and the San Francisco Bay Area*.

Hernán Cuevas Valenzuela received his PhD in government from Essex University. He is a CONICYT eesearcher and works in the Vice-Chancellor's Office of Institutional Relations and Outreach from Universidad de Concepción. His research interests include: ideology and discourse analysis, post-Marxism, post-stucturalism, citizenship studies, political economy, and cultural studies. His current research deals with city-ports in sociohistorical and comparative perspectives.

Niccolò Cuppini received his PhD in politics, institutions and history at the University of Bologna, Italy. His research is an attempt to urbanize political thought and to grasp the transformations of the contemporary city within a global perspective. He has also researched and published on the cycle of strikes in the logistics sector in Northern Italy.

Sheheryar Kaoosji is the founder and co-executive director of the Warehouse Worker Resource Center, USA. He worked as a research analyst and strategist in support of efforts to organize workers in the supply chains of major global manufacturers, retailers, and food companies. He has a Master's degree in public policy from UCLA and a BA from UC Santa Cruz.

Johnson Abhishek Minz is an assistant professor at the Tata Institute of Social Sciences (TISS), Mumbai, India. His primary research spans the areas of employment and labor, particularly looking at them from an interdisciplinary angle. He has been involved in projects with the International Labour Organization, and has also worked on various assignments for the Government of India.

Abu Mufakhir is a program coordinator at the Asia Monitor Resource Centre, Hong Kong. His recent publications analyze the new experiences of factory raids and general strikes of organized labor in Indonesia. He graduated from the Department of Mass Communication at the University of Indonesia with a thesis on labor publication.

Immanuel Ness is professor of political science at City University New York. He is the author of *Southern Insurgency* (Pluto, 2015), *Guest Workers and Resistance to US Corporate Despotism* (University of Illinois Press, 2011), and numerous other works. He is editor of the *International Encyclopedia of Revolution and Protest* and co-editor, with Zak Cope, of the quarterly periodical *Journal of Labor and Society*.

Peter Olney has been a labor organizer for 45 years. He is the retired organizing director of the International Longshore and Warehouse Union (ILWU). He was also associate director of the Institute for Labor and Employment at the University of California from 2001–04. He holds an MBA from UCLA.

Fahmi Panimbang is a labor activist with LIPS (Lembaga Informasi Perburuhan Sedane/Sedane Labor Resource Center) in Indonesia. Fahmi worked as a program coordinator on capital mobility at the Asia Monitor Resource Centre in Hong Kong from 2010–16. He recently published the edited book *Resistance on the Continent of Labour: Strategies and Initiatives of Labour Organizing in Asia* (AMRC, 2017).

Dimitris Parsanoglou is a senior researcher at the Department of Social Policy at Panteion University of Social and Political Sciences, Greece. He has worked as a sociologist on several national and European research projects, and has extensively published on the history and sociology of immigration to Greece with special emphasis on employment, urban space, gender, and migration policies.

Alfian Al'ayubby Pelu is a labor activist with LIPS, Indonesia. With his colleagues, he recently published an investigative report on worker's exposure to hazardous chemicals in electronics factories in the Batam industrial zones of Indonesia.

Carolin Philipp is a political scientist and a member of glokal e.V./

Berlin, who work in political education projects on postcolonialism and societal inequalities. Since 2009 she has lived mainly in Athens, Greece exploring social movements in crisis, the topic of her PhD (2017). She also works on a research project at the Panteion and Kapodistrian University on migration, racism, and neoliberalism, and reports for various media outlets in Greece.

Spencer Louis Potiker is a graduate student in the Department of Sociology at the University of California, Irvine. His research interests center on logistics and socioeconomic implications of prolonged occupation; the intersection of race, citizenship, and gender with labor positionality; and transnational labor movements.

Ellen Reese is professor of sociology and chair of the Labor Studies program at UC Riverside. She is the author of *They Say Cutback: We Say Fightback!* (Russell Sage Foundation, 2011) and *Backlash Against Welfare Mothers* (University of California Press, 2004), and co-editor of *The Wages of Empire*.

Bai Ruixue is a researcher on Chinese labor issues. She is also an editorial board member of the *Borderless Movement* website and contributed to the book *China's Rise: Strength and Fragility* (Merlin Press, 2012).

Çağatay Edgücan Şahin is an assistant professor at Ordu University, Turkey, in the Department of Labor Economics and Industrial Relations. He holds an MA and PhD in labor economics, both from Marmara University, Turkey. His research interests include the labor history of modern Turkey, social policy, unions, and political economy.

David A. Smith is professor of sociology at the University of California at Irvine, USA. His research focuses on global commodity chains, world cities, and the political economy of the world-system. He is editor of the *International Journal of Comparative Sociology* and was 2015–16 president of the Society for the Study of Social Problems.

Elizabeth A. Sowers is an assistant professor of sociology at California State University, Channel Islands. Her research interests are in the areas of globalization, economic sociology, and work, with a specific focus on investigating working conditions in the logistics industry.

Jason Struna is an assistant professor of sociology and anthropology at the University of Puget Sound, USA. His research focuses on transnational class formation, and the labor processes that make contemporary capitalist globalization possible. His work appears in *Globalizations*, *Labor Studies*, and *Perspectives on Global Development and Technology*. He is currently writing a book on shop floor life in Southern California's warehouse industry.

Pekin Bengisu Tepe is a PhD candidate in the Department of Anthropology, Ankara University, Turkey. He holds an MA in anthropology from Ankara University. His research interests include different dimensions of anthropology: human evolution, the relationship between humans and tools/machines, informal groups (especially in the working class) and their communication habits.

Au Loong Yu is a socialist writer based in Hong Kong. He is a founding member of *Globalization Monitor* and an editorial board member of the *Borderless Movement* website. He is the main author of the book *China's Rise: Strength and Fragility* (Merlin Press, 2012).

Index

Printed and bound by CPI Group (UK) Ltd, Croydon, CR0 4YY

13/04/2025

14656489-0005